LOCAL GOVERNMENT

Dollars & Sense

225 financial tips
for guarding the
public checkbook

LEN WOOD

© 1998, 2002, 2004 by Len Wood

10   9   8   7   6   5   4   3

ISBN 0-9634374-3-7 Hard Cover

Library of Congress Catalog Card Number 97-90605

Published by The Training Shoppe, Rancho Palos Verdes, CA
Book and cover design by Casa Graphics, Inc., Burbank, CA

I wish I would have listened a bit more,
questioned a bit more,
and trusted just a bit less.

Orange County Board of Supervisors Chair Thomas Reilly
after the County Filed Bankruptcy

I dedicate this book to my wife, June,
whose powerful suggestions, gentle critiques,
and tireless editing and proofing made this book a reality.

Acknowledgements

These public officials and community leaders have provided invaluable assistance and advice in the development and writing of this book. I wish to thank them all for their gracious help.

Debbie Ackerman, City Councilmember, Skagway, Alaska

David Aleshire, City Attorney, Rutan & Tucker, Costa Mesa, California

David C. Antonucci, General Manager, Tahoe City Public Utility District, California

Anita Bingham, Director of Finance, City of Camarillo, California

Ken Blake, City Councilmember, City of La Palma, California

Eva Minor Bradford, Mayor, City of La Palma, California

Gary R. Brown, City Manager, City of Tempe, Arizona

Scott P. Bryant, Trainer and Consultant, City of New York, New York

Judy Buchan, City Councilmember, Redwood City, California

Michael R. Capizzi, District Attorney, County of Orange, California

Gary Caporicci, Auditor, Caporicci & Larson, Newport Beach, California

Howard L. Chambers, City Administrator, City of Lakewood, California

Brigitte Charles, Human Resource Director, City of Rialto, California

Ken Farfsing, City Manager, City of Signal Hill, California

David Finigan, Assistant City Manager, City of Vallejo, California

Jim Hankla, City Manager, City of Long Beach, California

Roger Kemp, City Manager, City of Meridian, Connecticut

Pat Klotz, Attorney for Friends of Jackson Square, New Orleans, Louisiana

Margaret E. Langdon, Educator, Library Sciences, Seattle School District, Washington

Richard M. Langdon, Educator, Seattle School District, Washington

Wally Linn, Mayor, City of La Palma, California

Susan A. MacManus, Professor, University of South Florida, Florida

Martha Marshall, Management Consultant Supervisor, Prince William County, Virginia

Michael C. Moreland, Auditor, Moreland and Associates, Newport Beach, California

Dennis Murphy, Chief Administrative Officer, City of Bridgeport, Connecticut

Ernie H. O'Dell, City Treasurer, City of Redondo Beach, California

James C. O'Donnell, President, O'Donnell Management Consulting, Irvine, California

Paul Philips, City Manager, City of Artesia, California

Dave Ream, City Manager, City of Santa Ana, California

Debra Rich, Housing and Community Development Director, City of Signal Hill, California

Richard Riordan, Mayor, City of Los Angeles, California

Frank Rowlen, Deputy City Treasurer, City of Redondo Beach, California

Linda Dee Sarver, Mayor, City of Covina, California

Guy Santagate, City Manager, City of Chelsea, Massachusetts

ACKNOWLEDGEMENTS

Duane Schuster, Mayor, City of
La Palma, California

Mary Strenn, City
Administrator, City of San
Fernando, California

Ira J. Toibin, Ph.D., Assistant
Superintendent-Personnel,
Palos Verdes Peninsula Unified
School District, California

Maria Torres, Management
Analyst, East Bay Municipal
Utility District, California

James S. Wiggins, Community
Activist, Fort Walton Beach,
Florida

Keene N. Wilson, City
Administrator, City of Lomita,
California

June Wood, Executive Vice
President, Len Wood &
Associates

Michael L. Yoder, Executive
Assistant to the Mayor, City of
Indianapolis, Indiana

Ricky Young, Reporter, Orange
County Register, California

Special thanks to Ernie & Patty Weckbaugh of Casa Graphics, Inc.
His cover and interior design and their suggestions were very
important to the production of the book.

Introduction

Orange County California Supervisors William G. Steiner and Roger B. Stanton undoubtedly grimaced when they received subpoenas ordering them to appear before the grand jury.

What had they done? Certainly they had not embezzled or stolen money. Nor did they help a friend or family member gain a special privilege. Both Steiner and Stanton were charged with willful misconduct in office for failing to oversee the activities of Robert Citron, the Orange County Treasurer. Citron's poor judgement and faulty investment strategy resulted in the loss of over a billion dollars.

The Orange County District Attorney, Michael Capizzi was dead serious. He pursued the charges against the two supervisors all the way to the California Supreme Court before they were finally dismissed. The court ultimately held that the supervisors could not be held liable for their own bad judgment.

However, the overriding message was clear. Governing board members of counties, cities, districts and school districts had better spend time learning about their agency's finances. Before the Orange County bankruptcy, local officials could slight their agency's mundane finances and concentrate on what they considered the more interesting issues. This is no longer the case. Capizzi and others have brought governing board accountability for budget and finances to the front burner.

The Orange County calamity is not unique. The same financial problems and mistakes plague local governments across the country, whether it be Chelsea, Massachusetts, Bridgeport, Connecticut, Washington, D.C., Miami, Florida or California's Laguna Beach Unified School District.

Overseeing finances is not an easy job. When asked under oath about whether he questioned a financial matter, Supervisor Steiner candidly admitted that he did not know the type of questions to ask. Steiner is not alone, there are thousands of newly elected and seasoned governing board members who do not know how to review and analyze their agency's budgets let alone the financial reports. The warning signals are always there — it's just that they are not recognized or they are simply ignored. Financial disasters do not happen overnight, they are built on neglect, denial, poor judgment and faulty decisions.

This lack of financial knowledge is not entirely the elected official's fault. There is a dearth of easily understood budget and financial information. Much of the financial literature is written in a very technical and detailed manner. While the majority of administrators invest many hours in educating their governing boards, there are some who secretly admit that they prefer to keep legislators in the dark about important financial matters.

To many people, guarding the public checkbook is a simple task. All you have to do is stop the reckless spending and throw out the rascals. This simplistic view quickly changes after one is in office for a short period. As a member of a governing body you know that the problems are much more complex.

Yes, budgets and financial reports can be intimidating. But they don't have to be. This book is about the actual financial issues local officials face. It contains 225 tips for elected officials to make them more knowledgeable and less vulnerable. The numerous examples recount actual problems that local government officials have had to confront and resolve.

Local Government Dollars and Sense is written so that you can read it in the traditional manner of front to back or, you can skip to the chapter that most interests you. Each chapter begins with a relevant vignette that is followed by several tips.

LOCAL GOVERNMENT DOLLARS AND SENSE

Table of Contents

Dedication   v

Acknowledgments   vii

Introduction   xi

CHAPTER 1
Stop Campaigning and Begin Governing   1
    Don't be Hamstrung by Unrealistic or
        Uninformed Election Promises   4
    Keep on Top of Your Promises   8
    Brace Yourself for Information Overload   10
    Switch to Your Governing Mode   10
    Obtain the Key Documents   12
    Build a Positive Relationship with Staff   13
    Lay the Groundwork for Your Proposals   14
    Don't be Afraid to Ask Questions   15
    Don't be Reluctant to Say "I Don't Know"   18
    Get on a Budget or Finance Committee   18
    Protect Your Meeting Time Like the Last
        Potato Chip   19
    Don't Rely on Osmosis to Learn About
        Public Finances   19
    Get Used to the Sunshine   21
    You Must be Accessible to the Public   22
    Establish a Continuous Self-Education Program 23

CHAPTER 2

Know Your Financial Oversight Responsibilities   **25**

You Must Exercise Oversight   29
Maintain Your Independence   30
Public Finances Need Not be Boring   31
Avoid Micro-Management as an On-going Practice   32
Avoid Complacency Management   35
Elected Official Oversight Means Holding
    Administrators Accountable   36
Don't Accept Unrefined Data   38
Exercise Your Financial Oversight Responsibilities   38
Make the Mission Statement Your Own   39
Develop the Governing Body's Goals   40
If You Don't Set Your Agency's Goals, Staff Will   41
Agree Upon the Level of Detail in Goals   41
Update and Prioritize Your Goals   42
Develop Financial Policies   43
Review Your Agency's Financial Policies   44
Oversight Means Evaluating Programs Beforehand   45
Insist Upon Performance Evaluation Criteria
    for New Proposals   47
Make Sure of the Follow-Up   48
Hold Goal Setting Retreats   48
Set Retreat Ground Rules   50
Follow-up After Retreats   51

CHAPTER 3

How to Lessen Budget Anxiety   **53**

Budgets are More than Control Documents   56
Budgets are Plans of Action   56
Budgets Need Not be Complex   57
Budgeting is Irrational   58
Budgeting is also Rational   59
You Have Little Control Over the Total
    Expenditure Program   59
Determine What Type of Budget Your
    Agency Uses   61
Don't Ignore the Capital Budget   64
Focus on the Significant Budget Issues   64
Expect the Budget Message to Clarify the
    Big Picture   65
Public Accounting is Different from
    Commercial Accounting   66

Examine the Beginning and Ending Balances
  Table for the General Fund   67
Find the Personnel-Related Statements   69
Suggested Budget Questions   70
Ask Hard Questions Before Approving a
  New Program   72
Avoid Trivial Pursuit   73
Hold Separate Hearings for Major Public
  Proposals   74
Make Sure the Budget is Made Available to
  the Public   74
Recognize the Limitations of the CPI   76

CHAPTER 4
Disastrous Fiscal Practices   79
Know the Chief Administrator's Financial
  Skill Level   81
Don't Let Program Success Blind You   82
Fiscal Crises Do Not Develop Overnight   83
Be Aware of the Financial Crisis Warning Signs   84
Management Response to Warning Signs is Critical   86
Debt Issuance is a Poor Bail-Out Method   87
Look for Breakdowns in Management   90
Avoid Financial Gimmickry and Cut Your Losses   90
You've Got to Rein in the "Pleasers"   91
Be Aware of the Fiscal "Ambulance Chasers"   92
You Cannot Borrow Your Way Out of a Fiscal Crisis   94
Avoid Bankruptcy Filings   95

CHAPTER 5
When You Must Cut   99
Identify the Inhibitors to Solving the Problem   102
Determine Why Cutbacks are Really Necessary   102
Examine Revenue Estimates   103
Rightsizing is Not Downsizing   103
Develop a Cut Back Philosophy   104
Identify Your Core Services   105
Priority Rankings Require a Mature Approach   107
Examine Management and Administration Costs   108
Examine the Levels of Management   109
Make Sure Cutback Strategies are Affordable   109
Don't Cut Revenue Producing Programs   110
Avoid the Other Common Cutback Mistakes   110
Hang Tough on Budget Freezes   113

Determine Who is Lobbying You and Why 114
Create an Incentive for Departments to Cut
    Budgets 115
Small Cuts are Important 116
Establish Specific Parameters for Blue Ribbon
    Committees 117

CHAPTER 6
Sins, Omissions and Poor Judgment **119**
Don't Let Squeaky Wheels Reset Your Priorities 122
Don't Fight Citizen Requests for Information
    on Services 123
Government Cannot Always Operate Like
    a Business 125
Don't Flaunt Court Orders 127
Avoid That Little Retirement Bump for
    Good Ol' Sam 128
Get a Fiscal Impact Assessment for Benefit
    Packages 129
Don't Let Vacation Liability Accumulate 130
Check Overtime Usage 131
Monitor Use of Agency Vehicles 132
Oversee Off-Duty Use of Public Vehicles 132
Monitor Credit Card Usage 134
Don't Use Public Resources for Campaign
    Purposes 136
Don't Frolic and Fraternize with Consultants 137
Soliciting for Charity Can also Present Conflicts 138
Separate Contributions from Decisions 138
Don't Use the Register of Warrants for
    Political Games 139
Don't Get too Close to Employees 140
Monitor Litigation Costs 141
Assume That There Will be Leaks 142

CHAPTER 7
Where is the Money Hidden? **145**
Why Money is Hidden in the Budget 147
Budget Padding is a Common Hiding Technique 149
Budget Padding Can be Minimized 151
'Giveaways' in the Budget are Common 152
Even Governing Bodies Resort to Hiding 153
Don't Expect Hidden Money to be a Panacea 155
Unmonitored Slush Funds Grow in the Dark 157

Don't Plead Inability to Pay with Unions 159
Unions are Adept at Finding Hidden Money 160
How to Look for Hidden Money 161
Examine General Fund Revenue 161
Examine General Fund Expenditures 163
Check Fund Balances First 165
Favorite Resting Places for Surplus Monies 166
Check for Increases in Expenditures 166

CHAPTER 8
What is an Adequate Fund Balance? **169**
Understand Fund Balance Definitions 171
Find the Primary Fund Balance 172
Find General Fund Reserve Policies 173
Obtain a Historical Trend of Your Agency's
    Fund Balance 174
Get the Entire Picture 175
Things to Consider When Establishing the
    Reserve Level 176
Check Reserve Policies of Other Funds 178
Setting the Fund Balance Level 179

CHAPTER 9
Treasure Your Treasurer **181**
Treasury Oversight Deserves More Attention
    Today 189
Assess Your Treasurer's Current Competence 190
Train and Compensate Your Treasurer Adequately 191
Elected Versus Appointed Treasurers 192
Develop a Line of Succession 193
Don't Press too Hard for Yield 193
Be Cautious but Demand Performance 194
Insist Upon an Adequate Cash Management
    Program 196
Make Sure Safety is the Top Priority 196
Let Independent Third Party Custodians Hold
    Your Securities 198
Have an Independent Auditor Evaluate
    Internal Controls 199
Follow-Up on Requested Evaluation Reports 200
Make Sure Your Treasurer is Not Enamored
    by Brokers 201
Appreciate the Risk Involved in Leveraging 202
Make Sure Your Investment Policy is Followed 203

Require Market Value Reporting for all Securities ... 204
Nurture an Effective Investment Committee ... 205
Make Sure Investment Reports are Timely and
    Adequate ... 206
Monitor the Yield on Investments ... 208
Make Sure the Portfolio is Diversified ... 208
Know Your Investment Pool's Policies ... 209
Thoroughly Examine an Investment Pool
    Before Joining ... 209
Don't Let the Treasurer Buy if it Can't be
    Explained to You ... 211

CHAPTER 10
Performance Measurement: What's the Fear? ... **213**
Performance Measurement is Not New ... 217
Don't Settle for the Numbers Game ... 219
Have Staff Develop Outcome-Oriented Objectives ... 220
Be Ready to Focus on Results ... 221
Performance Measurement Works with
    Contract Services ... 222
Performance Measurement Will Improve ... 223
Make Sure Your System is Working ... 224
Use Objectives to Evaluate and Manage,
    Not Punish ... 225
Don't Settle for Vague Measures ... 226
Reinforce Well-Stated Objectives ... 227
Bring the Public Along ... 228
You Must Review Performance Results ... 228
Look for Unintended Consequences ... 229
Limit the Number of Objectives ... 230
Modify Objectives When the Situation Changes ... 230
Use Customer Surveys ... 231
Encourage the Use of Benchmarking ... 234
Insist Upon Periodic Audits of Performance
    Measures ... 235

CHAPTER 11
Where Do We Get the Money? ... **237**
Grants Can Undermine Fiscal Discipline ... 238
Don't Blame the Feds ... 240
Avoid the Grant Pitfalls ... 241
When to Apply for a Grant ... 242
When Refusing a Grant, Tell Them Why ... 242
The Property Tax is Still the Most Despised Tax ... 243

Determine the Full Cost of a New or
    Increased Tax   244
Avoid the Static Analysis Pitfall   245
Don't Bank on "Sin" Taxes   246
Don't Promise Tax Cuts Unless You are Committed   247
Don't Overreact to Tax Limitation Measures   247
Examine Self-Sufficiency Claims   248
Make Departments Responsible for Revenues   249
Watch the Growth in Public Debt   250
Don't Raid Enterprise Funds Without
    Documentation   251
As a Rule Staff Will Underestimate Revenues   252
Don't be Pack Rats — Dump Excess Property   252

CHAPTER 12
Sewers and Classrooms Don't Vote...Right Away   **255**
Devote Money to Repair and Maintenance   256
Be Aware of Deferred Maintenance Decisions   258
Deferred Maintenance Costs More   259
Budget Operating Expenses for Capital Projects   260
Question Before You Cut Capital Expenditures   261
Make Sure Proper Security Measures are
    Implemented   261
Make Sure Bond Promises are Kept   262
You Must Level with the Public   263
Line-up Support for Capital Improvement
    Programs   267
Be Especially Cautious Before and After a Bond
    Issue Election   267
Consider Using an Oversight Panel for Capital
    Projects   268

CHAPTER 13
Support Your Local Auditor   **271**
Be Aware of the Different Types of Audits   274
There are External and Internal Auditors   275
Auditors Must be Independent   276
Clarify the Role of the Auditor   277
What Makes a Good Auditor?   278
Auditor Red Flags   279
The Four Types of Auditor Opinions   279
An Unqualified Opinion Does Not Mean
    Everything is in Order   280

The Audit Report is Not the Same Thing
    as the CAFR   281
Your Agency May Not Prepare a CAFR   283
The Budget Does Not Tie into the CAFR   283
Obtain Copies of Management Letters   284
Use a Competitive Process to Obtain an
    Independent Auditor   285
Make Sure Audit Firms are Technically
    Qualified to Perform Public Agency Audits   286
Be Sure to Enter into a Written Agreement   287
Auditors Should Use Performance Measurement   287
Consider Using an Audit Committee   288

CHAPTER 14
Public-Private Ventures are Not for the Timid   **291**

Keep the Electorate Informed   294
Negotiate Hard and Don't Leave Anything
    on the Table   295
Conduct a Detailed Risk Analysis for All
    Entrepreneurial Projects   296
Question Projected Benefits and Costs for
    Entrepreneurial Ventures   298
Obtain Unbiased, Independent Studies   300
Add Up All the Incentives   302
Know When to Pull the Plug on Entrepreneurial
    Ventures   303
Get Ready for a Gutter Fight if You Steal an
    Enterprise   303
Don't Let Time Pressures Void Your Good
    Judgment   305
Be Ready to Take Over an Enterprise if it
    Defaults on a Loan   306
Don't Let the "Entrepreneurial Bug" Derail the
    Primary Mission   307
Know the Market   308
Start Asking the Important Questions Early   308

Afterward   311
References   315
Appendixes   317
Glossary   347
Index   353
Biography   359
Ordering Information   361

Stop Campaigning and Begin Governing

"I was wrong about the no-tax pledge. Maybe I was a little naive; I thought we could make the cuts to make up the difference. At least I'm big enough to say I was wrong and do what's best for the community."

Covina Mayor Linda Sarver

Exposure

Linda Sarver's entry into politics was not too different from many others. She was invited to the Covina City Council meeting by a good friend. When she got there, she found the chambers packed with over 300 angry people and a city council that was considering a new utility tax.

While Sarver did not have a strong feeling about the tax, she became appalled with the council's failure to listen to residents. She just couldn't accept that her local government would treat people in such an arrogant manner. Moreover, the city council was holding the meeting at 7:00 in the morning.

That day the city council adopted a 6 percent utility tax. In response, angry residents immediately formed the "Stop the Utility Tax Committee" and launched a recall effort against all five councilmembers.

Getting Involved
Sarver was invited to one of the recall meetings and consented to become a part of the committee. "I will get involved, but I am doing so because of non-responsiveness on the part of the city council. I don't know enough about city finances. I don't know enough about the utility tax. I haven't gotten into it, but I feel any citizen is entitled to have questions answered and be treated with respect."

Sarver worked hard on the recall and emerged as a leader of the effort. The recall was successful. In fact, history was made since this was the first time in the nation's history that an entire city council was recalled at one time.

Sarver thought her government work was completed and had no intention of doing anything further. However, the recall committee members convinced her to run for a city council seat. The field was packed, with 21 candidates running for the five vacant seats; and she was the only woman. Much to her surprise, she emerged victorious as the number three vote getter.

Although Sarver ran on an anti-tax platform, she admits that she did not examine the city budget or annual financial reports. She just assumed that there were a lot of places where fat could be cut out of the budget. Sarver confesses that she walked in totally "green." In addition, the recalled council had cleverly adopted a budget that was balanced by the utility tax; yet they had let it expire just before leaving office. This left the newly-elected council with a terrible dilemma: They could adopt the despised tax or make deep cuts in the recently adopted budget. The new city council kept faith with the electorate by opting to forgo the tax and cut the budget.

The budget was eventually balanced but at a very high price. Several positions were cut, and the reserves were virtually wiped out. In the end, the new council had carved $1.7 million from the Covina budget. The job was not done, however, as an additional $2.3 million deficit was projected for the next fiscal year's budget.

Political Courage

This is where the story becomes unusual. Linda Sarver and fellow councilmember, Tom Falls, also an anti-tax advocate, began examining ways to cut the budget. "I literally thought that they had money under every rock. Instead, I found that the staff was counting pencils," Sarver recounted. To these new councilmembers' dismay, this quaint suburban town of 44,000 would have to terminate another 15 percent of its remaining 213 full time positions and eliminate several important community services.

Linda Sarver summed up the dilemma with the following: "Oh my God, I can't do this. I can't live in this city and lay off seven cops, nine fire fighters, close one of three fire stations, shut down the library and eliminate parks and recreation. I'm not willing to do it. If that is done, I will resign and move because Covina is no longer a place I want to raise my family. This is when I had to say, I was wrong."

Covina Mayor Linda Sarver displayed courage by renouncing a no-tax campaign promise after examining city finances

Outreach

Sarver and Falls did not sit still. They identified other alternatives to cuts such as a special district to assess fees for fire services, permitting a card club or instituting the utility tax. Sarver and Falls then hit the road and forthrightly presented the dilemma at dozens of community meetings. They also consulted with their many campaign supporters. The response was conclusive, the utility tax was preferable. Convinced of citizen support, the city council imposed, on a 4 to 1 vote, a 8.25 percent utility tax. This tax was 2.25 percent higher than the original tax passed by the recalled city council. Most of the people attending the meeting spoke in favor of the tax.

Reaction

The anti-tax group's reaction was swift with about ten diehard members going what was described as ballistic. "Oh, she's now one of them. She converted. She's bought into the government's philosophy. She betrayed us."

The group mounted four recall attempts against Sarver, Falls and Mayor Thomas O'Leary, but each effort failed to reach the ballot for technical reasons. According to Sarver, it was an unbelievably difficult and stressful time. Insults, attempted break-ins at her house, threatening phone calls and anonymous letters were part of the harassment. "Letters full of lies and half-truths were sent to the local newspapers, and someone had actually picked the lock to my front door," recalled Sarver.

Reacting to the pressure, the city council put the utility tax on the ballot as an advisory measure. It was advisory because state law, at that time, did not permit the city council to make it binding. The vote was decisive; the utility tax was ratified. This took the wind out of the anti-tax group's sails, and the ugly treatment ceased. Later, Sarver was made Mayor by her colleagues. This story brings out the best and worst of local government. It also lays a basis for several elected official tips on guarding the public checkbook.

Tip No. 1:   ***Don't be Hamstrung by Unrealistic or Uninformed Election Promises***

By now, it is probably too late to advise you to avoid making campaign promises without thoroughly researching their practicality.

Assuming you have tendered promises, it is best to keep faith with the voters and try to make good on them. If you have made unachievable promises and commitments, let's hope they are of the venial and not of the "Read My Lips" type.

When announcing his mayoral candidacy on November 18, 1992, at the Sportsmen's Lodge in Los Angeles, millionaire Richard Riordan emphasized public safety. At that time he unveiled a plan to add 3000 police officers to the city's 7400 officer force. This 40 percent increase in personnel soon became the linchpin of his campaign. Slick campaign literature quoted Riordan as saying that the city must immediately "hire, train and deploy an additional 3000 officers." The promise took on more meaning when, at a public debate, candidate Riordan elaborated: "I promise that I will add 3000 police officers over four years. If not, I guarantee you I won't run again." Richard Riordan, rode his ambitious police expansion plan to victory as the new mayor of Los Angeles.

Mayor Riordan quickly learned about roadblocks that candidate Riordan did not know or fully appreciate. He found (what he termed) a stultifying city charter, overly cumbersome competitive bidding requirements, outmoded civil service rules and powerful advocates for the status quo. He also had to convince a skeptical police chief, Willie Williams, who was worried about such practical issues as testing, recruiting, training, equipping and housing 3000 new officers.

This was the moment of truth. Riordan could have used the Sarver approach and explained that he was uninformed about the inner workings of city hall when he made his promise. He could take the heat early in his honeymoon rather than at the next election. Mayor Riordan chose the path of doggedly pursuing his original promise. "As leaders, I believe we must have the courage to set high goals — and we must have an unwavering commitment to meet those goals. Making the promise is the easy part — having the courage to follow up is the challenge," Riordan explained.

Over the next few years, the majority of the Los Angeles City Council took issue with the seemingly overemphasis on the expansion plan. They increasingly began to question the logic of expanding so quickly and at the expense of all other city departments. Councilmember Richard Alatorree, referring to Los Angeles' $4 billion budget complained: "This is not the police budget; this is the budget for the entire city.....I'd like to have 12,000 police officers, but not at the expense of everything else. Everybody's going to say public safety is the most important issue, but at what price? Having safe parks and safe libraries is also public safety."

One-time ally Councilmember Laura Chick explained in a letter to her constituents that Riordan was trying to finance the police force expansion by relying on: "rosy assumptions, questionable borrowing, dubious financial transfers and unstable one-time monies." This letter was sent to constituents only after Riordan had asked Chick's constituents to put pressure on her to support the expansion.

Riordan was successful in his first two budgets and increased the Police Department according to his four year plan. In a third year showdown between the city council and Riordan, the city council prevailed and scaled back Riordan's annual addition from 710 officers to 450 officers.

Mayor Riordan was not going to quit his quest. In the next fiscal year's budget proposal, Police Chief Williams submitted a $923.6 million budget, which included $200 million to get the hiring plan back on track. This represented phase IV of the Mayor's program to hire 3000 more officers. Williams, caught in a bind, indicated that he was aware of the city's severe fiscal constraints, but he was "....nevertheless submitting the request per the Mayor's instructions."

The city council again felt the pressure and had to explain to the community why they were against expanding the police force. Councilmember Mike Feuer said the city is already projecting a $150 million deficit. Where are we going to get the additional funds?

Unlike Mayor Sarver, Mayor Riordan decided to stick to his campaign pledge, even after he found out the improbability of achieving it. "Leadership is setting a goal even if getting there is tough. We can't sit back and say we can't get there. We have to get there," explained Mayor Riordan.

Los Angeles Mayor Richard Riordan reneged on his promise to not run again if he did not add 3000 officers to the police force.

During February 1997, three months before the election, Mayor Riordan reversed himself and proclaimed his 1993 pledge as "irrelevant" and said that what was important was his administration's success in hiring police and building the Los Angeles Police Department (LAPD) into the largest, most diverse department in its history. His rival, Tom Hayden, wasn't about to let the issue slide: "He failed to get 3,000 police, and he said he would quit if he failed to do that. He should honor his pledge to the taxpayers."

Riordan was reelected notwithstanding his failure to achieve his campaign promise. The community recognized that he had made substantial progress toward his goal, but he had expended considerable political goodwill with the council on his dogged adherence to that promise. In the end, he still caught hell and was accused of being disingenuous by trying to redefine his original promise. The moral — don't be strangled by campaign promises that you made without sufficient information. People expect you to have a platform when you run because they want to know what you are going to do or not do. If you make a mistake or you are wrong, admit it early on. "I think the problem with government is people are afraid to say I made a mistake," says Mayor Sarver, "When I came out, people said are you crazy? I didn't understand what a gutsy move it was. Fortunately, the people understood. What's wrong with the truth?"

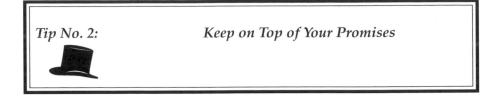

Tip No. 2:   ***Keep on Top of Your Promises***

While running for Mayor of San Francisco, Frank Jordan, ran a simple, yet very effective campaign. He had a brilliant idea — why not use post cards to get the message across to voters? Jordan created a series of eight cards that criticized the incumbent mayor, Art Agnos' performance. Each card was limited to one issue and included a message about Jordan's proven leadership, creativity or problem solving abilities. At his inauguration Jordan asked the voters to give him six months to deliver on his promises.

Showing unusual restraint, the *San Francisco Examiner* waited twelve months before publishing their "admittedly critical perspective" on Mayor Jordan's performance. Here are some of the original post card messages and the *Examiner's* assessment:

Jordan's Post Card Message: Mayor Agnos' solution to budget deficits has been to cut services and increase taxes. Closing libraries and raising Muni fares are unacceptable.

Examiner Comments: Jordan has decided to close libraries on certain days and presided over a raise in municipal fares. The main library is now closed every Sunday. Jordan cut the zoo budget, which now is in danger of losing accreditation. He eliminated one of the city's several emergency ambulances, reducing citywide response time by an average of 30 seconds. This is below state standards.

Jordan's Post Card Message: San Francisco's police department is short nearly 200 police officers. Frank Jordan has promised to bring back the police department strength in order to return safety to our streets.

Examiner Comments: San Francisco's murders reached a 10-year high in Jordan's first year, up 16 percent over Art Agnos' final year.

Robbery increased 21 percent, assault 16 percent, and burglary 12 percent. Jordan also cut the district attorney's budget. In his first year, Jordan went through four police chiefs.

Jordan's Post Card Message: Just try calling for a police officer, obtaining a building permit, getting an illegally parked car out of the driveway, finding a clean Muni bus or getting a pothole patched.

Examiner Comments: Emergency 911 calls in Jordan's first year took twice as long to answer, and Jordan has endorsed voice mail for non-emergency police calls. Police no longer respond to routine burglaries, car thefts or assaults. Instead, they mail the victim a form to be filed out and mailed back.

Jordan's Post Card Message: Not only are the deputy mayors overpaid, but many come from outside the city.

Examiner Comments: Jordan did not abolish Agnos's top paid positions. He put his own appointees into the same slots but changed their job titles. He then raised their salaries.

Frank Jordan, even though he had served as San Francisco Police Chief did not realize the difficulty of implementing change. He also had not counted on a severe recession and a massive deficit. The question is: How do you avoid a hit piece like the *Examiner's?* You probably can't, but you can take the initiative and establish the framework for your evaluation. Jordan let the *San Francisco Examiner* steal his thunder by using his post card concept against him.

While it is easy to sit back and be a Monday morning quarterback, Mayor Jordan should have immediately transformed his campaign promises into goal statements and then lobbied the board of supervisors to adopt them. This would have required some compromise, but it would have legitimatized his platform. Regular reporting on these items, using the same technique, may have preempted the *Examiner's* coup. The other tips in this chapter will help you make the transition from candidate to governing board member.

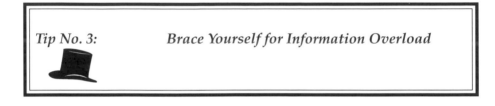

Tip No. 3:   ***Brace Yourself for Information Overload***

Linda Sarver, Richard Riordan and Frank Jordan, along with thousands of other newly elected officials, discovered that public business is much more complex than assumed by outside observers. It's much like an iceberg with only a small fraction visible to the public. Unless you have dealt with governmental finance, you are going to be momentarily stunned by the apparent complexity.

Gear your mind to process a lot of information. You are going to be introduced to financial terms like CAFR, GAAP, fund accounting and BANS (See Glossary for definitions). Since these terms and concepts will be dropped on you all at once, they will seem more overwhelming than they really are.

All newly elected officials go through a learning curve. Those with financial experience will tell you that it takes about six months. Others say that even after two years, they are still learning. As you assimilate the new language and learn the processes, things will become more clear. It just takes time and a probing mind. If you don't understand something, ask that it be explained.

Tip No. 4:   ***Switch to Your Governing Mode***

Seasoned elected officials will tell you that the skills they use to win an election are counterproductive as governing tools. In a campaign you must be competitive. You must stand out and in many cases, you wind up attacking your opponents. As an elected official you are part of a group, and to be successful, you must get a majority of them to support your positions. Collaboration, consensus building and compromise are your important new tools. Barbara Dye, Palos Verdes Peninsula Board of Trustee candidate, said it this way: "Unfortunately, the skills one needs to win a campaign are not the skills one requires to do the job of school board trustee effectively. Candidates must be pushy, thick skinned and ambitious, while the job of trustee requires one to be an effective listener and consensus builder."

Successful governing board members win their colleagues respect and confidence. Peter Hill, the very popular, newly elected councilmember of the City of Rocklin, California was convinced he had the right strategy. "I was sure that simply going to council meetings, pressing my ideas and pointing out the faults in everyone else's suggestions would make my colleagues see things my way." Hill, soon found that colleagues were not only ignoring him, they were beginning to shun him.

Former councilmembers noticed Hill's plight and decided to pull him aside and provide a little in-service counselling. "They suggested I remember that I was a member of a team (not the captain) made up of the council, staff and constituents, all working for a better community. They reminded me that, as a member of the council, I had only one vote; and since it takes a majority to approve an action, I had to persuade at least two others to vote with me. They also pointed out that it is difficult to get people to vote with you when they are mad at you."

Councilmember Hill summed it up when he said: "Clearly, there was nothing new in this wisdom, yet it is easily forgotten. Unfortunately, by forgetting it you become less effective as a councilmember to the detriment of the team and the community."

Tip No. 5:   ***Obtain the Key Documents***

Many agencies have formal or informal orientation programs for newly elected officials. At these sessions the key documents are explained and distributed. If you do not get your agency's key financial documents, don't hesitate to request copies from the management staff. However, getting the information is not enough. Request a one-on-one briefing of these documents. Put the burden on management to explain the significance of these documents in concise, understandable language. Don't be mesmerized or intimidated by the jargon, apparent complexity or sheer size of the stack. Ask staff to cut to the chase and focus on your information requirements. You don't want a laborious lesson in governmental accounting. You want bottom line explanations on what is in the documents and how the information will help you in your oversight responsibilities.

A list of the most important financial documents include:

1. Annual Operating Budget
2. Annual Capital Budget
3. Comprehensive Annual Financial Report (CAFR)
4. Capital Improvements Program (CIP)
5. Long Range Financial Plan
6. Interim Financial Reports on Expenditures and Revenues
7. Investment Reports
8. Register of Warrants

Tip No. 6: **Build a Positive Relationship with Staff**

First the downside. A quarrelsome elected official once confided to me that it was easy to attack staff in public because "they won't fight back." It was a devastating disclosure, but one that rang true. I shared this revelation with a savvy city manager who said: "Sure, I will not fight back in public, but you can be sure I'll get even." What the elected official didn't appreciate was the power staff exercises. Governing bodies adopt the decrees, budgets, policies, resolutions and laws. Staff implements them. As a directive makes its way down the chain of command, different things can happen to it. Its purpose, value, impact, and suspected motive are analyzed. If it is determined to be negative, it can be delayed, put on the bottom of the pile or lost forever.

Some agency staffs are so bureaucratic and self-serving that they have forgotten their role. They dispense minimum information and provide only the information they want the governing body to have. The thought process goes like this: "Elected officials are itinerants — we'll be here a long time after they have departed."

Mayor Sarver saw it this way, "In some cities I see an attitude on the part of city staff that the mayor and city council only need to know what we staff want them to know. Staff is really doing a disservice to the community and to themselves. Elected officials need information to govern."

Now the positive part. Your staff wants to work with you. They have the skill and expertise to help you achieve your goals. They will treat you with respect and try to please you.

Ron Gonzales, former Vice-Mayor of Sunnyvale, California expressed it this way: "The campaign was the easy part of the job. What you're about to learn is that you are now government. All those problems

---

which were so easy to point out during the campaign are now your problems which will haunt you during your whole term if not solved. There is one resource that can either be your biggest asset or liability as an elected official — your staff."

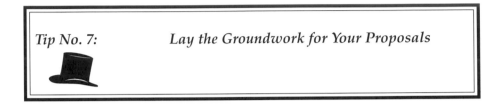

Tip No. 7:   *Lay the Groundwork for Your Proposals*

Frank Marley won a tough election victory and was elated. As the last light flickered and extinguished at his makeshift campaign headquarters, he savored his success.

He was now on top of the world and began counting the hours before taking office. Fortunately, he had two weeks before his term officially began, so he had time to prepare for the challenge of being a school board trustee.

Frank Marley mentally envisioned all the things he would accomplish. During the campaign, he met with scores of constituents who really opened his eyes. There are many problems to tackle. Not to worry. Marley had plenty of good ideas on how to solve every one of the problems.

The big night finally arrived. After deserving accolades were presented to the outgoing members, Frank Marley was sworn in and seated as a new trustee.

Marley was called upon to say a few words. As he proudly presented his well thought out ideas to his new colleagues he couldn't help notice that none were paying attention. In fact they appeared down right rude. The trustee next to him was reading her mail, another was reading his agenda packet, and the two next to him were whispering to each other. Even the chair appeared to be preoccupied. Only members of Marley's family and his campaign workers were listening. Marley was devastated.

Frank Marley made the mistake that many newly elected officials make. They assume office with a plethora of ideas and expect them to be embraced right away. Governing bodies do not operate that way. The governing body may have considered and rejected Marley's ideas before. Or they may be privy to confidential legal advice regarding the issue. One school board member put it this way: "You've got to earn your stripes before we will take you seriously."

New ideas must be planted and given time to germinate. Support must be garnered. It takes a lot more time to get things done when working with a group of people. It's like a round of golf. In the overwhelming number of cases, you will not get a hole in one. It takes several different shots to get the ball in the hole. Ginger Bremberg, long term member of the Glendale City Council expressed it this way: "The popularity contest is over after you win the elective position. Your new colleagues only know what you said during the campaign and are curious about how you will perform. Don't anticipate that you will be able to save the city during your first month in office!"

Tip No. 8:   ***Don't be Afraid to Ask Questions***

Most public officials cringe when they hear advice like "There are no such things as dumb questions; there are only dumb answers," or "The only dumb question is an unasked question." Unfortunately, there are dumb questions. There are also dumb responses such as Dan Quayle's misspelling "potato," or Bill Clinton answering a question about the type of underwear he wears. Elected officials learn very quickly that a dumb question or statement can be very embarrassing. They would rather be caught dead than be humiliated in public.

As a result, many newly elected officials play it safe and hold back from asking questions. To learn about finances, however, you must take the risk and ask questions. This is the best way elected officials get beyond the written material that is provided. Well stated questions are powerful. They allow you to deviate from the channeled approach laid out in financial documents and to develop your own perspective on what things really mean. They allow you to fill in the white space between the words and numbers.

The type of question you ask will dictate the response you will get. There are two basic types of questions, closed-ended and open-ended. Closed-ended questions can be answered with a yes or no, or with a simple statement of fact. Examples of closed questions include:

- How much did we collect in property taxes?
- When does the fiscal year begin?
- Who performs the organization's audit?
- Was notice of the budget hearing given?

Closed-ended questions like "How much is the total general fund expenditure budget?" will elicit a specific response, such as "$16,500,000." These types of questions work well for getting specific information in a hurry.

Open-ended questions are used to get more in-depth responses and cannot be answered with a simple yes or no. Here are examples of open-ended questions:

- Why wouldn't it be better to contract this service?
- What will this new program accomplish?
- What does the department manager think about the proposed consolidation?

If you ask an open-ended question like "What will the budget look like next year?" you can get any number of responses, such as "Well, that depends. If you are asking about the entire budget including all funds; it looks pretty good. The general fund does not look as good. Property taxes are up, but we expect sales taxes to decline. Other revenues are very flat."

Open-ended questions also help the questioner get the responder's underlying thinking and assumptions. These questions are very good for getting general information about the budget and financial thinking. Notice also that the responder to the second question preferred to couch the response in terms of revenues rather than expenditures and did not deem it necessary to provide specific dollar information.

Both types of questions have a purpose. The closed-ended will help you get specific responses to questions you need to answer for your constituents. The open-ended questions help you get to the thought processes behind a response. The information elicited helps build consensus. A question to a colleague like "What reservations do you have with the new aquatics program?" will help you identify concerns and possible alternatives.

In some cases, you can start with open ended questions and follow up with specific questions. Recognize also that you may not get the information you were looking for with your first question. If so, re-phrase the question. If you do not get a satisfactory answer, don't give up. It is staff's job to explain things in a clear, understandable manner. Judy Buchan, Redwood City, California councilmember put it this way: "Never stop asking questions, and don't be satisfied until your questions are answered properly."

Along with asking the right questions, you will get more useful information if you phrase questions so that they do not put staff or colleagues on the defensive. "How could you let such a dumb thing happen?" will undoubtedly get evasive and vague responses. "What were the assumptions leading to your decision?" will get a more helpful and less defensive response. Unfortunately, some elected officials never learn that using questions as a way to shame or blame makes people sufficiently suspicious and gun shy, so that only minimal information is provided.

Throughout this book, "safe" questions will be suggested to help you unravel the mystique of your agency's budget and finances.

> ### Tip No. 9:   *Don't be Reluctant to Say "I Don't Know"*
>
>

You don't need to give an answer to every question. While elected officials prefer to provide informed responses to constituents, it is not always possible or wise. Seasoned elected officials will tell you that if you don't know, say so. People will accept a response like "I don't have that information now, but I will find out and get back to you by today." By following up as promised, you will show diligence and responsiveness.

> ### Tip No. 10:   *Get on a Budget or Finance Committee*
>
>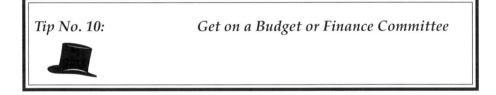

Many governing boards use subcommittees to handle budget and financial functions, such as examining budget proposals or reviewing the register of warrants. These subcommittees are great places to learn about local government finances. They are usually conducted in a more informal manner, and it is safer to ask questions. It is also easier to get into issues in much more depth. If you are not appointed to a budget or finance committee, see if you can attend these meetings as an observer.

Tip No. 11:   *Protect Your Meeting Time Like the Last Potato Chip*

The overwhelming majority of local governments do not meet on a daily basis. Statistics compiled by the National League of Cities show that the typical city meets two to four times a month, and meetings last an average of two to four hours. Most counties, school districts and special districts also meet as infrequently. If your government meets once a week for four hours, this amounts to only 208 hours per year.

Unfortunately, many governing board members forget how limited time is and waste it on minor items. This leaves less time for the important items. Since meeting time is a scarce commodity, you don't want it wasted on insignificant matters.

You should assume that you own a percentage of your governing body's meeting time. Your ownership share is equivalent to your percentage of the total vote. Don't let others pilfer your time and wile it away.

Recognize also that the most important time is at the beginning of the meeting. This is when everyone is fresh and unencumbered by meeting detail. Don't spend too much of this high quality time on mundane items like correcting minutes or questioning the register of warrants.

Tip No. 12:   *Don't Rely on Osmosis to Learn About Public Finances*

Tom Mathey was newly elected to the Water District. He ran on a narrow platform and garnered considerable community support. His platform was based upon his leading a successful fight against a high density residential development which would have required a costly new reservoir.

Mathey had very little organizational experience and absolutely no exposure to public finances. He privately expressed his apprehensions to other board members. The chair, Mike Gomez, told him not to worry and to follow his lead. "Vote on those items I come out strongly for, and vote against those I take a stand against," Gomez told Mathey.

Not satisfied, Mathey asked board member, Margaret Bates, how she mastered finances. "I would like to help you, Tom, but I just don't have the time. Why not do it the way I had to do it — just watch and muddle through. While I vote my conscience, I like the thought process that Gomez uses. You can't go wrong following his lead."

Mathey decided to go along with the advice. What he didn't know at the time was that Gomez and Bates were actually in cahoots with two local contractors and were funnelling hundreds of thousands of dollars worth of district contracts their way. When the scam was made public, Mathey came under suspicion with Bates and Gomez since his votes paralleled theirs. While this may be an unusual situation, it does point out the vulnerability that newly elected officials face. New officials need to know something about finances and budgets to avoid being victimized by other members who have their own agendas.

Sitting back and observing your colleagues discuss issues and make proposals used to be an acceptable learning strategy. Newly elected officials were not expected to know about budgets and finance. Many elected officials have become very proficient by sticking to the learn-by-watching strategy. Things have changed, however, and this strategy is no longer viable. Newly elected officials are expected to hit the ground running.

Tip No. 13:　　　　　　　　*Get Used to the Sunshine*

One of the first legal requirements newly elected officials are confronted with are the open meeting laws. Sunshine laws have been enacted because a few governing boards have acted illegally or made important decisions in secret with no public input. During the election campaign, you may have gotten used to caucusing and making important decisions in private with the key people surrounding you. As a governing board member, you must forgo the closed door approach to decision making. With a few exceptions, you must now make decisions, and the discussions leading to those decisions, public. Every state now has some type of sunshine or open meeting law.

It is important to learn the provisions of your open meeting law. Most states permit limited exceptions to their open meeting laws, such as meeting in private when evaluating the chief administrator or instructing negotiators on labor relations. Find out what is permissible and what is not; and when in doubt, err on the side of openness.

While some violations of the sunshine laws are blatant attempts to hide something from the public, most are innocent transgressions. For example, the governing body may go into a closed session for a legitimate reason. During or after the permitted deliberations, discussions may drift to prohibited subjects. You'll find that sitting in a closed session is much more comfortable than in a public meeting, and it is easy to inadvertently drift into the trap of discussing other issues.

When open meeting laws first went into effect, some governing boards complained about how these laws inhibit decision making. Full and free discussion are hampered, they said. However, with time, most governing board members feel that the laws have had no adverse effect on the public process and actually benefit it. Governing boards that are comfortable with their open meeting laws say it results in a more participative process and that the public develops greater confidence in their elected representatives.

Recognize that newspapers have a strong interest in enforcing the open meeting laws. A good deal of their information comes from public agencies, and they will go to court to force compliance.

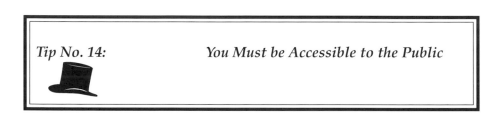

Tip No. 14:　　　　　　　　*You Must be Accessible to the Public*

Closeness to your constituents is the single most important difference between local and other levels of government. When people have a problem, don't be surprised to find them at your door step. Unlike members of a state legislature or Congress, you are accessible twenty-four hours a day. Most local officials have publicly listed phone numbers which result in late night and early morning calls. While you may have a formal meeting every two weeks, there are countless other meetings with community groups, neighborhood associations, and other jurisdictional representatives. You cannot go to the market, visit a school, or attend a youth event without becoming engaged in local politics.

As a side note, most of the people who attend governing board meetings have a specific problem or agenda. As people walk into your meetings you will find yourself watching very closely and asking yourself, who are they and why are they here?

Tip No. 15: **Establish a Continuous Self-Education Program**

The really effective elected officials have one thing in common — they continue to learn more about their job everyday. You will be bombarded by lots of information, and you must become selective as to what is the most important. You will be continuously challenged because of your accessibility. You'll find that you cannot buffer yourself like a member of Congress. You must develop your skills to spontaneously respond to difficult financial questions. This gets easier after you begin a self-education program. Elected officials do this by:

1.   Attending relevant classes.
2.   Reading professional magazines and books.
3.   Networking with colleagues in other governments.
4.   Establishing your own web page with a response section.
5.   Attending conferences and workshops.
6.   Obtaining in-house training and explanations from your agency's financial and budget officers.

Know Your Financial Oversight Responsibilities

"When I think of oversight, I look for red flags. I look for something wrong. I look for something to pry up and start asking questions about. The indicators were not there."

Roger Stanton
Orange County Supervisor,
cited by the Grand Jury for willful misconduct
and oversight failures

The Setting
The County of Los Angeles had been on the verge of bankruptcy for many years. It seemed like every penny counted, except for some departments.

Over the years, Sheriff Sherman Block told the Los Angeles County Board of Supervisors that he was running a lean operation with little or no fat in his billion dollar operating budget. Due to tight budgets, the sheriff decided to shut down several jails, creating a severe shortage of beds. This, in turn, left the sheriff with no alternative but to release inmates before they served their entire court imposed terms. Unfortunately, this helped Los Angeles County win a national distinction it did not relish — the jail system with the lowest percentage of prisoner time served. On average, Los Angeles County inmates wound up serving only 23 percent of their time.

Sheriff Block was an elected sheriff and a highly popular one. Over his eighteen-year tenure, he built up a tremendous amount of power. As a result, most county supervisors paid homage to him and rarely questioned his budgeting practices. When they did muster courage to question him, it was done apologetically. Moreover, they would back off quickly if the sheriff resisted. The most tenacious supervisor, Zev Yaroslavsky, complained: "Every elected official, including the President of the United States and a county supervisor, has to disclose how they spend their money and don't have to go on a wild goose chase to find it. The same level of fiscal scrutiny does not exist with the sheriff."

The Twin Towers Jail facility presents an example. For over 14 months, the new state of the art, $373 million dollar jail remained empty because Block said he did not have the money in his budget to operate and maintain the facility. Feeling community pressure, the board of supervisors seriously considered directing other departments and the sheriff to cut their budgets to provide for the opening of the facility. Block dug in his heels and threatened the board with taking more than 400 deputy sheriffs off the street to fund the jail opening. The supervisors, tinged by the political heat, relented.

Los Angeles County's $373 million, top-of-the-line jail sat empty for 14 months while the board of supervisors and sheriff tried to figure out where to get operating funds.

Public pressure, however, did not wane; and miraculously the sheriff announced at a board meeting that he had found $62 million from savings and outside sources to open and operate the jail. One person at the meeting observed, "The supervisors were so elated, they fell over themselves congratulating him. They should have been asking him the hard questions about not being able to find the money before."

The sheriff also refused to let the county executive, Sally Reed, institute a program budget approach in the department. The county executive's plan was to divide the sheriff's budget into five programs — administration, patrol, detectives, custody and court services, so that the supervisors could get a better idea of where money was being spent. The board, even though this budget improvement would have assisted them in their oversight responsibility, backed off and supported Sheriff Block.

Investigation
It took an investigative team of *Los Angeles Times* reporters however, to goad the Los Angeles County Board of Supervisors to begin exercising their oversight responsibility. This team identified wasteful spending practices and failure to follow fiscal controls within the department that could not be brushed aside by the supervisors.

Many examples were uncovered by the *Times*. Some notable ones included:

- Subsidizing a prisoner-operated bakery which could be privatized at huge savings.

- Purchasing a high grade of poultry for prisoners and jail employees that even the Defense Department did not provide to U.S. armed forces personnel. The chicken cuts were usually reserved for hotel catering and cost twice as much.

- Spending $861,000 for premium blend coffee, which the vendor admitted was among the highest grade of coffees they offered.

- Providing deputies and jail employees meals without charging for them as other police agencies do.

- Rejecting the lowest bid for materials and services, twice as often as other county departments.

State Auditor

Two weeks after the *Los Angeles Times* articles were published, the California State Auditor jumped on the band wagon and publicly suggested that the Los Angeles County Sheriff could save at least $44 million per year by hiring civilians for positions held by highly trained deputies and by cutting frills such as the inmate-run bakery.

The auditor's findings included:

- The sheriff's department operates a bakery that produces baked goods such as bread, rolls, biscuits, cookies and pastries for its inmates at all county jails. The auditor compared the cost to operate the bakery with the cost to purchase baked goods and found that the county could save more that $1.2 million by privatizing the operation.

- The department could save up to $4.3 million by using 141 more civilian employees. Many routine, mundane jobs were being filled by highly trained and well compensated deputies. Civilians generally require lower salaries, fewer benefits and less specialized training than sworn officers. This also applies to administrative and technical positions that do not require direct law enforcement activity such as budget, graphic artists and complaint desk.

- From $25.4 to $33.6 million could be saved by using civilian corrections officers instead of sheriff's deputies to staff its jails.

- The department "gold plated" its original estimate to open the new jail and should have been more forthright. The fact that they could come up with a plan after the heat came down shows that the management was not as concerned about taxes as they should have been.

The entire blame for the jail fiasco cannot be laid at the sheriff's doorstep, however. The board of supervisors authorized placing the $373 million bond issue to construct the jail on the ballot without ascertaining that money was available to open and operate it.

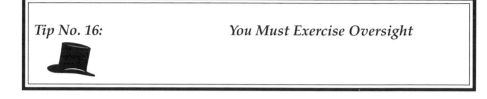

Tip No. 16:   *You Must Exercise Oversight*

How do you, as an elected official, guard the public checkbook? It's accomplished by providing financial oversight. Financial oversight involves setting policy, making sure that it is carried out, monitoring activities, and evaluating results. Guarding the public checkbook does not necessarily mean cutting back or freezing expenditures. If you don't spend money on some items such as capital improvements now, they may cost you more in the future.

A governing board must have the capability to monitor the fiscal management of staff. Oversight is a skill that must be developed and continually honed. Governing board members come from all walks of life such as school teachers, realtors, physicians, lawyers, homemakers, and business owners. Few have had exposure to governmental finance, and even fewer are formally trained in the field.

Elected officials are the first to admit that they need to improve their oversight skill. In a study of elected official perceptions conducted by the National League of Cities, elected officials rated overseeing program effectiveness and administrative performance among the lowest of the activities they do well (see Figure 1).

The governing body role is to establish policy and to make sure it is carried out. The management staff is charged with carrying out these policies. While the governing body is accountable to the voters, the management staff is accountable to the governing body.

Management staff has a great deal of power within the organization. Staff members are responsible for establishing and enforcing financial controls. They can also override controls when they consider it necessary. The governing body is the only entity that can exercise on-going oversight of the management staff and their activities.

Figure 1
City Council Effectiveness in Handling Major
Functions

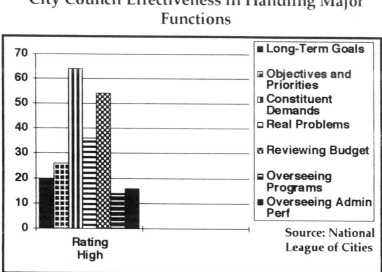

- Long-Term Goals
- Objectives and Priorities
- Constituent Demands
- Real Problems
- Reviewing Budget
- Overseeing Programs
- Overseeing Admin Perf

Source: National
League of Cities

Recognize that some staff members regard inquisitive governing bodies with trepidation, fearing that legislators will improperly interfere with the management of the organization. Such an attitude can frustrate the oversight function.

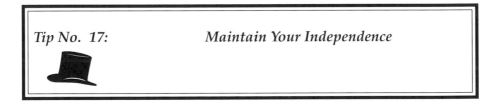

Tip No. 17:   *Maintain Your Independence*

In the case of the sheriff's department, a type of political deference existed which made supervisors clamor for the support of the sheriff. This contributed to their hands off approach to oversight. Shirking from political power, acceptance of stonewalling, unquestioned acceptance of the security argument and favorable treatment, all contributed to the breakdown in oversight. Ruth Holton, executive director of California Common Cause notes, "It is the role of the board of supervisors to know how the sheriff's department is spending its money, especially when money is extraordinarily tight. Just because you have a cozy relationship with the board of supervisors should not make you immune to scrutiny."

It is relatively easy to spot a governing body that tip-toes around a powerful department's budget. Typical behaviors include:

- Diverting attention to inconsequential items.
- Using rhetorical questions or questions that flatter the department.
- Being reluctant to ask penetrating questions.
- Failing to press when a satisfactory answer is not obtained.
- Accepting bold, unsubstantiated statements.
- Being obviously supportive in contrast to the treatment of other departments.

These approaches are used in an attempt to signal support for the favored department and at the same time convince the public that the elected official is carrying out the oversight function. To most people the effort is very transparent.

Every government has favored departments. In cities and counties, police and fire departments generally receive preferential treatment from their governing bodies. When other budgets are cut, public safety budgets remain untouched. This is understandable to a degree since public safety is generally felt to be the most important service provided by local government. However, failing to subject a department to scrutiny can only result in that department paying less attention to how dollars are spent. It should also be remembered that even the "favored" departments have administrative and overhead activities that can be bloated.

Tip No. 18:   ***Public Finances Need Not Be Boring***

In many organizations, the method in which financial information is presented to governing boards creates boredom. Laborious reviews of endless computer printouts or their equivalent can put anyone to sleep. The focus is put on the detail and not the big picture. Part of the problem results from allowing the accountants and financial experts to develop the reports. Another part of the problem results from governing body members not insisting that the reports be simplified or supplemented to help focus on the important policy questions.

Direct staff to use imagination in designing and delivering financial reports. If the report format is fixed and cannot be changed, ask that supplemental information be provided. Have staff put pizazz into them.

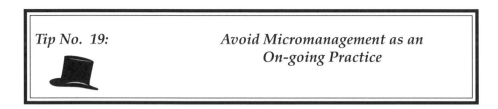

Tip No. 19:   *Avoid Micromanagement as an*
                            On-going Practice

Micromanagement generally refers to excessive focus on the details of implementation and a neglect of policy formulation. It means getting involved in the "how-to" rather than the "what."

Some micromanagement is innocent. Newly elected officials often come to their positions with minimal training in policy determination. They also are not used to having decisions carried out by others. They find a very complex system that has resulted from many years of regulations that have been layered over each other. The desire is to cut through the bureaucracy and get the job done. Only after they have delved into the detail, do they see how deep and counterproductive the micromanagement pit is. It happens over and over again, governing board members mess with the insignificant while the organization goes into fiscal crisis. The Washington, D.C. School Board was disbanded because board members failed to deal with the fiscal crisis before them. The oversight board, which was established by Congress to reform district finances, commented that school board members were spending more time on parking privileges and their own pay than the fiscal crisis.

Not all micromanagement is innocent. In some cases, governing board members want to keep their fingers in the detail so they can influence the award of contracts to friends, make purchases from supporters, or make sure that favored people are hired by the agency.

The Los Angeles Metropolitan Transit Authority Board, which was charged with building one of the largest subway projects in the nation, became so involved with internal meddling that the U.S. Transportation Department threatened to defund the project. In December 1996, Joseph Drew resigned as Metropolitan Transit Authority Chief Executive, complaining about micromanagement and infighting among board and staff members. His announcement was followed within a week by another resignation of a top official, the Construction Chief, Stanley Phernambucq. He revealed that he was quitting due to frustration with a board that had attempted to interfere with contracts and had humiliated his staff in public. "In public meetings they will look at you like you're the witness to a crime and treat you like you're never capable of doing anything right. It made our guys feel like hell," he said. "We call it playing 'Stump the Chump.' You can ask anyone a bunch a questions and sooner or later they'll get one wrong. Well, I was tired of playing the chump."

About the same time, Coopers and Lybrand issued a scathing audit report that characterized the MTA's operational management as "lacking basic leadership skills and clear goals, ruled by fear and had lost the trust of the board." The audit concluded that the board had also become too meddlesome: "Board members got to the point that their aides would call professional staff members directly and put pressure on to influence the procurement process and day-to-day construction activities."

Saying enough is enough, U. S. Transportation Secretary Federico Pena sought adoption of a five point plan to get the massive subway project back on track. One item required the MTA Board of Directors to develop a code of conduct that "lays out the appropriate role and behavior of board members as they deal with their oversight responsibility."

Whether innocent or not, micromanagement is destructive to the organization. When the governing body preoccupies itself with telling staff how to do something, it results in a demoralized and unproductive staff. Initiative is killed, and staff relegates itself to waiting for direction. More importantly, when the governing body immerses itself in detail, a policy vacuum is created. This inevitably results in staff filling the vacuum, and a reversal of roles occurs with the governing body tending the detail and the staff deciding the significant long range policy and financial issues.

Elected officials provide various justifications for getting into the detail, but few really stand up to scrutiny. Here are five common excuses:

1.   The public expects us to have the answers.

While the public expects you to get answers, it does not expect you to wind up doing someone else's job. Your responsibility as an elected official is to get the answers from staff. Adept elected officials fulfill this responsibility by holding staff accountable for finding answers.

2.   How can I make policy if I don't know the detail?

Knowing the detail does not help in policy formulation. In fact, detail can be so overwhelming that it obscures the big picture.

3.   It's the best way to make sure it is done.

There is a difference between monitoring management and actually trying to manage the organization. Your job is to set the standards and hold staff accountable for results.

4.   I have experience in the subject.

While you may be skilled in a particular area, you were not elected for that purpose (otherwise it would be a prerequisite to running for office). Telling staff members how to do something undermines the authority of the people responsible for directing the activity.

5.   We can't trust staff. They make mistakes or filter information.

If you cannot trust staff, you should confront them with your perceptions. In most cases, staff will work hard to resolve the problem. If not, your remedy is to remove staff — not bypass them.

Mary Strenn, City Administrator of San Fernando, California believes that the public fosters governing body micromanagement. "Ironically, the public often reinforces micromanagement by demanding answers about minutia such as travel costs, but does not demand answers about long-term financial conditions. While the former may be more interesting, the latter is much more important to the viability of the organization and community."

Another rub comes from the fact that no two elected officials agree upon what is excessive attention to detail. One may think that reviewing the individual items in expenditure accounts is legitimate oversight, while others insist that examining anything except the bottom line is excessive. Recognize also that some staff members do not want elected officials to monitor operations, and a tactic is to label legitimate inquiry as micromanagement. It is a good idea to talk to your colleagues, former governing body members, and staff to get their views on what is micromanagement. You'll probably find a wide divergence in views as to what micromanagement is.

Whatever, the results, do not cut back your level of inquiry for fear of being labelled a "micromanager." Legitimate questioning is not micromanagement, wallowing in the detail is.

Tip No. 20:   *Avoid Complacency Management*

The opposite of micromanagement is complacency management. Complacency management is not management. Rather, it is the abdication of oversight responsibility. It is just as dangerous as micromanagement and usually afflicts veteran governing board members. It is characterized by a general lack of inquiry and not spending time to review important financial documents. The largest bankruptcy in local government history, Orange County, California, was not caused by micromanagement or graft. It was caused by complacency. County Treasurer Robert Citron's very successful past performance mesmerized the board of supervisors and kept them from asking very basic financial questions.

Many governing board members who fall prey to complacency may have gone through an inquiry period and satisfied themselves that things were operating satisfactorily. They began relying more on trust and less on inquiry. They also confined their attention on issues of greater public interest instead of mundane financial items. (When finances are okay they are mundane. When there is a problem, there is nothing more important). Some tell-tale complacency signs include:

- Spending little or no time reviewing financial documents.
- Asking questions at public meetings that are answered in staff reports.
- Being reluctant to obtain outside help to develop or to examine financial systems or controls.
- Following an "If it ain't broken" philosophy.
- Accepting too much from staff and experts without asking questions.
- Encouraging only the good news. Don't bore us with problems.

Inquiry is your strongest oversight tool and the best antidote for complacency. When you ask a question about an item, it communicates to staff that this is important. You can be sure that if you ask questions in public about financial items, those items will get on-going attention from staff.

Tip No. 21:   *Elected Official Oversight Means Holding Administrators Accountable*

An important part of your oversight responsibility is making sure that those charged with management are held accountable for carrying out their responsibilities. In 1993, a study conducted by Arthur Anderson & Company for the Los Angeles Unified School District showed that the district could save several million dollars by replacing personnel with automated systems. The study indicated that costs would rise initially but would then decline appreciably.

A follow-up study five years later produced some unexpected news. While savings were starting to occur in some areas such as bus maintenance and energy expenses, overtime costs for the departments involved in the computerization had escalated 500 percent. The overtime budgets for the three departments of accounting, budgeting and computerization had increased from $399,940 to $2,538,081.

The school district's response was to ask for more overtime money. It was only after being confronted with the failure to control costs that Superintendent Sid Thompson admitted that he was not aware of the problem. "We need to have a formal evaluation. I didn't know this was occurring; but when you see overtime increasing five times, one has to ask the question: 'Is this the best way to do business?' I don't think so."

Even though Thompson may not have been aware of the problem he should have been. Being unaware meant that either he did not have competent administrators who could recognize a problem and report it or he had administrators who were deliberately keeping important information from him. The school board was not responsible for doing the superintendent's job nor managing the staff. The board however, should have held Thompson responsible for his failure to keep himself and the board informed about significant fiscal issues.

While, one would like to think that the problem was on the way to being resolved, that was not the case. The very next year, the school district staff asked that $2 million be set aside for overtime since the study on overtime had not been completed. Later, the school board received a consultant's report showing that average overtime usage per employee had been reduced approximately 33 percent over the previous year. Pleased with the progress, the board authorized $1.75 million in overtime. Had the board held firm, they may have been able to slash overtime another $100 to $200 thousand without impacting service.

Tip No. 22: **Don't Accept Unrefined Data**

Too much financial detail can be overwhelming. It also can obscure rather than clarify. An old bureaucratic trick is to respond to requests for information by providing mountains of detail. At first, the requestor is appreciative of the information — someone must have worked very hard pulling this all together. Appreciation quickly turns to frustration when the requester finds that the information is virtually useless. What the provider is banking on is that the requestor will give up and forget about it. Information must be summarized, categorized, and explained to be of value to an elected official. If it is not in a usable form, don't give up — ask that it be reformatted.

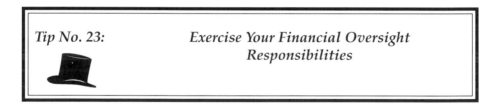

Tip No. 23: **Exercise Your Financial Oversight Responsibilities**

Listed here are some of the most important financial oversight responsibilities for local governing bodies. There are fifteen of them, and they are categorized by the frequency in which they are usually performed.

Long-Term: These financial oversight duties are considered long-term since their impact usually spans more than one fiscal year, and they do not necessarily have to be accomplished every year.

1. Establish and articulate the organization's mission.
2. Establish the organization's long-range goals.
3. Establish financial policies.
4. Establish the long-term capital improvement program (CIP).

Annual: These oversight duties are usually carried out annually.

5.   Set budget priorities, objectives and service levels through the annual operating budget.
6.   Approve the annual capital improvement budget.
7.   Establish salary, wage and benefit levels (sometimes implemented by multi-year contracts).
8.   Examine and question the Comprehensive Annual Financial Report (CAFR).
9.   Ascertain that audit management letter problems are dealt with and remedied.

Constant: These oversight responsibilities are carried out on a continual basis.

10.   Examine and evaluate financial and budget reports.
11.   Monitor the investment function and reports.

Periodic: These oversight duties arise at various times and are tied to specific issues, such as approving a bond issue to support a capital improvement program.

12.   Evaluate and decide upon requested budget adjustments.
13.   Closely review contracts, leases and bid awards.
14.   Analyze and evaluate all requests to issue or refinance debt.
15.   Insist upon periodic performance audits of agency functions.

These oversight responsibilities are discussed throughout this book.

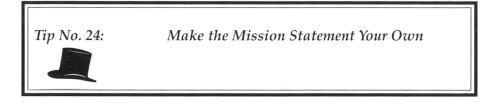

Tip No. 24:   *Make the Mission Statement Your Own*

City Councilmember Debbie Ackerman, of Skagway, Alaska, like many other elected officials, doesn't think much of her agency's mission statement. "Yes, the City of Skagway has a mission statement. The wording is generic. If you polled the councilmembers, nine will get you ten, none of us could tell you what the statement says. In my opinion, this renders the mission statement useless."

It's not too difficult to turn off on mission statements. You may find your agency's mission statement is pedestrian, trite and uninspiring. It may have been developed by another elected body, or it may have been developed by staff. In fact, it may have been borrowed from another agency. It doesn't have to be that way.

If your mission statement is dry and boring, spend the time to inject energy into it. A well stated mission statement should make you tingle with pride when you read or hear it. It should state the reason your organization exists, and it should apply to no other organization. It's needed because it forms the basis for your organization's goals, objectives and performance measures. It also communicates to the management staff where you want dollars spent.

Many people argue that the real value of the mission statement results from the process involved in developing it. Spirited arguments about your organization's core values, its purpose and the reason it exists can bring unity to your governing body. Examples of the City of Fontana's and the Tahoe City Public Utility District's mission statements appear in Appendix A.

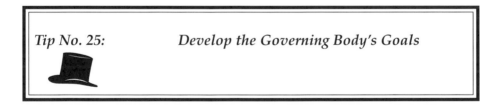

Tip No. 25:   *Develop the Governing Body's Goals*

Goals are leadership statements of the governing body and are directly connected to the mission statement. In fact, they interpret and give life to it. Goals communicate your visions, desires and promises. Goals can extend beyond fiscal years; however, they should be reviewed periodically to see if they still apply. All members of the governing body should participate in the development of goals.

Tip No. 26: *If You Don't Set Your Agency's Goals, Staff Will*

Some elected officials refuse to publicly state their goals. They may resent the loss of flexibility to change their minds when strong pressure is exerted. Or, they may fear that publicly expressing a goal will bring together diverse factions which would not have come together otherwise. Or, they just cannot agree on what the organization's top priorities are. Whatever the reason, the result is a policy vacuum.

Goals set the philosophical tone of the organization. The management staff needs to have an idea of what the consensus goals of the governing board are. What are the governing board's priorities? Where should resources and energies be allocated? This need is so fundamental that, if the governing body does not articulate its goals, staff will step in and fill the vacuum. These goals will not only be attributed to the governing board, staff will follow them until told otherwise. The failure to establish goals is an indicator of complacency management.

Tip No. 27: *Agree Upon the Level of Detail in Goals*

In *Partnerships in Local Governance,* Costis Toregas presents the argument that elected body goals should be broad and flexible, so that they offer multiple opportunities for fulfillment. Instead of a goal to "Build a new convention center," a government might express the goal as "Make the community an attractor of tourists."

Toregas says that this later goal statement might well suggest a new arena, but it also might create many other projects that could provide quicker returns on the investment or that could bring in needed outside revenue without plunging the city into a brand new business.

Toregas has pinpointed the disagreement and confusion over goals. His argument for broad goals is shared by many staff members. "Tell us what you want and leave the implementation to us." On the other hand, many elected officials are bothered by the lack of specificity. The goal of being an attractor of tourists could be interpreted to include unwanted river boat gambling, a card club or horse racing. It also leaves the elected official out of the decision loop.

The city of Rancho Palos Verdes, California, goals listed in Appendix B are broad statements that were developed after an extensive process that involved community surveys, focus groups and town hall meetings. Some of the Rancho Palos Verdes city councilmembers (especially those who participated in goal creation) believe the goals to be useful expressions of what the community wants. Said one member: "The goals and objectives are the best things we have done. I use them every chance I can to let the community know that we have vision and direction." Other councilmembers, who did not participate in the public process, however, cannot attach themselves to the goals. A newer member expressed his reaction to the goal statements by stating: "They are useless, non-actionable, and motherhood."

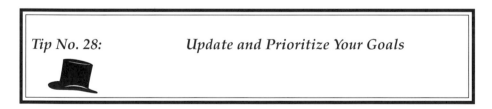

Tip No. 28:   ***Update and Prioritize Your Goals***

If your agency has adopted goals, make sure they are periodically updated. They always should be reviewed by the governing body whenever a new member is seated. This should be done as soon as possible. As noted in the Rancho Palos Verdes case, those members who participated in the original effort supported the goals and found them useful. New members had no part in their creation and did not buy into them. "I wasn't elected to implement someone else's agenda" one member confided.

Some elected officials resist establishing priorities. They may be reluctant to anger a person or group that supported them. Or they may not want to offend their colleagues for fear of losing support for an important program. If these reluctant elected officials prevail and priorities are not established, the management staff has nothing more than a wish list. Moreover, the governing body has abrogated its policy making responsibility.

One of the recurring complaints you hear from staff members is that elected officials will spend hours developing agency-wide goals, adopt them and then promptly forget about them the first time another issue emerges. Remember it takes time and resources to implement a set of goals that the governing body has adopted. Don't accept or approve goals if they do not represent the issues you want the management staff to pursue.

Tip No. 29:	*Develop Financial Policies*

Another important oversight tool is the financial policy. Financial polices establish standards that provide the guidance for the organization. These policies provide continuity in financial affairs and help staff understand the elected body's monetary philosophies. They also provide standards against which current budgetary performance can be measured and proposals for future programs evaluated.

Credit rating agencies love financial polices. They scrutinize policies to determine an agency's financial concerns and priorities. They also can assess an agency's actual financial performance in relation to the policies.

Another major benefit is the discussion that goes along with the development of financial policies. Rolling up your sleeves and considering individual policies puts you right in the middle of your policy making role. It also helps educate all the participants — elected officials, staff, the media and the public.

Financial policies cover such areas as revenues, grants, fees for service, debt, capital projects, enterprise funds, operating budgets, cash management and investments. Here are two examples of financial policies from the City of Dallas, Texas.

- The net (non-self supporting) general obligation debt of Dallas will not exceed 4 percent of the true market valuation of the taxable property of Dallas.

- Per capita general obligation debt will be managed so as not to exceed 10 percent of the latest authoritative computation of Dallas's per capita annual personal income.

Tip No. 30:   ***Review Your Agency's Financial Policies***

Many local governments have financial policies which were adopted over the years by previous governing bodies. These policies may be scattered throughout the organization in various documents, or they may have been brought together in one place. Being told that something is agency policy at a public meeting and not having seen that policy beforehand can be embarrassing. If you have not been provided agency policies, ask for copies.

An effective way to keep these policies in front of the governing body is to list them in the annual operating and capital budgets. The City of Tempe, Arizona budget not only lists the adopted policy, it reports how the city fared in relation to the policy. Here are some examples from the Tempe budget:

- Policy: Current revenues will be sufficient to support current operating expenditures.

  Status: Estimated general fund operating revenues are $95.1 million as compared to expenditures of $79.0 million.

- <u>Policy</u>: The City will establish an appropriate mix of bonded debt and pay-as-you-go financing in the funding of capital projects.

  <u>Status</u>: Funds for the capital budget consist of $9.5 million in pay-as-you-go financing or 27 percent of the capital budget, and bonded debt of $15 million which makes up 42 percent of the total. The remainder is financed by Capital Improvement Program fund balances.

City Manager Don Brown says that the policies help the Tempe City Council put the financial numbers in perspective when reviewing the annual budget. He also notes that the council pays special attention to the policies in cases where actual numbers or projections differ from stated financial policies or when policies need to be revised.

Make sure the policies are followed. Orange County, California, had a financial policy which required any expenditure in excess of $500,000 or lasting more than a year to be placed on the board of supervisors regular discussion agenda. While a substantial number of investments required checks in excess of this amount, they were routinely put on the consent calendar.

Tip No. 31:   *Oversight Means Evaluating Programs Beforehand*

The Los Angeles Unified School District is one of the largest in the nation. It has a $4.2 billion dollar budget and an enrollment of 667,000. It is also one of the most ethnically diverse in the nation.

Superintendent Sid Thompson developed a plan to make the district more manageable. The plan was to create 27 community clusters in which all of the district's schools would be aligned. Each cluster would be composed of several schools. A new position, cluster leader, would be created. Twenty-seven cluster leaders would replace six regional administrators. Salaries for the new positions would be somewhat below the regional administrator salary and on a par with school principals. The cluster leaders would be assigned to school sites where they could be in touch with local school issues and problems. The intent was to decentralize authority to local campuses and Thompson promised that this laudable goal would be accomplished without increased costs or expanding the existing bureaucracy. The school board adopted the program.

Twenty months later, Superintendent Thompson prepared a report and recommendation to increase salaries for several management employees including the cluster leader's pay to the level of the old regional administrators. He also proposed expanding their staff and providing each a vehicle, car phone and police radios. Thompson's rationale for the recommendation was based on the finding that the cluster leader post wound up entailing a lot more than he envisioned. Implementation of reforms, which was to be carried out by principals, wound up as cluster leader responsibilities. "We were into a reform where everything would happen at the principal level, but the public hasn't bought into it. If they aren't happy with what's happened at their school, they want to talk to the cluster leader, and those people are overwhelmed with requests."

Interestingly, cluster leaders did not wind up at the schools as was promised. Instead, their offices gravitated away from their cluster schools and ultimately were centralized at the district headquarters.

Helen Bernstein, President of the United Teachers of Los Angeles was incensed about the management increases. "What a sham. Thompson is sneaking it in during the last week of school, prior to knowing what the budget is really going to look like for other employees. What he's done has just re-created the old system — only it's bigger and more costly. This is great for morale...the teachers will be furious."

Another troubling issue surfaced regarding the salary increase requests. The salary increases and requests for more positions were based upon the argument that the school board was demanding a higher student achievement (Los Angeles City school students were ranked among the lowest in the nation) and, therefore, should be rewarded for it. "If we're going to make the changes we're saying we're going to make, we have to compensate people for it. "

The story did not end there. A few months later, Superintendent Thompson submitted a recommendation to increase staffing in cluster offices. The proposal would add 27 assistant cluster administrators, 27 secretaries and five additional assistants.

This is a classic and expensive example of a governing body not exercising its oversight responsibility of critically evaluating a new program before huge costs are incurred. It also indicates a failure to monitor program implementation. The board should have insisted upon evaluation criteria and more assurances before adopting the superintendent's illadvised plan.

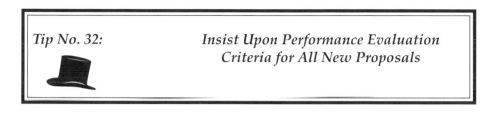

Tip No. 32:   ***Insist Upon Performance Evaluation Criteria for All New Proposals***

Patricia Hagler, the city of Signal Hill, California, Public Works Superintendent, wanted to change the work schedule for maintenance crews from a five day, eight-hour work day to a four-day, ten-hour work day.

Like most proposals, the anticipated benefits were outlined. "It is anticipated that the city will benefit from the alternative work schedule because of the extended availability of services, as well as a sig-

Patricia Hagler, Signal Hill Public Works Superintendent, leads maintenance personnel in early morning stretching exercises to reduce injuries.

nificant reduction in overtime. Higher productivity and a marked reduction in absenteeism also is expected."

Some of the city councilmembers however, were skeptical of the assertion that the program would save money. What sold this proposal was the inclusion of criteria which would be used to evaluate the success of the program. "The alternative work schedule will be implemented on a trial basis from April 15 to October 15. During that period, the Public Works Superintendent will evaluate the program using the following criteria: (1) reduction in overtime (2) increase in productivity and (3) reduction in absenteeism. After the trial period was completed, staff was able to show the city council success in all three areas

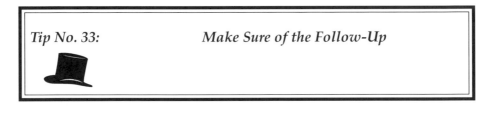

Tip No. 33:   *Make Sure of the Follow-Up*

Individual governing board members will sometimes request that an evaluation report be prepared and submitted to the board after a newly adopted program has been in operation for six to twelve months. This is a good technique as it gives the board a chance to appraise the success of the program. It is not uncommon that this request is lost or forgotten. To make sure that a report is prepared and submitted, obtain concurrence from the entire board and have it recorded in the minutes. You should also request staff to schedule it for a future agenda.

Tip No. 34:   *Hold Goal Setting Retreats*

Goal setting retreats are becoming more popular with governing bodies. It gives members a chance to step back from the day-to-day issues and think about the future of their agency. Where are we going? What opportunities and threats face us? What is our vision for the future? What goals, resources and action steps do we need to get there?

Try to hold the retreat at a location away from the governing board's usual meeting area. Leaving the building and all its distractions is crucial. When you retreat you want all members focused on the agenda and not the all consuming day-to-day problems.

It is critical that all governing board members attend the session. While some may resist, due to business, personal or political reasons, every effort should be made to work through the problem so they can join the group. If a member refuses to attend, however, the governing board should still hold the retreat. In many cases, a hold out will relent and attend the next session, especially if he/she feels they missed something important.

It is also important that the chief administrative officer attend the session. The CAO will add insights and be able to communicate the governing body's underlying thinking to staff.

A successful retreat must be well-planned, and preparing an agenda is one of the most important steps. It not only helps organize activities, it focuses the objectives of the retreat. What are we trying to achieve this year? What topics should be covered?

The process may flow as follows:

- Begin thinking about problems, issues and a general theme.
- Develop a draft agenda and circulate to governing board and staff members.
- Incorporate relevant suggestions and finalize agenda.
- Distribute agenda at least a week before the event.

While there is something to say for unstructured retreats, most governing boards find themselves being more productive and achieving higher quality results when an agenda is prepared. A well planned program allows for the accomplishment of multiple objectives. Here are some examples:

- Communicating critical elected official issues and concerns.

- Resolving interpersonal conflicts.
- Establishing governing board goals.
- Visioning and strategic planning.
- Checking alignment on agency-wide priorities.
- Reviewing accomplishments.
- Developing a mission and/or vision statement.

An underlying benefit of retreats is that they provide opportunities for governing board members to get to know each other on a personal level. This enhanced relationship pays dividends when the members face tough challenges and problems.

A successful retreat can be planned and conducted by staff and governing board members, especially if they work well together. If there is a split on the governing board or a few members tend to dominate the discussion, an unbiased facilitator is suggested. The facilitator can bring out all view points and free up the participants to deal with the issues at hand, rather than worry about process. A facilitator brings a refreshing viewpoint and information on what's happening elsewhere. Often a mayor, chairperson or chief administrator who tries to facilitate the session finds this role in conflict with the participant role.

Tip No. 35:   ***Set Retreat Ground Rules***

Agreed upon behaviors are necessary for a smoothly functioning retreat. Basic issues, such as punctuality, attendance, openness and participation, need to be agreed upon and enforced as group norms. These norms help set the tone of retreats and reinforce trust among the group. Here are some typical norms:

- Be open and honest.
- Be loyal to each other.
- Be helpful to each other.
- Listen actively.

- Bring a sense of humor.
- Show interest in other's issues.
- Disagree when necessary.
- Offer innovative thoughts.
- Be discreet and confidential.
- Trust each other.

Tip No. 36:   ***Follow-up After Retreats***

Follow-up is important so that issues are not dropped after the retreat. Minutes of the retreat should be compiled and distributed to the participants. The minutes can then be used as a topic list for follow-up meetings.

As part of the process, critique the retreat. This feedback is very important in planning the next session. It also helps focus on successful approaches as well as "bombs." Critiques can be held at the retreat or after everyone gets back to the office. These debriefings can be verbal or in writing.

Nine Guidelines
for
Successful Retreats

1. Leave the building. There are too many distractions in the office.

2. Prepare an agenda. It helps focus the retreat objectives.

3. Remain flexible. Change agenda at the meeting when necessary.

4. Use a neutral facilitator.

5. Use creativity in ordering subjects. Energy levels will be maintained longer.

6. Develop retreat ground rules. They help form a compact among members.

7. Critique retreat. This can be done during or after and verbally or in writing.

8. Prepare follow-up minutes. These become your guide to action.

9. Make it fun. Participants will learn and give more.

How to Lessen Budget Anxiety

"Four days was not enough for me to understand this document. I'm just not smart enough to understand this today."

Newly Elected Orange County Supervisor Don Saltarelli complaining about getting only four days to review the $3.5 billion Orange County Budget

Budget Stress

It's not that newly appointed Orange County Supervisor Don Saltarelli didn't try to understand the budget. The voluminous document of 500 pages was delivered to his house on Friday night. The transmittal memo advised that the budget would be considered by the board of supervisors on the following Wednesday.

Each day Saltarelli devoted a portion of his time to reviewing the budget, but it was not enough. As each day expired, he realized it more. Recognizing that he still had not reached a comfort level with the budget, he stayed up until a little before 3:00 a.m. Wednesday. Feeling tired and frustrated, Supervisor Saltarelli went to the budget workshop at 9:30 a.m. that morning and exclaimed his frustration about not being able to comprehend the budget document within such a limited time provided.

Saltarelli was somewhat comforted when the other supervisors expressed frustration about the budget. Supervisor William Steiner complained that he could not make one summary sheet balance with the next and that the budget contained no grand total. "How can anyone analyze this budget?" he asked. Supervisor Marian Bergeson could not tell whether positions were being added or deleted and in desperation about the budget's complexity, called for help. "A citizen's committee should be appointed to make sense of this confusing document."

The next day, the *Orange County Register* tried to communicate the essence of the budget, and, perhaps going beyond the call of duty, attempted to add up all the dollars. Guardedly, the *Register* announced to its readers that the 200 plus funds in the budget showed a 3 percent increase over the previous year. Three days later, the Orange County management staff finally unveiled the total budget figure. The budget had increased from $3.45 billion to $3.48 billion, a modest 1 percent increase.

Late Delivery

The Vallejo City Unified School District Board received the preliminary budget the night it was orally presented to them by the staff. The school board members complained that they did not have enough time to look at the budget before the meeting. Finance Officer Debra McClain explained that the intent was to distribute the budget at the meeting when a staff presentation could be made since the information was so lengthy and in depth that it filled up an entire binder. Then, she explained, "the information would lend itself to making it more simple and clear and easy to understand, rather than just seeming like a book full of numbers." McClain also asserted that she had advised the board of the budget presentation approach months earlier.

Board member Bill Pendergast not only disagreed he related that the board was miffed. Pendergast noted that typically, board members are sent information several days before the meeting so they can study it. In this case, they were not given the opportunity to do so. "To be here without prior information is totally unacceptable."

Staff Responsibility
Both the Orange County Board of Supervisors and the Vallejo Unified School District Board were victimized by their respective staffs
in the way the budget was prepared and presented. For example:

1.   Why wasn't the budget distributed well in advance of the
      public presentation? The Orange County staff erred by not
      giving supervisors enough time to study the budget.
      The Vallejo staff committed a bigger sin by assuming
      that the board could not understand it without staff's
      expert interpretation.

2.   Why is the budget so complicated that it requires a presenta-
      tion before it makes sense? The trend today is to include nar-
      rative and graphics to make budgets understandable. Is the
      governing board being presented a policy document or in-
      comprehensible accounting data?

3.   Why didn't the staff appreciate the basic principle that gov-
      erning bodies loathe surprises, and a budget that has not
      been reviewed before it is presented publicly could contain
      a bucket of "gotchas." Who knows what gremlins lurk in a
      budget? While staff may desire to present the budget at a
      time when they can answer questions, it puts the governing
      body in a vulnerable and untenable position.

4.   How can the staff justify submitting a budget without total
      figures? By presenting the budget without totals, the Orange
      County staff tacitly admitted that they still had questions
      about the budget they compiled. Governing bodies should
      avoid being sucked into making individual dollar commit-
      ments before learning the overall bottom line.

The operating budget is the most important annual document a
public agency prepares, and it is the first major financial document
newly elected officials must deal with. This chapter is devoted to
providing a better understanding of the annual budget — both the
document and the process. It suggests things to look for and questions to ask.

Tip No. 37:   ***Budgets Are More Than***
Control Documents

Why have budgets? The modern budget was created to provide control over public expenditures and taxes. Budgets provide the legal authorization to incur obligations and pay expenses. They are used as a means to hold administrators accountable for their management of public finances. While the original purpose of control is still the most important, other purposes have evolved. Budgets are used to plan the agency's spending program for the next 12 or 24 months. They allocate dollars for specific resources such as personnel, supplies and equipment to accomplish programs and activities. Programs that receive funding become the agency's priorities. Budgets also serve as evaluation tools. The governing body can compare the commitments made in the budget to actual accomplishments. Another evolving purpose is that of providing public information. Budgets used to contain little more than hundreds or thousands of numbers bound with interesting covers. Budgets now include more narrative and graphs to explain the agency's mission, goals, issues, problems and programs.

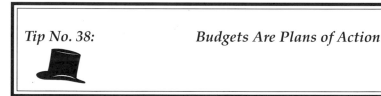

Tip No. 38:   ***Budgets Are Plans of Action***

The budget has been defined as "a plan of action" or "a plan of action based upon assumptions that is expressed in financial terms." This latter definition includes two important concepts related to the budget:

1.   The budget is only a plan and should not be viewed as something cast in concrete. If major changes occur, the budget should be changed to reflect the new situation. On the other hand, the budget should not be changed to accommodate every whim.

2.	The budget is based upon assumptions. Guesses are made about economic conditions, constituent needs, revenues and expenditures. Some of these guesses will be right on target while others will be off, either too high or too low. A good budget lays out the main assumptions for the governing body and community to see and evaluate.

Tip No. 39:   ***Budgets Need Not be Complex***

If you get an opportunity to view budgets from other agencies, you will notice very quickly that no two budgets are alike. Unlike annual financial reports, there is not a commonly accepted template for local government budgets. There are large budgets and small budgets. Some budgets include a plethora of graphs, photographs and tables, while others have a few standard pie charts. Some budgets include straight forth narrative, while others resemble phone books.

Your agency's budget size, composition and look has evolved over time. It includes items previous elected officials and staff members considered important such as a special fund to keep track of money donated for park purposes or an endowment fund for special student supplies. If you find the budget too complex, ask that it be changed to meet your information requirements. This might include adding or deleting information or presenting it in a different format. If you are told that the budget format is fixed by a state or local law or by some other mandate, request supplemental information in a format that is helpful to you. Make sure that staff is not using the law to avoid making the process simpler and more understandable.

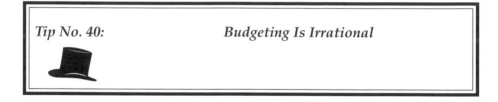

Tip No. 40: **Budgeting Is Irrational**

Budgeting being an art form, has its irrational aspects. Staff members, in a candid moment, will tell you that the way budgeting is carried out promotes destructive competition among departments. As long as a department gets its budget, it doesn't care too much about other department's needs. Staff may also tell you budgeting encourages spending, not saving; and it promotes game playing. They have learned that good budgeting is not rewarded and that too much emphasis is put on staying within budget and very little on attainment of objectives.

You may notice that some governing board colleagues have agendas that are not on the table and that these hidden agendas make it difficult to reach consensus. You may find that several of your colleagues do not really understand the budget, so they fake it. You may also notice that some colleagues get so hung up in the detail, they fail to see the big picture.

You'll soon find that higher levels of government have a tendency to mandate programs for your organization and that these directives take priority over your local needs. While your organization's top priority may be police protection, you find the federal government mandating your organization to divert efforts and resources to the homeless, even if your agency does not have a homeless problem.

Earmarking funds brings out the worst of irrationality. In the case of a county government, you may find the social services department making severe cuts in the mental health staff and at the same time, the sheriff's department is purchasing a new command center, patrol helicopters, and an exercise hall for officers paid for out of a restricted fund that can only be used for law enforcement purposes. All of these examples can lead you to conclude that budgeting is an irrational exercise.

Tip No. 41:   ***Budgeting Is Also Rational***

At the same time, staff members may also tell you that budgets are becoming more business like and focused on productivity. Goals, measurable objectives and performance measures are helping to change the emphasis from detailed examination of low significance purchases to dialogue on program outcomes. What are we trying to achieve with this expenditure?

Staff members may also admit that the budget process is becoming more participative and that departments are becoming more aware of other department's needs and that their fates are in reality linked. They may also concede that the trend for budgets to be developed and presented by teams, rather than by individuals, creates better budgets.

Staff may use very sophisticated techniques for estimating revenues and expenditures and determining demand for services. They also may have developed refined techniques for measuring constituent attitudes regarding the agency's service delivery. All of these suggest that there is also a rational aspect to budgeting.

You should expect staff to embody the rational side of budgeting. You should get reasoned, logical recommendations that are fair-minded and represent staff's best professional judgment. You should not tolerate biased or obviously slanted recommendations, but be careful to not call recommendations you do not like, biased.

Tip No. 42:   ***You Have Little Control Over the Total Expenditure Program***

Virtually all public agencies begin the budget process by determining how much it will take to continue existing programs.

What services are we now providing and how much will it take to continue to provide the same level of service to our clients? After existing commitments are met, any remaining money is used to fund new programs or increase existing ones. This approach is called incremental budgeting, and it guarantees that very few changes will be made in the program mix since the majority of the dollars are eaten up by existing programs. Incremental budgeting is based on the premise that the best usage of current dollars is to continue previously approved programs.

Figure 2 illustrates how little flexibility governing boards have over the annual operating budget. It also helps to explain why so few changes are made. Don't be put off by this. If you can only influence 3 to 5 percent of the budget, do a good job on that part. Also, look for ways to make more of the budget discretionary.

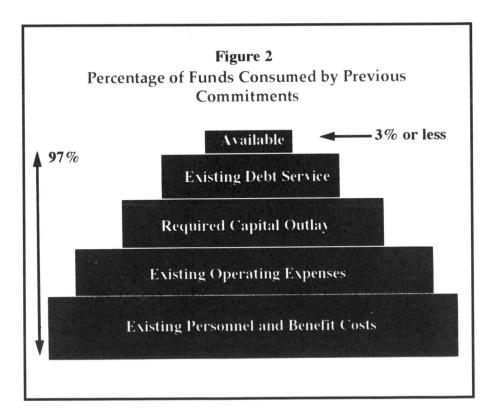

Figure 2
Percentage of Funds Consumed by Previous Commitments

3% or less

97%

Available

Existing Debt Service

Required Capital Outlay

Existing Operating Expenses

Existing Personnel and Benefit Costs

Tip No. 43:

Determine What Type of Budget Your Agency Uses

Local governments use different types of operating budgets. There are line item budgets, program budgets, performance budgets, program-performance budgets, zero-base budgets, expenditure control budgets and multi-year budgets. Confused? Don't be. Each of these budget types have common elements, and your agency may be using concepts from all of these.

While there are several different budget types, there are two basic budget formats that are used to present the operating budget — the line item and program format. The line item budget format is the most common way budgets are publicly presented by local governments. It is estimated that 60 percent of all local governments still present their budget in this manner. Appendix C displays a sample of a line item budget.

The line item format has many advantages for governing board members. It is familiar. Most family budgets are developed in a similar manner. It is also simple to prepare and to review. Once the concept is explained, it is easily understood. The approach is almost natural. Needs are determined, price estimates obtained, and all like expenditures are put in categories such as salaries, overtime, retirement, fuel, office supplies, utilities and equipment.

Many elected officials love line item budgets, and the more detail, the more love. Line item budgets lend themselves to such comfortable, yet inconsequential questions as:

- Why do you need so much for office supplies?
- Travel has gone up $100 between this year and last year, and it has gone up $300 over the last three years. Why?

The line item budget has some major weaknesses, and it can land governing board members smack into micro-management. First, it puts the focus on inputs such as what is to be purchased and not on outputs or outcomes, such as what services will be provided.

Historically, the focus has been on how many cops, firefighters, teachers or maintenance personnel are needed. The line item budget does not help answer the question about what these positions will be producing and whether they are really needed.

Second, the line item budget can be too restrictive. Managers wind up spending more effort and creativity to staying within the individual accounts than accomplishing the purpose for which the money was budgeted in the first place. In their effort to not overspend individual accounts, some managers will charge items to an inappropriate account. This distorts the cost of running an organization and accomplishes little. The questions about office supplies and travel may gain a governing body member points from the "lets guard every dime constituency," but these questions rarely have an impact on the budget one way or the other.

The other major format is the program format. Appendix D displays a typical program budget page for an operating department. The program budget was created to overcome some of the complaints about the line item budget. The concept underlying a program budget is to focus on the output side of the budget — what will the agency get for its investment? In this type of budget, all related costs — personnel, benefits, supplies and equipment — are compiled into one program. Thus, a fire budget may have such programs as suppression, prevention, rescue, and training.

Program budgets are easily linked to objectives and performance measures. Most program budgets now incorporate departmental objectives. It moves the budget review focus from paper clips and trips to what is to be done with the money provided. But program budgets can also become too detailed and complex if too many programs are created, and line item accounting is developed for each program. The trend is toward the program budget format. During the transition to a program budget, agencies sometimes print both types of budgets, until the governing body becomes comfortable with the new format.

Lakewood, California, City Administrator, Howard Chambers says that program budgeting is working very well in his city; but it wasn't always that way. Twenty years ago when he first came to the city; the council and staff would quibble over individual line item accounts. Questions like "I see you have $400 budgeted for office supplies, yet you only spent $350. Why are you asking for the extra $50?" abounded, and staff spent time and resources responding. Yet, this gut wrenching exercise that took anywhere from four to eight work sessions did not result in any significant changes in the budget. Money would be moved from one account to the next, but the overall bottom line changed very little. Moreover, it became an "us against them" exercise. Council felt that their job was to find "gotchas," and trap staff.

Over the years, Chambers convinced the city council that little was being accomplished; and valuable time was being wasted. "They would leave the process with no idea what the budget really stood for. They had no picture because they were so immersed in the detail and minutia of over 1,000 line item accounts that they couldn't possibly gain an understanding of the overall budget. Nobody was happy." Eventually, Chambers convinced the city council to try a program budget.

Chambers now presents a program budget to the city council, and they relish it. He focuses on the overall financial picture and then on the ten most important program areas. "This is a $30 million spending program. Here are the ten most important programs," Chambers reports. "The most important is public safety and the biggest chunk is in law enforcement, but it is also contained in the following activities: parks and recreation, public works, neighborhood watch, and the helicopter patrol program. Last year these programs totalled $5.8 million, this year $6.0 million. The difference is in negotiated salary increases. Here are the objectives of the program which you may wish to discuss." Chambers then moves to redevelopment which is the next most important program area, and eventually covers all ten program areas.

The program approach, coupled with a slide presentation, has reduced the time to a two and one-half hour work session; but more importantly, the council and public have an understanding of the budget and an overall picture of the city's priorities when they leave the meeting.

Tip No. 44:   ***Don't Ignore the Capital Budget***

In addition to the operating budget, your agency will probably have a capital budget. The capital budget contains funding for the big-ticket items such as buildings, roads, bridges and major equipment. The capital budget may be a separate document, or it may be included as a part of the annual operating budget.

Often, the operating budget takes most of the governing body's interest; and by the time the capital budget is up for review, there is little energy left. Don't let it happen. Give the capital budget the same effort as the operating budget. It contains some of your agency's most important expenditures.

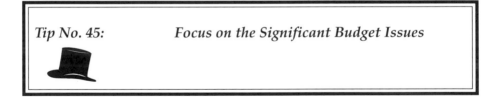

Tip No. 45:   ***Focus on the Significant Budget Issues***

The budget is a powerful document. It embodies literally thousands of decisions made at every level of the organization — from providing an air humidifier for a valuable long-term account clerk to setting competitive salary rates for employees to preparing plans for a new facility. The organization's programs and activities are initiated, extended or abandoned through your budget decisions. Your job is to concentrate on the significant issues and not be sidetracked by the insignificant ones. Significant decisions revolve around:

- Deciding whether or not to fund new programs.
- Deciding to increase or decrease service levels.
- Considering the tax impacts on various groups.
- Establishing employee compensation levels.
- Providing funding for infrastructure maintenance and expansion.

- Deciding to incur debt.
- Initiating programs that promote economic growth.
- Determining an adequate reserve level.

Don't waste your valuable time delving into whether a particular department should be allowed to purchase an inexpensive piece of equipment. You are paying your management staff lots of dollars to make those decisions. If you are overly concerned about an issue such as travel, go ahead and wallow in the detail, but don't do it too long or often. Spend your time establishing a travel policy and making sure it is implemented. When you are wallowing, you are not doing your policy job and your constituents are going to suffer.

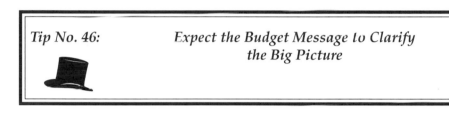

Tip No. 46:   ***Expect the Budget Message to Clarify the Big Picture***

The budget message or letter of transmittal is the most important section of the budget document and should be read after briefly thumbing through the budget. The big picture should be conveyed in the mayor or chief administrator's budget message. A well-written budget message should give you a good overview of your agency's issues for the ensuing year. It sets the overall tone — Is this a tight year or is a major expansion about to take place? More specifically it should:

- Reveal the major assumptions that the budget is built upon, such as population changes, inflation and interest rates.
- Highlight the major policy issues.
- Identify financial, economic, social and political problems facing the agency.
- Identify opportunities and the steps and resources needed to capitalize on them.
- Focus attention on changes from the last budget in terms of service and funding levels.

The budget message is the mayor's or chief executive's best, uninterrupted opportunity to communicate with the governing body and the public. Pride should be taken in its content and delivery. Lakewood City Administrator Chambers, prepares an eight to ten page message that focuses upon of all the significant budget issues. "If you read this message, it will tell you everything you need to know about the budget," Chambers tells new councilmembers. "You could actually feel comfortable adopting the budget based upon the message. It contains all the important information."

Tip No. 47:   *Public Accounting Is Different from*
Commercial Accounting

One of the first things you will notice is that public agency accounting practices differ from commercial practices. Accounting has two primary forms — commercial which is for-profit organizations and fund which is for not-for-profit organizations. All transactions in commercial accounting are presented as a "single economic entity" for the corporation or business. Everything is brought together in a single balance sheet. In governmental accounting, funds are used; and the number of funds may range from a few to well over 300. These funds are set up to comply with regulations or laws and must be treated as separate entities. Instead of one single balance sheet, a public agency is required to maintain balance sheets for every fund.

There are seven fund types, and the most important is the general fund. This fund is the chief operating fund of any governmental entity and there can be only one general fund. This is the fund you want to spend time understanding, analyzing and evaluating. Refer to Appendix E for a definition of the seven different fund types.

Don't get too confused with funds and fund accounting. Think of keeping your household expense money in different pots — rent, utilities, clothes and recreation. This is essentially how governmental funds evolved. While cash is now pooled for investment purposes, the funds into which these cash accounts evolved, are still used for financial reporting. Perhaps the most important thing to remember about fund accounting is that dollars earmarked for specific purposes in a fund, usually cannot be used for other purposes. Thus, money from a water fund cannot be used for police protection.

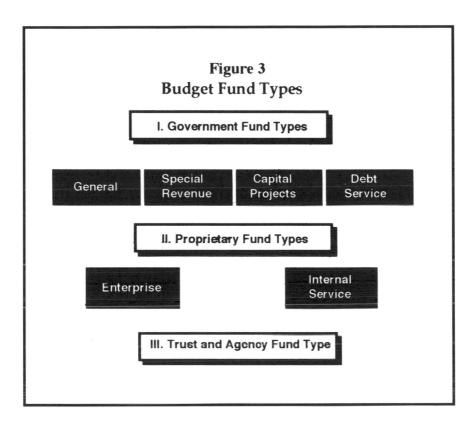

Figure 3
Budget Fund Types

I. Government Fund Types

General | Special Revenue | Capital Projects | Debt Service

II. Proprietary Fund Types

Enterprise | Internal Service

III. Trust and Agency Fund Type

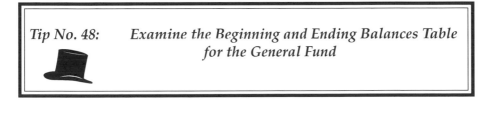

Tip No. 48:   *Examine the Beginning and Ending Balances Table*
for the General Fund

The "Changes in Fund Balance Table" provides one of the best snap-shots of overall fund activity. While the name of the table may vary it includes items similar to those in the following example (Table 1):

Table 1
Changes in General Fund Balance
FY 97-98

Estimated Fund Balance July 1, 1997	Estimated Revenue	Transfers In	Funds Available FY 97-98	Estimated Expenditures	Transfers Out	Estimated Fund Balance June 30, 1998
$4,799,027	$94,979,445	$5,900,000	$105,678,472	$99,774,311	$4,163,914	$1,740,247

Don't shy away from this table. If the budget includes this table or something similar and you don't understand it, have staff explain it. If the budget does not include it, ask staff to prepare one. It will give you several valuable insights about a fund's finances such as:

- Whether reserves are being used to balance the fund. In this case, the agency is using $3,058,800 from the general fund balance to balance the budget (difference between the beginning balance of $4,799,027 and the projected ending balance of $1,740,247). This may represent an unhealthy financial condition.

- Whether general fund expenditures exceed general fund revenues. In this case they do, with expenditures totalling $99,774,311 and revenues totalling $94,979,445. This again, may represent an unhealthy financial condition.

- How much money is being transferred in and out of the fund. In this example, transfers in exceed transfers out by $1,736,086.

Even if you understand the table, it is a good idea to have staff walk you through it. You will get additional information on the reasons why things appear as they do. Also, once you have learned to read this statement, the others will be a cinch.

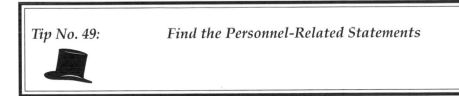

Tip No. 49:   *Find the Personnel-Related Statements*

Most local governments are labor intensive. In fact, most have personnel expenses that represent 60-80 percent of their operating budgets. The overall organizational chart gives a cat's-eye view of the entire organization. This chart is usually displayed in the form of a hierarchy. However, some organizations have dumped the traditional chart, for a chart showing a number of loosely connected boxes or even overlapping circles to show a more flexible organization. Whatever the form, you want a chart or table to provide basic organizational and personnel information such as:

- Number of departments
- Relative budget size of departments
- Number of employees per department
- Departmental reporting relationships

Another important personnel budget indicator is the "Changes in Personnel Summary" table. Again, it may carry different names, but this chart shows additions or deletions of positions by department.

These are some of the typical budget sections. Appendix F suggests eleven steps to tackle a budget. If your budget does not include some of these items, discuss it with staff; perhaps they are listed under different titles or sections. If you are not getting this type of financial information, ask why.

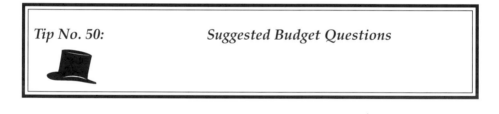

Tip No. 50:   ***Suggested Budget Questions***

Here are some safe, smart and open-ended questions to ask to get an overall feeling for the budget.

1. What are the underlying assumptions such as inflation, interest rates, population changes, grants, building activity?
2. What are the three most important problems? Opportunities?
3. How does this budget compare to last year's adopted budget?
4. What is the percentage change for the general fund as compared to last year's adopted budget?
5. What are the most significant dollar changes?
6. How do recurring revenues compare to recurring expenditures?
7. How have general fund balances changed?
8. How have general fund reserves changed?

9.   How have other reserves changed?

10.   What funds are subsidizing other funds (such as the Water Fund subsidizing the General Fund).

11.   Are capital improvements being maintained at an adequate level?

12.   How much have revenues increased from last year's adopted budget?

13.   What budgetary policy limits have been exceeded? What policies have not been met?

14.   Is the general fund budget balanced?

15.   Is there a deficit in any fund? Why?

16.   Are major revenues estimated conservatively or liberally? Explain.

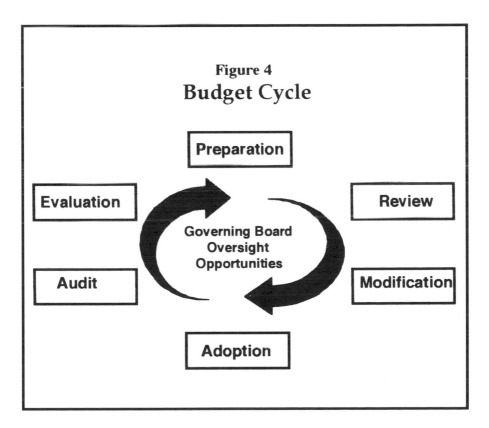

Figure 4
Budget Cycle

Preparation

Evaluation

Review

Governing Board
Oversight
Opportunities

Audit

Modification

Adoption

Tip No. 51: **Ask Hard Questions Before Approving a New Program**

New programs add to the base budget and will become an on-going obligation of the organization. Recognize that once a program is funded, it inevitably creates or enlivens a constituency that will fight to continue the program in the future. Make sure that the organization can pay for a program now and in the future before approving it. Here are some questions to ask before approving a new program or activity.

1.   What is the purpose of this program?
2.   Why is it needed?
3.   Why is this program being submitted at this time?
4.   What are the specific intended outcomes of this program?
5.   What are the measurable objectives?
6.   What do you intend to measure to determine whether the program is a success?
7.   What alternate service delivery approaches did you consider? Why were they rejected?
8.   Where will the money come from to pay for it? How will costs be recovered?
9.   Is this the full cost of the program or will it cost more in the future?
10.   What other costs will be incurred such as equipment and building space?
11.   How did you get by so long without it before?
12.   What will happen if the program is not funded?

Questions five through seven are directed to identifying measures of success before a program is adopted. Too often measurable objectives and outcomes are not developed until someone asks if the program is meeting its goals.

Staff should be able to answer these questions to your satisfaction. If you are still concerned about a major new expenditure, request a study and/or a special workshop to consider the item.

Tip No. 52:   ***Avoid Trivial Pursuit***

Governing boards are notorious for wasting their precious time on inconsequential items such as the type, style or even color of office furniture. This dalliance is usually done at the expense of significant items. I saw this phenomena occur at my first budget hearing. The council was struggling through the electric utility's budget. They were obviously uncomfortable with the technical items so they latched on to the first familiar topic — the typewriter. The next two hours were spent in a spirited debate over whether to purchase IBM or Underwood typewriters. At the conclusion of the debate, little time remained: so the purchase of new electric generators, costing over a million dollars, skated through without question or comment.

Trivial pursuit is a natural phenomena that can pop up at any time during the meeting. It is also highly contagious. Surprisingly, even skilled chairpersons fall prey to it. Staff members are well aware of the malady. Some even admit to salting budget hearings with well-placed trivial pursuit items to divert attention from more questionable items.

Elected officials, who recognize meeting time as a precious commodity that can easily be wiled away on the mundane, are the most successful in combating trivial pursuit. Some suggestions are:

1.   Review budgets beforehand to identify the most important items. Then prioritize them.

2.   Before the meeting, alert the chair and staff about the items you want to cover.

3.   At the meeting, keep your priorities in front of you and monitor the clock. Remind colleagues that quality time is needed for your items.

4.   Suggest that mundane items be moved to the end of the agenda.

Tip No. 53: *Hold Separate Hearings for Major Public Proposals*

The City of West Hollywood, California, was facing a $600,000 deficit; and staff included a proposal in the operating budget to remedy the problem. The proposal was to install additional parking meters along the city's main commercial boulevard. The plan also called for extending meter enforcement into the evening hours from 6 p.m. to 10 p.m.

Staff, believing the proposal was approved as part of the budget, began enforcing the extended hours immediately after the budget was adopted. It didn't take long for councilmembers to hear the outrage from the public. "How could you possibly do such a dumb thing? Did the city really expect someone watching a play or eating at a restaurant to run out every hour to feed the meter?"

The city council reacted quickly and put the plan on hold. Mayor Pro Tem Sal Guarriello said, "This should have been discussed many, many times. I don't know why they (staff) were jumping the gun on this all the way down the line." Mayor Paul Koretz stated, "I don't think any of us knew this plan would be implemented without warning or a public hearing. We approved it as a concept and expected it to go forward through the process."

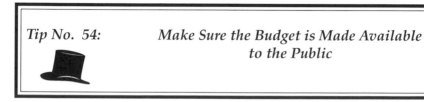

Tip No. 54: *Make Sure the Budget is Made Available to the Public*

The operating budget should be made available to anyone who desires a copy. It is a common practice of many cities and counties to provide copies of the complete budget document to community libraries. Copies of special district and school district budgets are found less frequently in public libraries. (This may be due to less interest in district activities or the district's desire to remain obscure).

Some agencies charge a fee for a copy of the annual budget. The idea behind this charge is to offset the cost of materials and printing. Several agencies that have adopted fees indicate that the net result has been fewer budgets being distributed to the public. The irony is that while budgets are being made more understandable and user friendly for the public, fees are discouraging circulation of budget documents.

To encourage public review, many agencies print a budget in brief or provide a summary version of the budget. These summaries usually utilize attractive graphs and tables to highlight key trends, assumptions and programs.

Recently, the City of Sacramento, California, decided to get input from citizens on how to balance the city's budget. The budget gap was approximately $11 million in a $144 million budget. Every residence in the city was asked to participate in balancing the budget. This was done by mailing budget work sheets to all dwellings in the city. The budget dilemmas were outlined, and residents were invited to balance the budget. What combination of service cuts and revenue increases would you select? The city received over 1000 responses. Opinions varied as to helpfulness. Participant Ed Weeks said, "I'm not sure I got into it. It's like Monopoly. Sure they have to make hard decisions. My thought is how many of their decisions are made in their own self-interest?"

May Fell liked the process, "It's like in your own household budget; you pay your bills before you go to the movies." Jim Arnold said, "I appreciate the opportunity to participate, but don't take the results too far. The work sheets did not provide enough information to really make informed decisions."

Not satisfied with just a survey, the city then invited residents to role play as elected officials. The Sacramento Community Convention Center was reserved for all those who wished to act as city councilmembers and to help resolve the budget deficit. Willing participants were divided into city councils of seven members and given the charge to balance the budget. Participation was much lower;

and while city councilmembers found the exercise fun, it was less helpful.

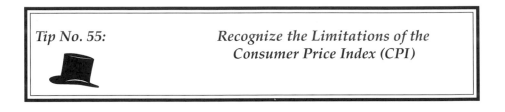

Tip No. 55: *Recognize the Limitations of the Consumer Price Index (CPI)*

In late 1996, an independent commission appointed by Congress reported that the government was overstating the inflation rate by 1.1 percentage points per year, costing it billions of dollars in inflated Social Security and other entitlement payments.

Just how significant was the overstatement of the CPI? Senator Daniel Patrick Moynihan, who was instrumental in setting up the review commission, put it in perspective, "The CPI's overstatement of inflation could be considered the fourth biggest federal program in terms of dollars, after Social Security, Health and Defense.

The Consumer Price Index (CPI) is compiled by the Labor Department's Bureau of Labor Statistics. It purports to measure changes of prices over time by tracking the prices of a "market basket" of 207 categories of products and services meant to reflect typical consumer purchases. The government surveys Americans about what they buy and consume. Each month, the government surveys a sample of stores and outlets to find the price for the items in the basket. Approximately 95,000 prices are collected each month. The change is suppose to be the measure of the inflation rate. However, it is now acknowledged that the CPI overstates the cost of living. The distortion results from the premise that the current CPI does not sufficiently incorporate improvements in goods and services over the years.

What is wrong with the CPI? The problem is that the basket of goods and services that make up the index are only revised every ten years. Ten years is a relative life time in today's world. Milestone breakthroughs are not picked up until the next adjustment period. VCRs and cellular telephones had not been added to the basket as of 1998.

Economics Professor Jerry Croskry explains it this way, "If the price of apples rises, a family is worse off; wages will purchase fewer apples and this is reflected in the CPI. However, if the crime rate goes up and the family feels compelled to purchase a burglar alarm, the decline in the family's welfare is not reflected. CPI calculations will always be imperfect. There is no perfect index of cost of living."

At the local level, CPI is used in a number of ways. Unions push for a cost of living increase to keep up with inflation. They argue that this is not a salary increase, only an attempt to keep up with inflation. Some of your local government's revenues change automatically with increases in the CPI, and many contract rate adjustments are based on changes in the CPI.

Disastrous Fiscal
Practices

*"Two, four, six, eight, now it's time
to terminate."*

Angry parents shouting for the dismissal of the
Laguna Beach Unified School District
Superintendent Paul Possemato

For many years there was nothing particularly distinguishable about
the Laguna Beach Unified School District. It was a small district in
an affluent area of Orange County, California, with 2500 students, a
budget of $13 million and reserves of $11 million.

The Transformation
Then Paul Possemato, an acclaimed educator with a history of educational successes, was hired as superintendent. For five years he
worked his magic and transformed the school district into one of
renown excellence. Superintendent Possemato implemented over
28 different "educational innovations," such as a mandate to make
community service a high school graduation requirement, a citywide AIDS education program, and foreign language classes for
elementary students. Under Possemato's charismatic leadership,

Laguna Beach High School won the National Blue Ribbon School of Excellence Award; and Thurston Middle School was named a California Distinguished School.

Blemishes
However, during this five year period, a number of events took place that undermined the district's financial viability.

- First, wildfires burned over 440 homes, causing more that $500 million in damage. The fires, followed by floods and mud slides the next winter, resulted in a drop of over $1,000,000 in property taxes.

- Second, the district had all its reserves invested in the Orange County Investment Pool and lost $340,000.

- Third, the Southern California recession resulted in devaluation of residential and commercial properties. Many of these properties requested and obtained lower valuations from the county assessor. This reduced property taxes even further.

- Fourth, the educational enhancements increased the on-going costs of the district. The district expenditure per student became the highest in the county at $5,682 compared to the county per student average of $4,308.

- Fifth, the district exhausted it reserves to renovate Laguna Beach High School and to pay for classrooms lost during the fire.

During the fourth year of Superintendent Possemato's tenure, the problems began to surface. The district addressed the problem by cutting $350,000 from the budget and raising $150,000 in new bus fees. These, however, were short-term measures that didn't solve the underlying financial problem — the district was spending more than it was receiving.

The Fiscal Crisis
Going into Superintendent Possemato's fifth year, the district was now aware of a severe financial problem. Parents, teachers and school officials all worked as a team and came up with what appeared to be a balanced budget by cutting $1.1 million in teacher and staff

member reductions, along with cuts in several popular programs.

Then, the next shoe dropped when a financial consultant reported to the board of trustees that the district had a $1 million shortfall caused by bookkeeping errors, falling property taxes and unexpected expenses. The revelation was not taken lightly. People were in an uproar. The superintendent and management staff had lost the confidence of the community. Within a week, the chief financial officer and Superintendent Possemato were fired. The budget deficit continued to grow, and it took a five percent cut in teacher and other district employees' pay to close the gap and keep the state from taking over management of the district.

Grand Jury Findings
The Orange County grand jury later concluded that the Department of Education, which was required by law to review all local school district budgets, began issuing warnings of fiscal problems to staff in 1993. However, these admonitions were not passed on to school board members. To avoid such crises in the future, the grand jury recommended that warnings be sent directly to the school board.

Reflections
Possemato had worked wonders for the school district by improving academic and science programs, but he failed to exercise proper oversight over the district's finances. Later, he candidly admitted that his skills were on the academic, not the financial, side. This story's ending is sad, but it identifies several tips for governing board members.

Tip No. 56:   *Know the Chief Administrator's Financial Skill Level*

While it is desirable to have a chief administrative officer whose skills include government finance, there is nothing wrong with having one who is not. Like Superintendent Possemato, Ernie Schneider, Orange County Chief Administrative Officer admitted that he was not a finance person. The key is to know it beforehand — not after a fiscal disaster has occurred.

If you have not participated in the hiring of the chief administrator ask for a copy of his/her resume; and after reviewing it, request a one-on-one briefing. The administrator will be flattered, and you can then ask financial-related questions, such as:

- What is the administrator's skill level and comfort with finances?
- How does the administrator compensate for a lack of financial background (if that is the case)?
- What things does the administrator look at to be satisfied that finances are okay?
- What is the administrator's experience in dealing with financial issues and problems?

Tip No. 57:   ***Don't Let Program Success Blind You***

No one was asking the hard questions regarding ability to pay when everything was going well with the Laguna School District. After the financial crisis was made public, parents started questioning what the "nice-to-have" programs, such as the "surf-board building" class, really cost.

The district PTA Council President, Barbara Norton, summed up the failure to ask questions "I think it is real tempting, when you're in a wealthy district to say 'Yes' to parents who are used to having state-of-the-art programs. Unfortunately, nobody said No! Nobody said, 'We can't afford it,' and that's hard to do sometimes when you have parents beating down the door."

While the community and special interest groups can be excused for getting carried away and not thinking about the price tag, there is no excuse for governing body members failing to monitor finances and asking "How are we going to pay for this?"

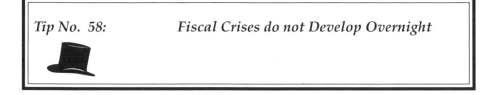

Tip No. 58:   *Fiscal Crises do not Develop Overnight*

It can take years of fiscal mismanagement and denial to get to the point where the Laguna School District found itself in deep trouble. Here are some of the stages a government may go through:

- **Equilibrium State:** This is the stability point. Finances are in satisfactory condition with on-going revenues exceeding on-going expenditures. The government is solvent, cash flow is sufficient, reserves are stable, and program needs are met on an annual basis. The budget is balanced. The agency takes whatever actions are necessary, no matter how painful, to maintain equilibrium. They not only deal with current problems, they anticipate future ones. Most local governments have been in equilibrium for their entire existence. Fiscal prudence is the norm.

- **Problem State:** An event or a combination of events takes place that disrupts the equilibrium. Perhaps the problem is caused by an external factor, such as a major industry closing down or a hurricane destroys important retail businesses or an extended recession emasculates the revenue base. The problem may be self-inflicted. The agency embarks on a large capital improvement program without ascertaining where operating and maintenance funds will come from or the agency agrees to a costly salary and benefit package it cannot afford. At some point, a cross-over occurs where on-going expenditures exceed on-going revenues. All of a sudden, the governing board finds itself in a political dilemma. To deal with the fiscal problem head-on may offend strong constituencies, such as unions, residences or businesses. However, to not directly deal with the fiscal problem permits it to worsen. Temporary measures, such as relying upon reserves to get through the fiscal year offers the easy out for people whose highest desire is reelection, but it exacerbates the financial problem. Moreover, the easy out is addictive. Expediency is the norm.

- **Crisis State:** The agency has not been able to reestablish equilibrium, and the problem continues to grow. Temporary remedies, such as using fund balances or borrowing money, are no longer viable options. In many cases, theft, graft, or corruption is discovered. The governing board must now consider drastic remedies, such as severely cutting budgets or raising taxes. It may mean rolling back previous salary and benefit increases. Those agencies that still refuse to deal with the problem and continue to hope for the magic bullet, gravitate to the next state. Denial and finger pointing are the norms.

- **Implosion State:** This is the state where virtually all control over the situation has been lost and the only alternatives are bankruptcy, government dissolution or relinquishment of local control to the state. The sad part is that when an external party is brought in, they implement the same actions that the governmental body found too painful to act upon. No-nonsense, prudent decision making becomes the norm.

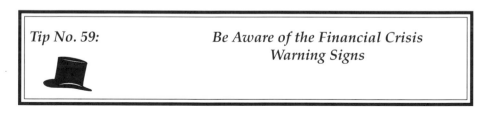

Tip No. 59:   *Be Aware of the Financial Crisis*
              Warning Signs

After the New York City financial crisis that nearly led to bankruptcy, the Advisory Commission on Intergovernmental Relations published a study entitled, "City Financial Emergencies." The Commission identified several danger signals:

1. Outstanding short-term debt at the end of a fiscal year.

   It is common for local governments to borrow money to get over temporary revenue shortfalls during the fiscal year, but most repay the debt before the fiscal year ends. Failure to repay accumulated short-term loans was cited as the single most important signal of a fiscal crisis.

2.   Poor budgeting, accounting and reporting techniques.

Advisory Commission Director Philip Dearborn stressed the importance of adequate and timely reporting. "Good municipal accounting and reporting are more important than they sound. The governments that got into trouble did not have good reporting techniques." This problem continues to exist, and the numerous crises cited in this book were accompanied with inadequate and/or late reporting.

3.   Municipal expenditures that exceed revenues by more than 5 percent in one year.

This danger signal refers to a comparison between on-going revenues and on-going expenditures. If a one-time expense such as major capital expenditures create the imbalance, the danger signal may not apply.

4.   Expenditures exceeding revenues for two consecutive years with the second year's deficiency being larger than the first year's.

Again, this danger signal refers to on-going revenues and expenditures. This sign is considered more telling than number 3 because it indicates the spiraling of an adverse trend.

5.   Interfund loans that are outstanding at the end of the fiscal year.

A temporary cash shortfall in one fund is sometimes covered by a loan from another. For example, the retirement fund may be tapped for a temporary loan to cover a general fund shortage. The danger develops when these interfund loans are not repaid before the fiscal year ends.

6.   Failure to provide full funding for currently incurred pension liabilities.

For those agencies that provide their own pension system, it is sometimes politically more expedient to put available dollars in salaries and current expenses rather than into an obscure retirement fund. Some of the governments that have had fiscal emergencies have attempted to or actually raided retirement funds.

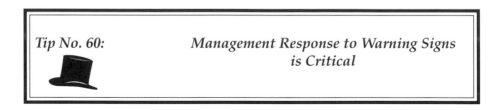

Tip No. 60:   *Management Response to Warning Signs is Critical*

Anthony Authur, vice president of Standard and Poor's Corporation, indicates that a local government in financial distress is one that cannot maintain existing services because it cannot meet payrolls and current bills or it cannot pay debt service on long and short-term debt. Early warning signs, according to Authur, are a declining population base, change in age or income of the population, impact of collective bargaining, impact of inflation on labor-intensive services, erosion of the tax base, slow growth in revenue from on-going sources and management's response to these trends. This last one is one of the most important. According to Authur, "A governing board's response to these trends is often a major factor in determining whether the agency avoids the problem, works its way out of difficulty, or surrenders entirely to the rising tide." The key negative indicators the company looks for include:

- An operating deficit for the current year.
- Two consecutive years of operating fund deficits.
- A current year operating deficit that is larger than the previous year's deficit.
- A two-year trend of increasing short-term debt outstanding at the fiscal year end.
- Property taxes greater than 90 percent of the tax limit.
- Debt outstanding greater than 90 percent of the debt limit.
- Total property tax collection less than 92 percent of the total levy.
- A trend of decreasing tax collections (two consecutive years in a three-year trend).
- Declining market valuations (two consecutive years in a three-year trend).
- Expanding annual unfunded pension obligations.

These are some of the warning signs of a pending local government fiscal calamity. The presence of even one signal should sharpen the governing body's scrutiny. Standard and Poor's also looks for positive signs such as effective budget controls, realistic budgeting, and willingness to raise taxes when required.

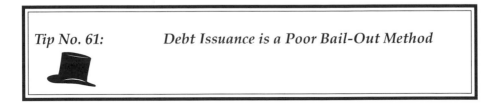

Tip No. 61:   *Debt Issuance is a Poor Bail-Out Method*

Miami is a central city of 375,000 people, rated the fourth poorest city in the United States. For many years, the City of Miami relied on its tourist attractions and the resultant sales tax that flowed into city coffers. When business growth slowed, the city did not take prudent steps to assure long-term solvency. Instead, the city relied on short-term measures, such as using reserves to balance budgets. The city also used imprudent practices, such as using bond proceeds to cover operating deficits. "Over the years, we'd float a bond issue whenever we ran out of money," one city official explained. "The hope was that downtown development would kick in, and the tax base would start growing again."

The tenuous financial situation began to unravel when the Unisys Corporation complained to federal officials that the city's finance director tried to extort $2 million from the company. Unisys provided computer services to the city and had a $20 million contract. The federal government instituted an investigation colorfully, albeit tragically, dubbed operation "Greenpalm." The investigation resulted in the finance director pleading guilty to embezzlement and extortion. The investigation also resulted in City Manager Caesar Odio resigning after he was charged with trying to shakedown Cigna Healthcare for $12,500 per month. The veteran city manager, who held his post for 11 years, plead guilty to obstructing justice. In return, federal prosecutors dropped several counts of taking kickbacks. A Miami city commissioner was also snared in the investigation after he was caught with $25,000 in marked bills. He pleaded guilty of trying to extort a $200,000 piece of the Unisys deal.

The city commission appointed Merrett Stierheim, interim city manager on a Friday. That night he took the budget home to examine the city's finances. "By Saturday night I knew something was terribly wrong because they had taken $25 million from a $72 million bond issue and moved it to the prior fiscal year to balance the books," Stierheim revealed. "Tax revenues levied for sewers were used instead to fund garbage collection. Cash reserves were moved around in an elaborate shell game to pay for many things for which they were weren't intended, including vacation pay."

After completing his analysis, Stierheim reported that the city faced a projected budget deficit of $68 million, or 20 percent of its overall general fund budget. How did it occur? While the corruption was a contributor, the major causes resulted from poor financial management practices. Dr. Robert Bradley, Director of Florida's Office of Planning and Budgeting, identified a litany of problems including:

- Continual underbudgeting of expenditures, debt interest and pension costs.
- Consistently overestimated revenues.
- Approving capital expenditures without knowledge of funding source.
- Constantly co-mingling enterprise and general funds.
- Mixing bond money with general funds.

Bradley said that the accounting system was so bad that the city had to rely upon its banks to tell it how much money it had on a daily basis. "People just didn't care if the accounting system provided a correct picture of the city's finances."

Mayor Joe Carollo reluctantly notified the State of Florida that the city was in a "financial emergency." While the board of commissioners had the power to deal with the problem, they could not bring themselves to implement simple steps like raise fees and service charges. The week before, city commissioners rejected a plan to double garbage fees to help close the gap. Moreover, the unions refused to make any wage or benefit concessions. During a meeting with Governor Lawton Chiles, Carolla raised the possibility of Miami declaring bankruptcy. A bankruptcy filing would allow the city to void union wage and benefit contracts.

Reacting to the city's failure to bring about fiscal stability, Standard and Poor's rating service downgraded the city's bond rating to 'B' from "BBB." The new rating is close to junk bond levels and resulted in making it more expensive for the city to borrow to meet short-term cash needs. Robin Prunty, a S&P spokesperson, indicated that the city had the capacity to address its financial problems but lacked the political will to do so.

A state oversight board was appointed by Governor Chiles with the charge of monitoring the financial situation and bringing Miami back to fiscal solvency. This was the first time the State of Florida had appointed an oversight board for a city government. The oversight board, chaired by Lt. Governor Buddy MacKay, was empowered to make adjustments in union contracts and cuts in services. However, its powers were limited as it could recommend a tax increase, but not order it.

Distraught with what was happening to its local government, a group of citizens circulated petitions and obtained 10,000 signatures to call a referendum on abolition of the city. These petitions were certified, and an election was held during September, 1997. Even though less than 25 percent of the electorate turned out for this momentous event,

Miami's fiscal problems and corruption threatened its survival as a city.

the proposal to abolish the city failed by a 85 to 15 percent vote. But the message was clear — clean up the corruption and mismanagement.

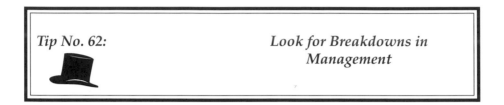

Tip No. 62:   ***Look for Breakdowns in Management***

Aside from the financial problems, lackadaisical attitudes had permeated the City of Miami personnel practices. Management had completely abrogated its responsibility to manage the workers compensation system, resulting in one-third of all employees filing claims. In the sanitation department, 60 percent of the refuse workers had claims pending. The incentive to file is strong as successful claimants receive full salary with no income tax. The cost, however, is borne by the city in terms of higher premiums.

Just as distressing, Dr. Robert Bradley noted that management rolled over in the collective bargaining process. The tendency was to accept the salary and benefit demands of the employees. This left the city commission without the buffer that the governing body needs from management to keep salaries and benefits at a reasonable level.

Tip No. 63:   ***Avoid Financial Gimmickry and Cut Your Losses***

When financial stress is first encountered, some governing boards resort to expedient techniques to balance the budget or to get through the fiscal year. This approach may be based upon a genuine feeling that things will get better, or it may be based upon fear of alienating service receivers. Whatever the reason for avoidance, it must be remembered that the majority of the damage that occurs from fiscal disasters results from a failure to deal with the problem once it surfaces.

After the near bankruptcy in New York City, Robert E. Merrian, Chairman of the Advisory Commission on Intergovernmental Relations, stated it this way, "What happened in New York City is what we are feeling at all levels of government. In their desire to get re-elected, public officials are unwilling to tear into tough problems involving the level of services and taxation because of the political consequences."

Here are some of the financial gimmicks that a local government may use to make a budget appear balanced. They do nothing to solve the underlying problem and usually compound it .

- Inflate Revenue Estimates
- Underestimate Expenditures
- Extend the Fiscal Year
- Raid the Reserves and Enterprise Funds
- Fail to Repay Interfund Transfers
- Misappropriate Grants
- Divert Bond Monies
- Change the Books or Method of Accounting
- Defer Costs to the Future

Tip No. 64:   *You've Got to Rein in*
                                            the "Pleasers"

San Francisco residents love their library. They financed a new high tech main library and to insure its fiscal viability, passed Proposition E in 1995, which guaranteed a portion of the general fund would be devoted to library uses. This increased the library budget by approximately 50 percent.

Within a year, library officials reported that the $35 million, 27-branch operation faced a deficit of $2.8 million. Library officials blamed the projected 8 percent deficit on inefficient management and increased labor costs, resulting from the popularity of the new main library. "We were more popular than we thought we would be, and that has created the problem. In a way, our librarians have been too anxious to provide good service. We haven't had the proper controls in place," conceded Commission President Steven Coulter. The library had been reducing permanent positions through an attrition program; however, the current year savings were eaten up by the extension of part-time hours to meet the demand at the main library. Circulation at the new main library was up 71 percent.

To deal with the problem, the library commission voted to freeze all budgeted book purchases and request a $1.1 million supplemental appropriation from Mayor Willie Brown. They also requested a financial recovery plan from City Librarian Kenneth Dowlin. The commission also promised to submit to a full audit of its finances.

"It's nuts. This is a city department that had a 50 percent budget increase because of Proposition E, and they already have a deficit," said library critic Timothy Gillespie. Jan Hargrove summed up this fiscal tip when she said: "Good service is important, and I'll bet anyone can provide it by throwing money at the problem. Is it too much to ask our highly paid professionals to provide good service within an already generous budget?"

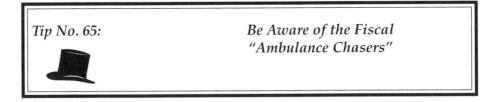

Tip No. 65:   ***Be Aware of the Fiscal "Ambulance Chasers"***

Los Angeles County had developed an eclectic budget balancing package that relied upon using fund balances, excess retirement fund earnings and a transfer of monies from other funds. After a considerable amount of wrangling, the board of supervisors adopted the plan.

Just when the supervisors thought that they were home free, Attorney Richard Fine filed a lawsuit, challenging a state law that was passed specifically for Los Angeles County to divert $50 million in Metropolitan Transportation Authority funds to the general fund. Later, a superior court judge declared that a state law that just benefits one county, is unconstitutional.

This ruling knocked the pins out from under the delicate budget balancing program and sent Los Angeles County officials scrambling for ways to fill the hole. The supervisors were not happy with Fine and accused him of exploiting the system. "We may end up having to close some of our clinics and reduce beds in our hospitals," said Supervisor Yvonne Brathwaite Burke. "There could be many victims as a result of this lawsuit."

Fine saw it differently. He believed that the only reason his lawsuit was possible was because the politicians failed to do their job in the first place. "Only when the government stops misappropriating the people's funds will my business fall off," lectured Fine.

Right after his success in the Los Angeles County case, a citizens group retained Fine to challenge the Orange County Bankruptcy recovery plan. The Orange County plan used bus, parks, flood control and redevelopment money to pay off the bankruptcy debt. Fine's argument in this case was that by changing the use of the tax money, the county had in effect created a new tax without getting voter approval. The remedy sought in this case was to return the money to their respective funds.

Fine has found a very lucrative field as he has filed numerous lawsuits which have resulted in various governments returning over $200 million to originating accounts. One of Fine's favorite targets is the use of special funds to balance the general fund such as the City of Los Angeles diverting over $90 million from a parking meter fund.

Whether you feel that Fine is a fiscal ambulance chaser or serving a legitimate public purpose, the fact is that many bailout plans that rely upon transfers and one-time measures present inviting targets.

Tip No. 66:   ***You Cannot Borrow Your Way Out***
                            of a Fiscal Crisis

For many years, Los Angles County borrowed heavily to mask the fact that it had a severe negative imbalance between revenues and expenditures. While many public agencies borrow money to build capital facilities, Los Angeles County violated the primary rule of borrowing — never use long-term debt to finance operating expenses. It got into the habit of doing so and borrowed to excess.

Beginning in the 1990's, the county tax base had been ravaged by a number of factors including the recession, mandates, and state raids on its revenues. Rather than cut back services, the board of supervisors elected to maintain high cost services, such as health and welfare programs at their current levels, in the hope that the economy would rebound. They also expected that the state and federal governments would step in and bail the county out of the mess.

By using certificates of participation, the county was able to avoid public votes and obscure the magnitude of the borrowing. Only through a series of articles by the *Los Angeles Times* did the public learn of the extent of the problem. In order to secure the debt, the county mortgaged or pledged as security, 99 percent of all its assets, including its hall of administration, courts, sheriff's stations, fire stations, golf courses, parks and world famous Marina Del Rey yacht harbor. Debt service payments became the county's third highest expense, just behind the health and sheriff's department.

Wall Street watches the debt service ratio closely and considers 10 percent as the danger threshold. The county debt payment ratio topped 15 percent before the warning bells went off. Here is how the county continued to use debt to try to deal with its deficit:

Year	Debt Ratio
89-90	7.7%
90-91	8.5%
91-92	6.4%
92-93	7.0%
93-94	10.6%
94-95	15.6%

Said Supervisor Zev Yaroslavsky (who was not part of the board that made borrowing decisions), "The problem here is not that they have borrowed, although they have borrowed far more than is prudent. The problem is the reason for which they borrowed. The board of supervisors borrowed in order to avoid tough decisions."

After the debt ruse was exposed, county supervisors promised to quit using debt as a crutch since it was threatening to result in a lower bond rating which would make borrowing even more expensive. Chairwoman Gloria Molina articulated the belated change in attitude of the board by declaring: "You cannot continue to finance operations with one-time borrowing."

Tip No. 67:   *Avoid Bankruptcy Filings*

Bridgeport, Connecticut is the largest city in the state and was home to Phineas Taylor Barnum, of P.T. Barnum fame who once served a term as mayor. When hard times came, however, Bridgeport became notable for coming under the watch of a state-appointed financial review board in 1988. It was a city caught in the vise of not enough money for required services, no place to get funds without a major property tax increase and no state or federal assistance available.

In 1992, the city was unable to fill a $18 million gap in its $304 million budget. It's not that city officials didn't try. Street sweeping, snow removal, two senior centers and virtually all recreation programs were eliminated. Property taxes were also raised 5 percent.

Since labor costs constituted 65 percent of the budget, labor unions were asked to do their part and renegotiate contracts; but the unions refused to give an inch.

The state-created Financial Review Board, which had no real power, recommended the traditional method of meeting a deficit budget — hiking taxes and in this case a hefty 18 percent. However, taxes had already been raised to the highest in the state. The City's Common Council balked at an increase, fearing that such an action would drive even more businesses and residents from the town. "People would refuse to pay 18 percent more. They'd just board up their homes," Mayor Mary Moran proclaimed.

On June 6, 1992, however, Mayor Moran made an announcement that surprised residents, union members, and state legislators. Because Bridgeport could not fill the budget gap, it was seeking protection from its creditors under the Chapter 9 provisions of the Federal Bankruptcy Code.

The reactions by the rating agencies were swift. Moody's Investors Service, Inc., suspended the rating on the city's uninsured general obligation debt, while Standard & Poor's lowered its rating on $77.7 million in bonds to CCC (below investment grade) from BBB. While the mayor insisted that the city would meet its debt obligations and the bankruptcy was merely a way to nullify expensive labor contracts, rating officials were unmoved.

State legislators were aghast. The city had acted illegally, they said, since Chapter 9 filings required state approval, especially since Bridgeport's fiscal affairs had come under the watch of the State Review Board.

The Mayor's action, however, was renounced by the community and Mary Moran became the first one-term Bridgeport mayor since the 1920's. Joseph P. Ganim was elected Mayor in 1994 and immediately withdrew the bankruptcy petition.

The new mayor and Chief Labor Negotiator Dennis C. Murphy renegotiated all 12 of the city's collective bargaining agreements that had since expired. Unpaid furloughs and 0 percent wage increases were negotiated. Staffing on sanitation trucks was reduced from 3 to 2 persons and overtime was slashed from over $800,000 to under

$250,000 per year. The city's 36 hole golf course was privatized, resulting in triple the revenue and better golf. A labor-management cooperative was formed to enhance dialogue and help get union acceptance of this bitter pill that had to be swallowed if Bridgeport was to pull itself up.

It took two years to resolve what was dubbed the Moran deficit. Since then budgets have been balanced with modest surpluses; and taxes were reduced in 1996 and 1997 despite the addition of more police officers. Moreover, bond ratings have steadily improved to investment grade, (BBB-) allowing the city to borrow up to $78 million for capital projects including a minor league baseball stadium and entertainment facilities. Says Dennis Murphy, who was appointed Chief Administrative Officer, "Municipalities should not avoid bankruptcy, they should never file bankruptcy. There's always a better way. "

When You Must Cut

"I don't have much hope for the survival of this City. Chelsea will never be able to raise anywhere near the level of local revenues it needs to become financially stable."

Former Alderman Donald Jordan reflecting on Chelsea's financial future

Receivership
Chelsea, Massachusetts, is an ethnically diverse community of 28,000 people and 1.8 square miles, located just five minutes from downtown Boston. In September 1991, Chelsea became the first city in Massachusetts, since the great depression, to be placed into receivership. Faced with a $10 million deficit and an inability to meet its payroll, the Chelsea Mayor appealed to the state government for relief. Previous efforts, such as grants and loans from the state and the establishment of an emergency finance board, had failed. So rather than further bailout the city, the governor proposed, and the legislature passed, special legislation to permit a receiver to take over the administration of the city's finances and services.

Remarkably, Chelsea's financial problems developed during the mid-

1980's, when the rest of Massachusetts was enjoying an unprecedented economic growth period. A spiraling recession, mismanagement, corruption and lethargy were the apparent reasons for Chelsea's failure to participate in what became known as the "Massachusetts Miracle." The *Boston Globe* described the Chelsea stagnation "as a period when bagmen could reach out and touch police and elected officials but competent financial managers and record keepers were far away."

Cutbacks

Before receivership, the two groups which could do something about the city's financial plight spurned pleas for help. The city went to taxpayers to obtain more revenue raising flexibility. Massachusetts Proposition 2 1/2 requires an election to override revenue limits but lacking confidence in its governing board, the voters flatly rejected the proposal. Labor unions were asked to abrogate existing wage and benefit agreements. They, too, rejected the pleas, believing that the city wanted to balance the budget on their backs.

To overcome political roadblocks, the receiver was given broad powers and responsibilities at the expense of the elected mayor, aldermen and administrators. The receiver utilized fee increases, cuts and one-time measures, such as a $5 million advance in-lieu of taxes from the Massachusetts Port Authority to get the city into a positive cash position for the first time in years. Long-term measures, however, were necessary to get the city back into a state of self-sufficiency.

Problems

Chelsea's labor practices were so political, archaic and rule bound that prior governing boards were stifled from making any meaningful changes. Some examples of problems included:

- Labor contracts contained minimum staffing clauses which established the number of firefighters required for each shift.

- Past practices permitted overtime abuses, unlimited sick leave and a very generous vacation program.

- Department heads were underpaid but granted virtual lifetime tenure in exchange for their low wages.

The receiver enacted numerous changes to bring about long-term solvency. The city staff was reduced by 28 percent from 309 to 224 positions. Minimum staff clauses were modified, overtime abuses rectified, and senior management positions eliminated. In the police department, 23 percent of the low producing, senior management positions were cut. Several department heads were also eliminated. The remaining department heads were given competitive salaries and higher accountability. Privatization, use of volunteers, technology, and updated user fees were also part of the long-term strategy to bring about self-sufficiency.

New Government
An 18-member Charter Preparation Team was also established to create a new charter for the community. Susan Podziba, a public sector mediator, utilized public meetings, surveys, interviews, call-in-public TV programs, and focus groups to involve community members in the development of a new charter for Chelsea. The process worked. In June 1994, the citizens of Chelsea approved the new charter by a 60-to-40 percent vote. An important element of the charter was the establishment of a council-manager form of government. Shortly thereafter, Guy A. Santagate was appointed the first city manager. In August 1995, the receivership ended; and the City of Chelsea became self-governing again. Many were worried that the days of graft and fiscal mismanagement were just around the corner. They need not have worried. In his 1997 State of the City Address, Santagate pointed to the following accomplishments:

1. Over $250 million in new private and public investment had been attracted to Chelsea during the previous two years.
2. Financial reporting deficiencies were corrected and accounts reconciled, thereby locating $423,000 in new revenue.
3. Fiscal Year 1996 ended with a $1.1 million cash surplus.
4. A $27 million, five year capital improvements program was formulated to address over 40 years' of deferred maintenance.

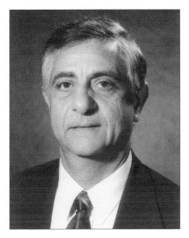

Guy A. Santagate, first City Manager of Chelsea, Massachusetts, focused on fiscal conservatism and staff professionalism.

The financial community's judgment was perhaps the most important. Chelsea's bond anticipation notes were assigned Standard & Poor's highest rating for short-term securities. Santagate summed up Chelsea's resurgence with the statement, "We're not out of the woods yet, but I'm more confident today than I was a year ago; and I am now sleeping nights."

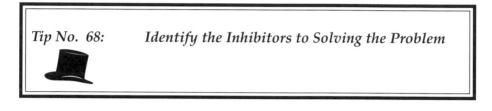

Tip No. 68:   *Identify the Inhibitors to Solving the Problem*

Why didn't the Chelsea governing body take the steps necessary to keep the city from being taken over by a receiver? The receiver did nothing that the city hadn't already considered. In virtually all of the agencies facing extreme emergencies, there appears to be a similar reluctance to make the tough decisions.

This is where governing body leadership is vital. Unions, businesses, homeowners and other special interest groups whose help is needed to solve the problem tend to sit back and wait for others to commit. Elected officials have to exercise political courage by telling it like it is and recruiting these groups to make the needed sacrifices.

Tip No. 69:   *Determine Why Cutbacks Are Really Necessary*

Cutting budgets is much more difficult than increasing them. This holds true for staff, as well as elected officials. Once you start to cut, you will be impacting people — their jobs, their livelihood, and their basic needs. Often, cuts are made during a crisis period. Quick action is required; and the same degree of analysis that goes into implementing a new program may not be exercised during the downsizing.

Knowing the underlying reason for the cutbacks helps elected officials make the type of decisions that are required. Has the problem been caused by a slight reduction in revenues, such as when the local economy dips during a temporary recession? This type of problem can be dealt with by using temporary bailout measures. Or, has the problem resulted from what is termed a structural imbalance — on-going revenues are insufficient to pay for on-going expenditures. This is a much more serious problem and requires some major reductions in on-going programs or acquiring new revenue sources.

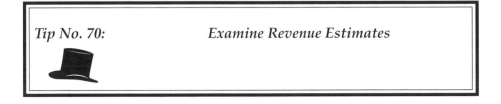

Tip No. 70:   ***Examine Revenue Estimates***

Too often elected officials will make major expenditure cuts without checking revenue projections. It could be that while the expenditures are estimated fairly, the revenues are estimated conservatively. This may force the elected body to make unnecessary cutbacks.

As a general rule, staff members "low ball" revenue estimates. This is because the penalty is much greater for failing to achieve a revenue estimate than it is for exceeding the estimate. The press rarely criticizes conservative revenue estimation practices.

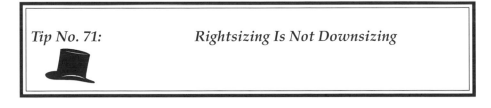

Tip No. 71:   ***Rightsizing Is Not Downsizing***

Downsizing is a means of balancing the budget during a crisis period. It usually means across-the-board spending cuts. It is an expedient strategy in that the basic package of services are continued but with less money. In downsizing, every department takes a proportionate hit. Downsizing approaches include deferral of maintenance and capital expenditures, delay in paying bills, and personnel furlough programs. Downsizing is based upon the assumption that once the crisis is over, the old programs will be restored.

Rightsizing, on the other hand, means shifting resources from low priority programs to high priority programs. This requires a ranking of programs by their importance and value. Units of government may be consolidated, management levels eliminated, and services dropped. It is considered a long-term strategy in that changes are considered permanent. While some budgets may shrink or disappear, other high priority programs may increase. Gerald Seals, former City Manager of Corvallis, Oregon distinguishes between rightsizing and downsizing this way, "If there's a business we should no longer be in, rightsizing says, lets get out of it. Downsizing doesn't get out of a business."

While the two concepts are different, they are not mutually exclusive. Some agencies believe that a year of downsizing is a necessary prerequisite to an effective rightsizing effort. Other agencies, such as Prince William County, Virginia applied both concepts at the same time.

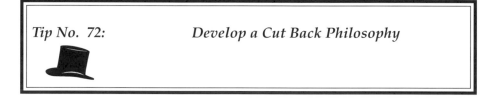

Tip No. 72:   *Develop a Cut Back Philosophy*

In 1992, faced with a growing imbalance between on-going revenues and on-going expenditures, Charlotte, North Carolina, City Manager O. Wendell White presented a rightsizing philosophy to the city council at its annual budget retreat. After much debate, the city council adopted the rightsizing concept with the provision that no layoffs would be made and a progress report would be submitted to the city council after one year. The idea underlying rightsizing is to reallocate resources from lower to higher priority areas. The Charlotte staff approached this by asking the question, "If we were to design city services anew today, what would they look like?" Answers to four follow-up questions were sought from this organization of 5000 employees in order to provide information necessary to make restructuring decisions:

1.   What services should city government provide?
2.   How should these services be financed?
3.   How should resources be organized to deliver services effectively?
4.   What is the most efficient method of providing city services?

Several strategies were used by the city to achieve the rightsizing objective, including a hiring freeze and job bank, a retirement incentive program, guidelines for reducing layers of management, and a process for prioritizing city services. A key part of the program was the continuing involvement and training of employees.

One year later, City Manager White presented the following accomplishments to the city council:

- Reduction of 272 positions with no layoffs.
- Innovations and productivity improvements totalling $2.8 million.
- Reductions in layers of management in 12 city departments.
- Position reduction of 20 percent or greater for six departments.
- Reduction in total management positions by 10 percent, as compared to labor and trade of 7 percent.

Charlotte's success was due to many factors; and a key one was the adoption of a coordinated rightsizing philosophy, as opposed to a piecemeal approach to cutbacks or outright denial of the existence of a problem, as was the case in Chelsea.

Tip No. 73:   ***Identify Your Core Services***

Over the years, your organization has undoubtedly added functions and services. Some of these were added to meet the needs of a growing constituency. Some were added because a public or private grant was made available for a new service, such as the senior nutrition programs or a traffic enforcement bureau for a police department. Once the grant expired, the service was continued with agency funds. Others may have been added because of pressure from a special interest or a powerful governing board member.

The City of Santa Ana, California, after projections revealed an impending financial crisis, decided to deal with the problem in the initial stages. Dave Ream, City Manager, concluded that the only way the city could get through the 1990's recession was to focus on preserving its core services, while cutting back on all other programs.

The city council decided what the core services were — police, fire and maintenance of the infrastructure. These were determined to be the most important services the city provided to its residents, and these would be the ones preserved. Other programs and services, while important, were cut. The city manager started in his own office by reducing a staff of 34 to 7, by cutting out several desirable but non-core programs, such as cable television production and affirmative action. Ream helped sell the core program concept to the organization and the community by displaying the old organization chart of the city manager's office on a large poster board showing 27 red "X's" where positions used to exist.

Santa Ana City Manager Dave Ream, displays organizational chart of a drastically cutback City Manager's office which was reduced from 34 to 7 positions.

Charlotte used a services assessment process to identify their core services. The city categorized city services into 41 service activities such as transit, rescue, fire suppression, police patrol, landscape maintenance and street maintenance. The governing board, a city management group, and a 44-member citizens' assessment panel participated in a paired comparison program, where the 41 service categories were compared with one another by responding to the following question: "In your opinion, which of the following two services is of more importance and value to the community of Charlotte?" After each participant made 1640 comparisons, the results were compiled into a priority listing of all 41 programs. The top five services were:

1. Police patrol
2. Firefighting/rescue
3. Criminal investigations
4. Police street drug interdiction
5. Recycling

Participants were then asked to respond to another question to determine the relative effectiveness of programs: "From the customer's point of view, which of these two services is being provided better?" This question was designed to help identify customer service improvement opportunities.

The results of the two questions were then plotted on a matrix, with the relative importance of the service on the horizontal axis and the relative effectiveness on the vertical axis. Without the assistance of personal computers, the process would have been overly cumbersome.

Tip No. 74:   *Priority Rankings Require a*
                       Mature Approach

The heart of a rightsizing program is the ranking process. It requires the governing body to publicly vote to reduce or to eliminate dollars from weak programs. While it makes sense in theory, it requires a mature governing body to make the hard decisions to eliminate a popular highly visible program that ranks low in value and importance. Elected officials will naturally prefer an across-the-board cut to having to take money from the tiny tots program and put it into sewer maintenance. Another obstacle to the ranking approach arises when final rankings of programs by order of importance are used by members to embarrass other members. A typical ploy is to give the results to the newspaper with choice comments about the other member's indifference to constituent needs.

The ranking process is logical and presents a method for dealing with difficult financial problems. To use it effectively, however, governing body members must downplay politics and think of the entire organization. Those that lack the will to do so, as was the case in Chelsea, may wake up and find a state appointed receiver making the hard decisions for them.

Tip No. 75:   *Examine Management and*
              Administration Costs

Vice President Al Gore seized a popular complaint when he began urging state governments to examine whether too much of the school district budget was being consumed by administrative costs. According to the California State Department of Finance, administration expenses (superintendents, curriculum experts, school-board members, purchasing and personnel, etc.), on average, consume 9 percent of a school district budget. "Let's take the money from the bureaucrats and put it in the classroom," urges John Perez, Vice President of the United Teachers of Los Angeles. Perez was the main backer of a state initiative to limit administrative expenses to 5 percent of school budgets. Administrative budgets may be too fat and should be examined, but some key questions should be answered:

1.   What is your agency's definition of administration? Is it the same as other districts?

2.   Will teachers and other direct service providers to students wind up performing these administrative duties if administration is cut? Will this increase the teacher's administrative load?

3.   Is the administrative percentage higher because your district is participating in special programs that require a higher administrative cost?

4.   Are small districts mandated to have many of the same personnel as larger districts? If so, smaller districts will show a higher student administrative cost.

A district must also determine the dividing line between administration and direct benefit for students. Dennis Myers of the Association of California School Administrators asked the question, "What about the legal costs for getting rid of a bad teacher? That can cost hundreds of thousands of dollars. It's administrative, but it results in a direct benefit to students."

The relationship between administrative and service delivery expenses is not confined to school districts. Cities, counties and special districts can become bloated at the top with supervisory and support services personnel.

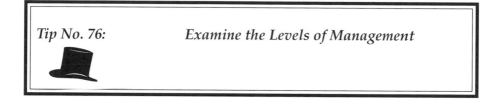

Tip No. 76:   *Examine the Levels of Management*

A way to decrease administrative burden is to reduce the levels of management. One of the Charlotte rightsizing strategies required each department to reduce its layers of management. "Those departments with more than 125 employees will have a goal of five layers or less; 50 to 125 employees, three or less; less than 50 employees, two or less." This was one of the more controversial aspects of the plan, but it resulted in 12 departments reducing their levels of management by one or more. Departments were allowed to require an exemption from the guidelines if they could provide convincing justifications. According to City Manager White, several exemptions were requested but none were granted.

Tip No. 77:   *Make Sure Cutback Strategies*
Are Affordable

During the rush to reduce costs, many agencies adopted early retirement programs. These programs varied, such as providing an employee one to three years of retirement credit or a dollar incentive such as $10,000 to $20,000 to retire. Long-term employees command high salaries and benefits, and the intent was to reduce costs by replacing these positions with entry level positions or eliminating the positions altogether. Many organizations found that their early retirement programs were very popular, but they failed to project the one-time start-up costs. In some cases, the budget deficit was actually exacerbated because these employees carried years of accrued benefit costs that had to be paid off all at once. Agencies also found that the work the veteran employees were doing sometimes required more than one replacement position.

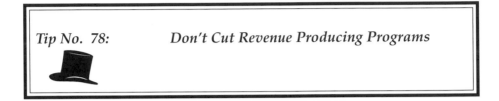

Tip No. 78:   ***Don't Cut Revenue Producing Programs***

Some programs are tied to revenues, and a cutback or hiring freeze can cost the agency sorely needed revenue. Such was the case pleaded by Ventura County, California, Assessor Glenn Gray. During an extended economic downturn, property values dropped severely and resulted in thousands of assessment appeals. Due to shrinking revenues, the assessor's office lost 53 positions through cuts and attrition. With the increased workload and a decreasing staff, the assessor faced a dilemma. By law, if the assessor is unable to process the appeal within two years, it is automatically granted and the county loses the property tax revenue. It took several forfeitures before the board of supervisors relented and decided to provide the assessor with four additional personnel in order to process over $21 million in appeals.

Does it really help to treat a revenue producing program the same way as a non-revenue producing program? One administrator responded this way, "Yes. I know we lose money; but by treating all departments the same, we cannot be accused of favoritism." Obviously, a business would not last long using this type of logic.

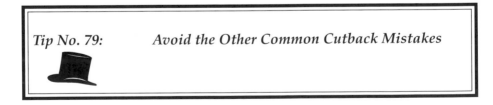

Tip No. 79:   ***Avoid the Other Common Cutback Mistakes***

Here are some of the other common "mistakes" elected officials make when faced with budget shortfalls.

- **Let's Exhaust the Reserves**

  While politically appealing, reserve depletion is a short-term strategy that can have long-term detrimental consequences. The reliance on reserves can help an agency get through the crisis period, but their use should be discontinued as soon as possible. While financing on-going programs with reserves delays the day of reckoning temporarily, it exacerbates the overall problem since the interest income from reserves is lost, and the gap between on-going expenditures and revenues increases.

- **Let's Freeze All Vacant Positions**

  While seemingly a very caring approach, freezing vacant positions can be one of the most counterproductive strategies. It is based on the assumption that all positions carry the same priority for the organization. This is simply not true; some are more critical than others. Some departments have been severely hurt by the freezing of positions, requiring highly technical skills that cannot be picked up by untrained personnel. The City of Charlotte, North Carolina, was able to overcome the weakness of a position freeze by linking it with a job bank. The job bank concept was used so that critical jobs would still be filled, but other vacancies were banked and evaluated for elimination or transfer to a higher priority city need. A placement committee was established which evaluated whether a vacant position would be filled.

  The hiring freeze and critical review prior to filling positions was based on the premise that each vacancy is an opportunity to downsize the organization. To give the system teeth, the job bank required that once a vacancy was created, an adjustment in the organization had to take place. Each vacancy that was approved to be filled could only be filled by another city employee. As a result, each vacancy that was filled created another vacancy that would go through the same review process. While exceptions were permitted for highly skilled or technical positions, these exceptions were rare.

- **Let's Make Across-the-Board Cuts**

  Equal cuts across-the-board such as 5 percent per department seems fair, but it reinforces poor budgeting practices.

If one department has padded its budget by 10 percent and another has submitted an unpadded budget, the padding department will be rewarded for its apparent cleverness. Most governing bodies would never build budgets on the same premise — everyone gets an equal percentage increase without justifying why the money is needed.

To avoid this trap, identify those departments that have shown the ability to manage a budget. What has been the department's history in dealing with cutbacks? Has the department:

- Offered real rather than cosmetic cuts?
- Combined or eliminated functions or activities?
- Privatized any functions?
- Demonstrated quantifiable productivity improvements?
- Found new revenue sources?
- Improved revenue collections?
- Achieved their revenue estimates?

Two other things to examine is the change in budget in real and constant dollars during the last five years and the changes in number of employees as compared to population and clients served.

- **Defer Equipment Purchases**

It doesn't make sense to keep expensive positions and not provide them with the relatively inexpensive equipment needed to carry out their functions. There are numerous horror stories about positions that were saved from the cutter's ax only to set idle for lack of required equipment, such as the accountants who were not given calculators, let alone computers.

- **Cutback Capital Expenditures**

Reduction in the level of capital expenditures is a popular way to deal with cutbacks. However, this is a short-sighted and expensive strategy. During cutback periods, the proportionate share of capital investment should be maintained. Some questions to ask before cutting capital expenditures.

- Will the action result in property value reduction?
- Will it exacerbate community deterioration?
- Will the reduction create a hazard or safety problem?

- • Will the reduction impact the preservation of other capital assets?
- • Will it impact community values?

- **Eliminate Training and Workshops**

  While politically popular, eliminating training and workshops from the budget is one of the most typical, yet most short-sighted strategies. Local governments are in the service business and 60 to 80 percent of their budgets are composed of salaries and benefits. Employees must have the skills and technical training to carry out their tasks effectively. Poorly trained employees cost the agency money in terms of mistakes, lower productivity, and accidents.

- **Direct Staff Where to Cut**

  The governing body should resist the desire to roll their sleeves up and begin cutting individual budgets. This undermines the accountability from staff. The staff knows where cutbacks can be made without serious harm. It is better to give them a target and let them make the cuts.

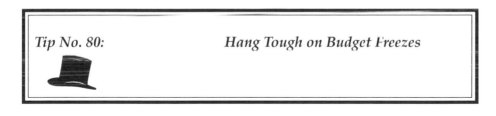

Tip No. 80:   *Hang Tough on Budget Freezes*

To combat an estimated $120 million deficit, the City of Los Angeles City Council imposed a freeze hoping to cut 1600 positions and save one-half of the amount needed. Despite this freeze and five others, the city wound up hiring an additional 1200 employees in the 11 months after the first freeze was adopted. With the 244 additional positions added during the first six months of the next fiscal year, the number of authorized city employees hit an all time high of 32,350 during the freeze period. Keith Comrie, City Administrative Officer, argued that "the freeze was for real. The departments, including this one, are bleeding." He pointed out that the freeze was slow to materialize since there were many positions in the pipeline, and the city could not withdraw offers and commitments that had been made.

Councilmember Ernani Bernardi saw it differently, "I think it's a fraud. It's a lack of priorities and commitment to hard nose management." Said Councilmember Zev Yaroslavsky, "We didn't have a real freeze until January, eleven months later. It was a phony freeze. The mayor and council were not willing to start telling department heads that we were in a crisis mode."

The problem resulted from two main factors. First, a significant number of positions in the Department of Water and Power, Department of Airports and Harbor Department were exempted from the freeze because their agencies were enterprise funds and had their own revenue base. Second, the freeze rules continued to be weakened. One job freeze lasted two weeks before being replaced by a totally different program. The new program allowed departments to fill vacant positions as long as they found other ways to reduce their budgets by six percent. If all else failed, department managers could go to the city council and plead their case. The city council was reluctant to enforce the freeze as evidenced by the fact that over 88 percent of all requests for exemption were approved.

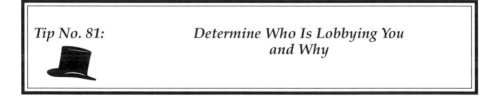

Tip No. 81:   *Determine Who Is Lobbying You and Why*

In 1995, the Heritage Foundation examined who was testifying in front of congressional committees and subcommittees during budget cutting sessions. The findings provided revealing insights. More than 35 percent of congressional witnesses were federal employees; and of the remaining witnesses, more than one-third represented organizations that received federal funds. While lobbyists must register and political campaign contributions must be divulged, no policy requires those receiving federal contracts or grants to divulge their stake in federal spending when they testify. Congress is starting to recognize that they may not be getting a balanced view and that a good proportion of those testifying have a vested interest.

A similar situation occurs at the local level when a group fills the meeting chamber to pressure the governing board to support or oppose an issue. It is not uncommon to hear recall, referendum, and lawsuit threats. The pressure from this tactic can be so intense that public officials forget about those people and groups that are not at the meeting and whose views are not being added to the dialogue. Elected officials who have gone through a difficult budget cutting session attest to the skewing that occurs when a group of residents, employees, customers or contractors puts the heat on to preserve their vested interests. Some thoughts on countering this tactic include:

- If you know about the situation in advance, be sure to invite representatives of the opposing view to attend.

- If you are blindsided by a pressure group, consider trying to get the item continued so that a more balanced deliberation can take place.

- Ask staff to provide the pros and cons of the issue at the meeting.

- If your colleagues have a good perspective on the issue, ask one of them to provide their insights. A question like, "Board member Johnson, can you provide some background on this item, along with the arguments for and against?

- If people do not divulge their vested interests in a matter, ask them to do so.

- Try to remember that you represent your entire constituency and not just those in the meeting room.

The fact that a person or group has a vested interest, does not necessarily discount their arguments; it's just that you can make a more informed decision by knowing about it.

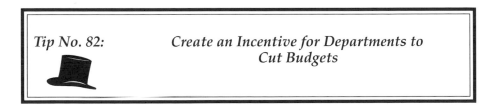

Tip No. 82:   *Create an Incentive for Departments to Cut Budgets*

Even during a severe fiscal crisis, why should a public manager offer cuts? What is the incentive to cut one's budget? Virtually none. To offer or to permit cuts to one's budget makes a department manager appear weak and uncaring toward his/her employees and clients.

Sherman Block and Gil Garcetti both publicly threatened to file lawsuits to thwart cuts to their budgets by county supervisors even though Los Angeles County faced a $1 billion deficit. Both men are two of the most influential, recognizable, and highly paid public employees in the United States. Block runs the Los Angeles County Sheriff's Department. Garcetti manages the Los Angeles County District Attorney's Office. How can this happen? Rule number one for the public manager is to protect and increase your budget at all costs.

To do otherwise shows weakness. This will continue to be the case until rewards are provided for good budgeting and sanctions enforced for poor budgeting.

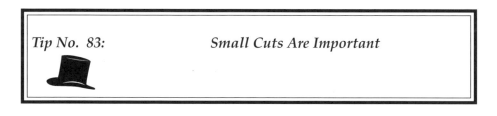

Tip No. 83:   ***Small Cuts Are Important***

The banner of the California State Police was lowered for the last time in 1994, after a 108-year history as a separate state department. They fought hard to maintain their identity and made convincing arguments like the State Capitol needed professional policing from its 271 specially trained officers. However, in the end, the state legislature decided to consolidate the State Police with the California Highway Patrol, thus saving taxpayers $835,000 annually.

Opponents to the merger argued that the less than $1 million savings was peanuts when compared to the state's $40 billion plus budget. "You're swatting gnats when you should be chasing alligators out of the pond," one partisan complained. While it was a small amount, it was a significant statement. There was an obvious duplication of effort; and as many legislators said, "You've got to start somewhere."

Opponents to cutting programs love to argue both sides of this issue. If you skip the small programs and go after the big ones, you will be accused of favoritism or discrimination. If you focus on the small ones, they try to condemn you for wasting time on insignificant issues.

Tip No. 84:   ***Establish Specific Parameters for***
                             Blue Ribbon Committees

Establishing citizen committees to obtain advice on cutbacks has become a popular approach for many governments. If not used carefully, however, the approach can bring unwanted problems to the agency. Problems include members using the committee as a political platform to embarrass the governing board, members springboarding into unauthorized areas, and members getting involved in too much detail. One such committee actually increased the work of staff with their constant requests for detailed salary, benefit, current expense and travel information for individual employees.

Things to clarify when establishing a blue ribbon committee to provide cutback recommendations include:

- Clearly define the mission and expectations in writing.
- Specify how and when the committee will report to the governing body.
- Set deadlines for reports.
- Establish a sunset date for the committee to end operations and stick to it.

Recognize that if you do not like the results, it may be politically difficult to ignore blue ribbon committee recommendations once they are publicized. If however, the committee is composed of thoughtful, qualified members and they stick to the mission, your governing body can reap tremendous benefits. Moreover, the committee members can help sell difficult proposals to the community.

Sins, Omissions and Poor Judgment

"The City Treasury is not your personal piggy bank, the money belongs to the people."

Judge Gordon Ringer sentencing City Manager
Aurora (Dolly) Vollaire to prison

The Quiet Little Town

The Bradbury, California, city council was convinced that their government was operating satisfactorily and that city manager, Aurora (Dolly) Vollaire kept a tight fist over the budget. The city had expenditure controls — three signatures required for every check, monthly review and approval of all expenses by the city council, and a final review by the mayor of all monthly expenses. An annual audit was conducted every year, and the city always received a clean bill of health.

Sure there were occasional complaints that Vollaire exercised too much control, but that was understandable for someone who had managed and operated the city with very little help for two decades.

Besides serving as city manager, Vollaire was the planning director, city clerk and finance director.

But then one day a city credit card statement was erroneously delivered to a resident's house. Something was definitely amiss — why was the city manager purchasing fine china, designer sunglasses and other luxury items with a city credit card? Armed with the credit card statement and receipts, community member Robert Penny confronted the city council and requested that an audit be undertaken immediately. Within days Vollaire had resigned, and the district attorney and the *Los Angeles Times* were investigating what was unofficially referred to as "Dolly's Little Shopping Spree."

The Shopping Extravaganza
Over a ten year period, Vollaire was able to divert over $84,000 in city funds for personal use. She dined in fine restaurants and shopped in high end stores from Beverly Hills to Newport Beach, New York City, and even Barbados. She used the city credit card, petty cash and city checks to purchase personal items like sneakers and socks at discount stores and dresses and blouses at designer shops such as Adrienne Vittadini.

Safeguards
Even though the city had checks and balances in place, Vollaire blatantly, albeit clumsily, got around them. Techniques included:

* Requiring that all credit card statements be delivered to her unopened.
* Cutting receipts in such a way to eliminate the vendor name and item description.
* Obtaining pre-signed checks from the mayor since he was often out of town.
* Adding checks to the list of warrants that had already been approved by the city council.

As the story unfolded, an outraged community demanded that the city council resign for letting the pilfering occur on their watch. Mayor Audrey Hon and Councilman Thomas Melbourn were recalled. Mayor Hon, who had only held the position for a year, bore the brunt of the attack for presigning checks and approving the altered demand list without verifying it. "When I go in to sign the list of demands, I'm assuming they're exactly the same as what we saw in the packet. Why would I go over them again? We all trusted the city manager," Hon argued in defense.

Vollaire pleaded no contest to the misuse of public funds and was fined $10,000, ordered to pay $100,000 in restitution, and sentenced to two years in prison. She served her term and made complete restitution to the city from her retirement funds. Councilman John Richards later reflected: "Dolly ran the city as her own principality, and she was the only city official who really saw the details of the financial operation; but she always had acceptable answers."

Aftermath

Finger pointing and denial reigned after the discovery of Vollaire's misdeeds. The mayor and city councilmembers believed that the auditor would uncover any improprieties. The auditor indicated that the city was not paying for an audit that would uncover fraud and that the city was responsible for putting controls in place. The fact was no one was really checking on Vollaire. Had they done so, they would have easily noticed the odd looking invoices that had no store name or item description or that the list of demands on the agenda was very different from the demand list signed by the mayor.

After Vollaire resigned, the city council hired Keene Wilson as city manager. Wilson, a professional administrator, with a strong financial background, immediately implemented a series of internal controls that segregated duties and closed the holes in the city's financial procedures. He also opened the communication lines so that the council had an understanding of city finances.

After Wilson moved on to become city administrator of Lomita, California, he was asked whether it could happen again in Bradbury. Wilson thoughtfully responded, "Not right now. The city council is very sensitive to oversight; but in a few years after the current council is gone, Bradbury, like any other city, will be vulnerable."

This chapter is about the indiscretions that cause embarrassment to the organization and the governing body. While they are not generally life threatening to the organization, they cause embarrassment, impede or even end an aspiring elected official's career.

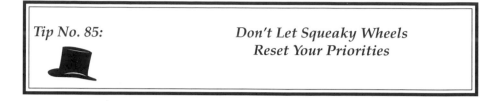

Tip No. 85:   ***Don't Let Squeaky Wheels***
Reset Your Priorities

The U.S. Department of Transportation's 19-page audit was an embarrassment for the Los Angeles City Council and Public Works Department. The audit accused the city of diverting federal road funds to construct "questionable, low priority drain projects that benefitted a few vocal constituents." To respond to complaints about standing water in streets caused by leaky water lines, the city used its street maintenance funds to construct storm drains. According to the report, important street maintenance projects were delayed and the backlog of streets requiring resurfacing increased from 42 percent of the city street system to 54 percent. City Councilman Nate Holden, who had just been elected to the city council, agreed with the findings about the street system. "It's an accurate finding that streets have been neglected. There is a pothole for every vehicle in the city and then some."

"While the diversion was not illegal, it showed poor judgment on the part of the city council and senior management," said Pat Myers, spokesperson for the Department of Transportation. "The delayed projects will cost the city millions of dollars because construction costs have escalated during the past year."

The report concluded the city's management of the street maintenance system was not up to federal standards. The report also criticized the city for making funding decisions on expediency and not on a broad assessment of highway needs. Holden said, "The squeaky wheel gets the grease, but we have to make sure that money for street maintenance is used for street maintenance."

Tip No. 86: *Don't Fight Citizen Requests for Information on Services*

Citizens in the French Quarter of New Orleans were convinced that crime was increasing, but their pleas to the city for crime statistics was repeatedly rejected. Two French Quarter groups, the Friends of Jackson Square and the St. Peter Street Neighborhood Association hired attorney Patrick Klotz, who submitted a freedom of information request to obtain the information. Under the New Orleans law, either the information or the reason why it cannot be released must be provided within five days. Six weeks later and after several unanswered calls, Klotz filed a writ of mandamus with the civil district court.

In the writ, the community groups requested the following information:

1. Type of emergency reported by the caller.
2. What the emergency turned out to be once police arrived.
3. Response times as calculated by the time the call was received and the time the officer arrived.

After the writ was scheduled for hearing, the city administration advised that the information would be provided if the groups paid a $16,000 fee for copying and processing. This was still unacceptable, so the French Quarter groups proceeded with their writ.

The civil district court judge ordered the city to release the data and to provide it on computer disk to reduce costs to $1,000. The statistics were eventually provided in what was described by the New Orleans newspaper, the *Times-Picayune*, as a "cluster of characters, indecipherable were it not for the legend supplied to interpret them." Moreover, Mr. Klotz, charged that in 90 percent of the listed emergency calls, no response times were provided. This made it very difficult to determine what the real response times were and whether police responses were disproportionately high due to inadequate staffing.

Nevertheless, in the 10 percent of calls which showed a response time, the average was nine minutes. Klotz indicated that the average response time should be between two and five minutes. The statistics also revealed that during the previous year, crime in the French Quarter went up 98 percent.

French Quarter outcry about increasing crime.

When the French Quarter groups released their conclusions regarding the crime increase and response times from the data provided, the police department expressed doubt about accuracy of the information.

What is hard to understand to the observer is that once the police department was ordered to provide the data, they didn't process it themselves. Instead they provided incomplete data, let an outside group process police department data, and then sat back and criticized the results. "We think their numbers are suspicious." said New Orleans Police Department spokesman Lt. Marion Defillo. "It's very difficult to interpret exactly what they have."

For many years the city had operated with a shortage of police officers. It took a tragic triple killing at a restaurant within the French Quarter two months later to focus upon the problem. While violent crime had been increasing dramatically, it had been downplayed for fear of driving away tourists; but after hundreds of murders, merchants and residents decided to take action. Throughout their beloved French Quarter, they posted signs like "Warning - This is a High Crime Area" or "Losses: Tourists 327, Murderers 0." "We've reached the point with the massacre that something has to be done. We're dying in New Orleans, and tourists are dying," complained a disgusted merchant.

The City of New Orleans was trying to keep this problem under wraps, so that it would not impact its valuable tourist trade. This attempt to push the issue under the rug had the opposite effect. French Quarter residents, frustrated by the failure of its government to provide information, appealed to the media, which was more than happy to air the problem nationally.

Too often, local governments try to solve the problem themselves instead of partnering with the community. The French Quarter groups were interested in setting up a foundation that would solicit public and private funds to help pay for additional police services, but they found an unreceptive city government.

Tip No. 87:   *Government Cannot Always Operate Like a Business*

Local governments are continually criticized for being too bureaucratic to provide the caring, responsive customer service that private companies give. Why can't local governments provide the same type of customer service as the leading private establishments such as L.L. Bean or Nordstrom? There are many stories out there about how Nordstrom takes care of its customers. There is the story of a husband and wife who brought a defective tire into a Nordstrom's store and wanted their money back. The sales person politely insisted that it could not be from Nordstrom, but the couple insisted that they purchased it from Nordstrom even though they couldn't produce a sales receipt. The sales person relented and politely accepted the tire even though Nordstrom does not sell tires. Another legendary word of mouth marketing story was born.

Then there is the Nordstrom's story about a man who purchased two suits and was promised them by a certain date because he had to attend an important event in another city. When he came to pick up the suits, the sales person apologized profusely that only one suit was ready. Not to worry, the salesperson obtained the address of the man's destination and promised to have the suit delivered free of charge. Sure enough when the man checked into his hotel room, he found a large package. When he opened it, he found not only his suit, but a white shirt and beautifully matching tie to complement the suit.

The tax collector of Colchester, Connecticut apparently felt that good customer service should not be confined to the private sector. It seems that over her 18-year tenure as tax collector, she often forgave interest penalties on delinquent property taxes for the elderly and the poor.

Then an owner complained when the tax collector refused to forgive her penalties, and the lid blew off in this quiet little town of 11,000 people. The tax collector was very well liked and was the town's highest vote getter. Newspapers across the country got hold of the story and played it to the hilt, pointing out how government has no compassion. One editorial began, "What disqualifies you from being a tax collector in Colchester, Connecticut? Apparently being too compassionate, too caring, too much of a soft touch. Too willing to bend the rules to do things such as forgiving the interest on taxes owed by elderly or poor people." Other newspaper editors across the country had a field day, extolling the virtues of a modern day "Robin Hood."

Then the resident who had complained started talking, "When I asked the tax collector for a tax abatement, I was told it was against the law. Well, I want to know who got abatements and why."

Forced to the wall, the town council hired an auditor who disclosed, among other things, that within a one month period, $15,000 in delinquent taxes were forgiven for 11 property owners. When pressed for an explanation, the tax collector refused to comment on whether the lucky property owners were indeed needy. The press then got into the act and asked hard questions including, who she had forgiven taxes for and how many times. Refusing to answer these questions and not wanting to battle anymore, the highly popular tax collector resigned.

The nation's press literally backflipped on the story. The editorials, some tongue in cheek, but most serious, raised an important question for local government. Just how far can appointed officials go to satisfy customers?

Tip No. 88:   ***Don't Flaunt Court Orders***

Not flaunting court orders sounds like straight forth advice. In 1985, a majority of the members of the Yonkers, New York City Council didn't heed this advice and brought the city and themselves to the verge of bankruptcy. After a long battle with the U.S. Justice Department over subsidized housing, the Supreme Court refused to hear a Yonkers appeal of a federal court order to locate 800 low and moderate income housing units in a predominately white, middle-class neighborhood. Shortly after the ruling, the city council voted 4 to 3 to defy the court order.

Within two days, a federal district court imposed a fine of $100 a day with the fine doubling every day. Simple projections showed that if the city did not comply within 22 days, its general fund reserves of over $330 million would be completely wiped out. After fines had accumulated to over $12,000, the New York State Emergency Financial Control Board stepped in and imposed decision making control over the city's finances and operations. Personal fines of $500 per day were also levied against the defiant councilmembers. It took all of these actions plus a few days in jail for the majority to relent. Councilmember Paul T. Kirner, of Parma, Ohio, whose city had a similar fight with the U.S. Justice Department but relented, summed it up, "Laws are there to be obeyed. The Yonker's councilmembers have a right to take their case to the highest court in the land, but once a decision is made they have to obey the law."

Tip No. 89:   *Avoid That Little Retirement Bump*
for Good Ol' Sam

When Richard B. Dixon was the chief administrative officer of Los Angeles County, he recommended that the dollar value of health insurance, sick leave, overtime and unused vacation time be included into the formula for computing retirement pay. The end result tended to increase retirement benefits for management personnel about 20 percent. This is called retirement spiking, and Dixon's efforts bumped his own pension from $105,000 to $130,000 per year when he retired.

The county board of supervisors, who also benefitted from the retirement bump, approved the plan without a public airing of the program. Moveover, they failed to require a fiscal impact statement. After the program was adopted, they asked for an assessment of the costs and found out that the program would cost $400 million over 20 years. After the media put the heat on, the board sought legal advice from the Los Angeles County Counsel (also a beneficiary of the program), who advised the board that the lavish benefit was a vested right that could not be rescinded.

City Manager D. J. Thompson earned $88,968 during his final year with the City of Manhattan Beach, California. Before retiring, Thompson convinced the city council to add unused vacation, sick pay and other benefits, totaling $148,907 which he accumulated over his 16 years, to his final pay. This spike boosted his retirement pay to $139,000 per year, $50,000 more than his final salary. Councilmembers claim that Thompson did not advise them of the impact of the change. One year later the city council was stunned to hear what Thompson was making. The press picked up the story which put additional pressure on the city council. Ultimately, the council was able to reduce the retirement pay by negotiating with Thompson.

These are just two examples of this pension spiking practice that unfairly increases retirement costs. In several cases, employee unions have successfully negotiated spiking provisions. State and local government plans are already short $100 billion of what they will need to meet their pension obligations, and pension spiking adds to this liability. When Richard Dixon was asked about his spiking efforts in Los Angeles County, he said, "We were only doing what savvy employers do — thinking in terms of a total compensation package rather than just salary." Sylvester Schieber, a Washington D. C. benefits consultant, sees it differently, "Spiking is legalized theft."

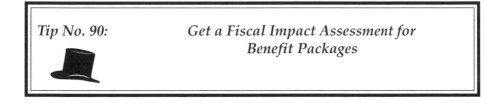

Tip No. 90:   ***Get a Fiscal Impact Assessment for Benefit Packages***

In both Los Angeles County and Manhattan Beach, the governing body did not ask for a fiscal impact assessment of the proposed package before approving it. While the chief administrator officer and city manager should have provided one, they did not. Only after the press and taxpayer groups began asking questions were studies ordered.

In the Manhattan Beach case, Councilmember Larry Dougharty charged that the finance officer, Merle Lundlberg, and other staff members failed to advise the council of the implications and costs of the package. "Lundlberg should have known the financial implication of Thompson's peculiar salary, but chose not to inform the council," claimed Dougharty. Lundlberg responded, "We were not privy to the negotiations that went on. When the agreement was given to us, we just went through and verified the figures that Thompson had computed and made sure we understood it and went ahead and made our payroll adjustment accordingly." Bill Smith, the new city manager, who was not involved in the retirement pact, defended the finance officer. In his response to the charges, Smith provides valuable insights for elected officials, "The finance director did nothing improper. He had no reason to believe the council had not asked those questions, and they had been answered. How many of us would question our boss's pay at the level of the board of directors if we didn't like it?"

Tip No. 91:   *Don't let Vacation Liability*
Accumulate

When the superintendent of a suburban Texas school district retired, he cashed in his 2100 hours of unused vacation leave time for a total of $122,000. His retirement was followed by the assistant superintendent who cashed in vacation time for $86,000. The school district had not budgeted for the payments; and when the board of trustees was confronted by the local newspaper, they had to plead ignorance of the district's policies. As it turned out, the district had a policy limiting accumulation to 160 hours per employee unless the limit was waived by the superintendent. Within this district, the waiver became routine — all an employee had to do was submit a written request.

This problem is not unique. Many local government employees take a minimum or no vacation and let the bank build up. One department head confided, "It makes a great savings account. I earn vacation at a lower salary and let it go up each year with cost of living and merit increases. My investment is safe, and it provides a great return."

During the lean years, local governments grant employees more vacation and leave time instead of raises. Unfortunately, many employees simply bank the vacation and leave time, creating a huge future liability for the organization. Putting a cap on the amount of vacation and leave time that can be accumulated is good management. Vacation time is provided for employees to get away. By permitting employees to bank the time provides a great employee financial incentive but defeats the underlying purpose of a vacation benefit.

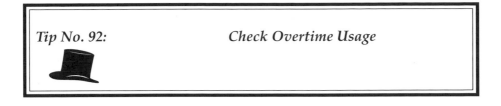

Tip No. 92:   ***Check Overtime Usage***

It is not unusual for agencies to resort to overtime to fill holes in staffing. This is especially true if the agency has undergone cutbacks in personnel or incurred some new responsibilities. In some cases, the agency can prove that it is less expensive to use overtime rather than hire new employees. Recently, the *Los Angeles Times* ran a series of articles on overtime in the Los Angeles Fire Department and found that the city spent a much higher percentage of its budget on overtime than New York, Chicago, Philadelphia, Houston or Orange County. Firefighters earned an average of $19,000 per year in overtime, and one firefighter earned $102,945. Los Angeles spent $50 million a year on overtime. The city could have hired an equivalent of 704 firefighters for the $50 million.

It takes courage and political will to reign in costs in a public safety department. The Los Angeles Firefighters Union president not so subtly warned, "If the council wants to cap the number of hours of overtime we work, no problem. All you have to do is tell us which ambulances you don't want to run, which fire companies you want us to close, which calls you want us to skip."

The governing board should ascertain that overtime has not become a type of entitlement upon which employees depend. The key is to commission an objective study. It may cost more the first year to fund the start-up and operating costs, but what about after year one and year five? The study should also evaluate the costs associated with fatigue, sick leave, workers compensation and disability retirements. After conducting scores of overtime studies, auditors have found that a sizable percentage of overtime is for administrative projects and other non-emergency tasks.

Tip No. 93:   *Monitor Use of Agency Vehicles*

An anonymous caller left the new Ten Washoe School District Superintendent, Mary Nebgen, a cryptic message. District officials had been driving unmarked district cars with what are known as "cold plates." District cars, according to the caller, clearly should have been marked as district vehicles. More importantly, local government license plates in Nevada should be marked with an "EX" meaning exempt. In most states, city, county and district cars are exempt from motor vehicle taxes and usually have an indication of such on the license plate such as an "E" or "EX."

Beau Wiseman, a member of a school district watchdog group, said that there is no way to know if the administrators have been using the cars for personal trips. "There's only one reason to have cold plates on a car, and that's deception of the public. It's a pretty good indicator there are some deeper problems."

As is the case with many practices, this one started ten years before. School administrators qualified for a district car when their job demanded travel "to a great extent" around the district. At some point, cold plates were approved and the practice grew after that, with little administrative oversight. District watchdog leader Jim Clark, who found out about the plates, called for more district accountability. "It's obviously an incident we happened upon by accident that indicates a real need for a truly independent management audit."

Tip No. 94:   *Oversee Off-Duty Use of*
Public Vehicles

"I've observed in other bureaucracies that the use of these cars is a perk that kind of creeps into the system," said San Diego County

Supervisor John MacDonald as he called for a study of the use of off-duty vehicles by county employees.

Ten months later Chief Administrative Officer Norman Hickey presented a study to the board which found that off-duty use of cars cost the county an estimated $1.26 million for the 4.3 million commuting miles that were driven (17 percent of all miles driven resulted from off-duty use). Hickey's report also found that there was not an overall county policy governing off-duty use of 537 county vehicles and that individual departments set their own policies.

The county paid for the gasoline, maintenance, depreciation, and insurance for vehicles. Based upon an average 32-mile round trip commute, the chief administrator estimated that the benefit to an employee was $2,350. The range was $268 for the shortest commute of four miles to $7,800 for the longest commute of 118 miles daily.

Most of the county departments did not allow off-duty use of vehicles. Those that did, justified the practice by saying it is was economical and more efficient for their specialized operations. The county administrator challenged these previously unchallenged assertions.

- **Assertion:** It allowed quicker emergency response by enabling off-duty personnel to report directly to a location such as a scene of a crime, water main break, or disaster.

  Analysis: Departments could not produce records showing the frequency of call outs. Had they done so, the actual benefit could have been determined. The conclusion was that the vehicles were called back into service infrequently.

- **Assertion:** Employees who work in the field can remain there longer by not having to drive back to the office to get their personal cars.

  Analysis: Records indicated that in the majority of instances, field employees had to come back to the work site to complete paper work.

- **Assertion:** Parking fees and repair costs caused by vandalism are reduced.

- **Analysis:** Parking fees were insignificant; and since most vehicles had county facilities to garage vehicles, the incidence of vandalism was low.

- **Assertion:** There is also higher police visibility because the vehicles were out in the public instead of being locked away in county facilities.

   Analysis: Most of the cars were not marked as law enforcement vehicles, so the benefit was questionable.

The county administrator also noted that the county was legally liable for accidents by the vehicles, even when they were being driven during non-working hours. The cost of defending against lawsuits and paying adverse judgments made any savings insignificant.

Hickey's recommendation resulted in an overall policy governing the use of off-duty vehicles. This policy laid out the criteria for assigning off-duty vehicles and called for the clear marking of all county vehicles, except undercover cars, to reduce unauthorized use and potential abuses. Perhaps the most important part of Hickey's study was the challenge to the traditional justifications put forth by the departments that wished to continue the practice unfettered by policy. There are valid justifications to take agency vehicles home, and these arguments should be discerned from the sham arguments.

It should also be recognized that some management positions have been granted the use of official vehicles as part of their compensation package. This is a legitimate contractual arrangement between the agency and the employee and should not be altered unilaterally.

Tip No. 95:   *Monitor Credit Card Usage*

Credit cards first came into massive use as part of the federal government's effort to cut the cost of buying goods and services.

Officially known as the International Merchant Purchase Authorization Card (IMPAC), it allows agencies to use a commercial Visa card to purchase goods and services.

Since the beginning of the purchase card program, the use of cards has skyrocketed. During Fiscal Year 1990-91, the first full year that cards were available government wide, the cards were used for a about 271,000 purchases worth about $64 million. Over the next five years, card purchases increased by 1500 percent. The average purchase was $375. A cost benefit study conducted by the General Accounting Office of 17 agencies found that purchase cards were less expensive than purchase orders. For 15 organizations, costs were cut by half. Per transaction savings for the 17 organizations ranged from $1.42 to $150, with an average savings of $54. The GAO also found that fraud had not increased with the use of purchase cards: "Although purchase card use has greatly increased, we found no evidence that this has led to increased abuse. In fact, with the electronic data maintained on all purchase card transactions, card use can be closely monitored."

Many public agencies have followed the federal government example and are issuing credit cards to employees to make minor purchases of supplies and materials. Howard County, Maryland, has given approximately 5 percent of its employees credit cards to make purchases costing less than $300. In the past, government agencies would require employees to obtain a purchase order before making the purchase. In many cases, the cost of issuing the purchase order would exceed the cost of the item purchased. Preparing, reconciling and filing multiple copies of purchase orders cost Howard County approximately $60 each.

While credit cards are cost effective, they are subject to abuse if control is not established and exercised. In contrast to the IMPAC program, the government American Express card program, which is intended to cover federal employees travel-related costs has been plagued by abuse. They have been used for personal items such as clothing, dining and travel. An important part of credit card control is to train employees on the card usage and limits. Stiff penalties for abuse should also be established and enforced.

Tip No. 96:   *Don't Use Public Resources for*
Campaign Purposes

In December, a county affirmative action officer received a call from an obviously distressed woman who refused to give her name. "If, um, my supervisor is forcing me to do work on county time, that is of a political nature, that is supporting campaigns, is that appropriate?" asked the anonymous caller. When the affirmative action officer replied that it was inappropriate, the caller wondered out loud what might happen if she refused to do the work but then hung up. The next call came in February. The anonymous caller said things had deteriorated and said, "It's about ten times as bad as it was when I talked to you earlier." At this point the caller identified herself as the chief of staff of a county supervisor.

A meeting was arranged at an out of town coffee shop the next morning. The chief of staff brought along three other staff members. They told the affirmative action officer that they had given a letter to the county supervisor saying they felt it was wrong to be doing the supervisor's campaign work on county time. "When we gave her the letter, she freaked out," they explained, "She really berated us and made us feel like we had done something wrong."

At this point the district attorney picked up the case. After completing the investigation the case was submitted to the grand jury. A few months later, the county's civil grand jury handed up an accusation against the supervisor comprised of 12 acts constituting willful misconduct in office. Charges included directing aides to write and edit political campaign statements, obtain political endorsements and compile a mailing list used for campaign fund raising purposes. The supervisor abandoned her office thus avoiding a criminal trial and possible fine.

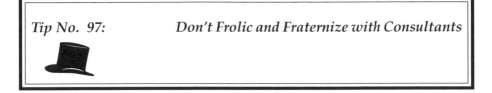

Tip No. 97:   *Don't Frolic and Fraternize with Consultants*

The Metropolitan Transit Authority (MTA) was embarrassed when it was revealed that transit chief Joseph Drew played in a charity golf tournament with contractors who were bidding for multi-million dollar MTA contracts. Drew recognized his transgression, called it a dumb mistake, and vowed to not do it again. Drew's failure to counsel staff members to avoid similar conflicts led to another black eye for the MTA.

The *Los Angeles Times* revealed that 60 top MTA staffers and an alternate board member belonged to the Pacific Transportation Golf Association whose membership included 25 MTA contractors, consultants and lobbyists. This group of staffers and special interests had long weekend outings at least six times during the year at luxurious golf resorts. The trysts were not illegal, and the employees paid their own way; but it raised significant ethical issues about the fraternization of public officials with those who benefitted financially from the officials' decisions. Staff members defended the practice by saying that it was of benefit to the agency. The MTA's chief financial officer expressed it this way, "There is no conflict of interest, and it benefits the public. If you accept these positions of responsibility, should you go into a shell and not talk to anybody?" he said. "It's better to know people rather than just seeing them as a sheet of paper." However, it appears the golf association itself became a cozy shell. City of Gardena Councilman James Cragin, called the golfer's club ill-advised. "They (staffers) should join another club where there aren't any lobbyists," Cragin said. "It doesn't look good. It's an abuse of common sense."

Michael Josephson, of the Josephson Ethics Foundation, felt it wasn't even a close call. It is "clearly wrong" he said. Focusing on the issue, Josephson said, "Lobbyists make a living not by bribing officials but by getting officials to like them. These MTA folks, even if unknowingly, are allowing those contractors unreasonable access to them."

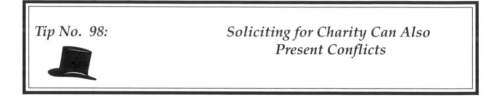

Tip No. 98: *Soliciting for Charity Can Also Present Conflicts*

When Los Angeles Councilmember and MTA Board Member Richard Alatorre acted as honorary chairman for the El Serano Youth Development Center's annual charity golf tournament, the results were very good. The charity received individual donations of $17,000 from contractors who, at the time, held large contracts with MTA. While there was a $250 legal limit on individual contributions to councilmember election campaigns, there was no such limit on donations to the non-profit organizations. One major contractor admitted that he would not have donated money if the councilmember was not involved in the charity. "When an elected official is involved, we pay more notice," he said.

When asked about the situation, ethics guru, Michael Josephson, was troubled. "People solicited to give money to charitable causes ought to feel 100 percent comfortable that their decisions will not be held against them or used to their benefit by a public official.

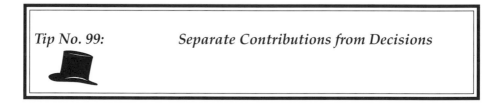

Tip No. 99: *Separate Contributions from Decisions*

Disclosure records showed that over 30 law firms having contracts with the city contributed to Los Angeles City Attorney James K. Hahn's 1997 reelection campaign. Over a five-year period, $15 million was donated to the city attorney by these firms. Suspiciously, many of the contributing firms were directly chosen by Hahn. Several others were selected by his top deputies. While the donations and their acceptance is legal, the perception is that there is a conflict. Hahn's challenger, Ted Stein, called them a "flat-out conflict of interest." Stein promised he would remove himself from contract decisions if he was elected.

Hahn denied the claim saying that the award of contract decisions was truly a decision based on merit. He also said that every contract award process is subject to competition.

Craig Holman, co-director of the Center for Governmental Studies, commented on the situation, "People contribute for a reason. They're not contributing out of some altruistic motive to better educate voters or promote a democratic system — they're contributing to have access, or have influence, on the office holder."

"Not only do some contributors give money to buy access, they also give money out of fear of losing access. You'll find many people give to both sides in order to avoid any possibility of being viewed as the enemy by whoever wins."

As part of their investigative reporting, the *Los Angeles Times* interviewed an attorney who spoke off the record for fear of losing lucrative contracts. His comments were revealing, "It's almost a requirement. I've decided that under the circumstances, the best strategic position for me is to give a modest amount to Jimmy (Hahn) because he's the city attorney, and he's giving out requests for proposals."

Reinforcing trust with the electorate includes, exposing and eliminating connections between contributions and decisions that benefit a person or group. Taken at face value, Hahn's failure to distance himself from the contract award process suggests at best, that his staff was incapable of doing it competently.

Tip No. 100:   ***Don't Use the Register of Warrants for Political Games***

The register of warrants is a report that lists every check written by the agency during a two-week or 30-day period. This listing includes the payee, the amount, and a brief description of the purpose. Governing board members find the register helpful in keeping up with how agency money is being spent.

Many agencies place the register of warrants on the agenda for adoption by the governing board. This affords some members an opportunity for grandstanding about agency spending. Individual governing board members have also used the opportunity to embarrass colleagues about their travel expenses. Members who take a cheap shot usually wind up being victimized themselves. Don't do it. If you have questions, ask them of staff before the meeting.

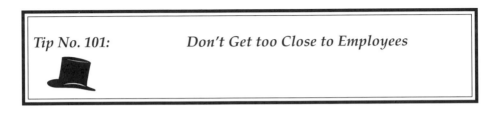

Tip No. 101:   ***Don't Get too Close to Employees***

Ted Grandson was a very popular community member and local business person. When he ran for the Simi Valley, California, City Council, he won by a large margin. Even though Grandson was appointed mayor, he saw no reason to break off his friendship with his police officer acquaintances.

When asked about a weekend trip to Las Vegas with members of the police union, Grandson retorted, "Just because I am now mayor doesn't mean I have to give up all my friends and activities." Shortly before the trip, the city council met in executive session with the city manager and management staff to provide direction in the negotiations with the police union. Grandson, whether deliberate or inadvertent, wound up revealing the city's entire strategy, including initial offers and the absolute bottom line, to the union.

As a result, negotiations did not go well. The union failed to give on any points and refused to move toward settlement. The knowledge the union gained enabled them to push to the limit. Management, not knowing what was happening, held strong with the city council direction. This resulted in an impasse and ultimately in a police slowdown. It was only at this point that the mayor recognized that his friendship was in conflict with his responsibility as a governing board member. Grandson, learned a valuable lesson — public employees cannot be your friends while you are in office.

Tip No. 102:   *Monitor Litigation Costs*

Litigation expenses are becoming a bigger part of local government budgets according to a survey of the National Institute of Municipal Law Officers (NIMLO) by Susan A. MacManus, Professor of Public Administration and Political Science at the University of South Florida, Tampa. In her survey, MacManus found that litigation costs for municipalities during a recent two-year period, have increased at an unusually high rate:

- Ten percent and above for more than half
- Thirty percent or more for approximately one-fifth
- Fifty percent or more for seven percent

Many local governments settle cases, even apparent winners, as a cost containment strategy. In the survey, MacManus found a disturbing correlation between "the propensity to settle cases to save money and the reported increase in frivolous lawsuits. Among the jurisdictions settling more than half of their cases to save money, nearly two-thirds (64 percent) identified an increase in the number of frivolous cases as a driving force behind rising litigation costs. In contrast, among those reporting that they settled less than 15 percent of their cases to cut costs, only 38 percent said their jurisdictions had experienced an increase in frivolous suits."

Pressures to settle lawsuits can be great. In one instance, the city manger and police chief of the City of Claremont, California were directed under a threat of contempt to meet with a superior court judge in his quarters concerning alleged brutality on the part of a police officer. The judge tried to persuade the city officials to settle for, what he described as a mere $5,000, to avoid huge litigation costs.

Fortunately, the city council backed the city manager's refusal to settle. In this case, support of a police officer was more important than litigation costs. (The city eventually prevailed). The police officers were very happy about the decision to stand firm and the court's ultimate decision.

As part of guarding the public checkbook, elected officials should insist upon periodic briefings by the agency's attorney regarding the status of various lawsuits. Settling or not settling lawsuits is an important governing body policy matter that should not be decided solely by the agency's attorney.

To keep litigation expense from adversely impacting the operating budget, many local governments have established litigation reserves to pay for attorney fees, court costs and settlements.

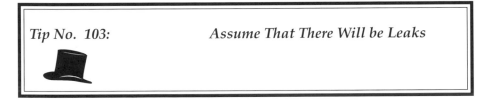

Tip No. 103: *Assume That There Will be Leaks*

The Los Angeles City Attorney was determined to keep his top secret report on how to prevent the leaks at city hall from leaking. Extensive security measures were implemented such as supervised reproduction, coding to prevent duplication, and storage in locked cabinets away from city hall. The police commission secretary had to sign an oath of secrecy before she was allowed to read a draft of the document. A messenger sent to transport the document had to produce identification before the documents were released. However, all of these precautions were for naught. Before the ink dried, the newspaper had a copy and was calling city officials for comments.

Councilmember Joel Wachs lamented, "If hypocrites could fly, this place would be an airport. It's a joke. Anything that's marked 'confidential' the press always has it." Councilmember Laura Chick added, "I don't know if there is a fool proof way to keep a document under wraps. It's a sorry state that we can't respect confidentiality." City hall observers felt differently, however, believing that most documents should not be classified as confidential in the first place and that more of the public's business should be conducted in public. "So long as the government controls the amount and character of the information that is released to the public, the public will be disempowered," said attorney Douglas Mirell.

Slapping a confidential stamp on a document is one of the best ways to increase interest in it. In fact, the more one attempts to suppress information, the greater the force to divulge it. A good operating policy is to assume that nothing will remain secret for very long.

Where Is the
Money Hidden?

*"If we played the game the city wanted us to,
we would get chicken feed for children's
programs. It took guerilla warfare to unearth
the hidden pots of money and make the
supervisors sit up and really listen to us."*

Sally Thomas, Leader of Save Our Children (SOC)

Sally Thomas cared very deeply about the children of San Francisco.
She felt that the city was not putting enough resources toward
children's services and programs. She also had become down right
frustrated about the budget process the city followed.

The Stacked Budget Process
The previous year, Thomas and her recently formed group, Save
Our Children (SOC), had followed the process laid out for residents
and groups who wanted new programs funded. She waited until
the budget hearings and made her pitch about the problems children faced and the need for more funds. Her presentation at the
public hearing was well-spoken and moving. She received a lot of
head nodding from the board of supervisors, which she interpreted

as positive. When the department head in charge of children's programs was asked to respond, he expressed concern about children's issues and then proceeded to eloquently and convincingly argue that the limited dollars available were allocated for other needy programs. His persuasiveness and knowledge of the budget won the day; SOC received less than 20 percent of what they had requested. The board of supervisors expressed what Sally believed was sincere reluctance; they wanted to give more, but there just didn't seem to be anymore money to go around. One supervisor, displaying a copy of the proposed budget said, "Look, we really care about children, and we want to help you. As you can see, all the money is taken up by these other programs. Our hands are tied." And then he inadvertently issued the challenge that would eventually spur SOC to victory, "If you can find money in this budget, we will be happy to fund more children's programs."

After reflecting about the budget meetings, Thomas concluded that the process was inflexible and stacked from the beginning. By the time the public was allowed to provide input, deals had been made, and the blueprint had been established. While the slick City of San Francisco budget document was stamped proposed, it was in reality cast in concrete. The system was not only closed, said Thomas, "It was oppressively technical and intimidating to outsiders." It was also virtually impossible for the public to compete with department heads who knew the process and had all the facts.

The Treasure Hunt

Some groups would accept what they received and go about their business, but not Sally Thomas and SOC. They retained a consulting firm to map out a public campaign to develop awareness and support for children's issues. SOC then started looking for money that could fund children's programs. Supervisors and staff members, sympathetic to children's issues, were more than happy to help. They gladly pointed to hidden money in programs and accounts that could be tapped for funding. They made a special point to identify the sacred cows.

SOC then developed what they called an alternate budget. Just as official looking as the city's proposed budget, the alternate budget not only requested funding, it boldly identified where the city could get the money.

Success

SOC didn't wait for the public hearing this time. They initiated what was termed a hard ball campaign to convince citizens groups of their cause. The media picked up the issue and played it for all it was worth. The alternate budget was a hit. By the time the public hearings came around, supervisors felt boxed in and compliant. They found the funds to grant SOC their requested budget.

SOC was successful, in part, because they uncovered some of the budgetary secrets of the organization. They learned the process and threatened to unearth the hidden money caches. This chapter is about hidden money, padding and some of the other games and strategies used by budgeters.

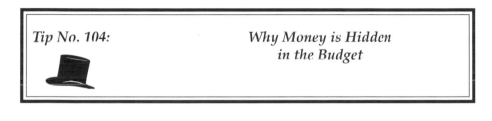

Tip No. 104:   ***Why Money is Hidden in the Budget***

Elected officials have the general feeling that money is hidden in the budget, and there is reason to support this conception. Richard C. Karney, in a survey of 23 Iowa cities in the 1980's reported that 26 percent of the budget officers acknowledged that they hid money to take care of unanticipated wage and benefit increases. Hiding activity was also detected in a study of 24 suburban San Francisco bay area school districts. In a multi-year study, 182 (86 percent) of 212 budgets analyzed had under estimated revenues; and 42 percent of the school districts always under estimated revenues. On the expenditure side, 57 percent of the budgets' projected expenses exceeded actual expenses. Between the years 1990 through 1996, the author conducted a budget behaviors study by surveying 365 city, county and district management personnel about 20 different budget practices. Of those surveyed, 72 percent conceded that it was acceptable to hide money in some form (see Figures 5 and 6).

Money is usually concealed in the budget for several reasons:

1. To Provide for Unanticipated Events

Money will be stashed away if the governing body or top management has the habit of imposing unbudgeted programs on departments without providing supplemental funding. After this happens a couple of times, the department will secret away some money, so that they do not have to use funds committed for other items to meet the unplanned request. Administrators like to have money available to provide funds for an unbudgeted program the governing body comes up with during the year.

2. To Keep the Governing Body from Spending It

Administrators and mayors have hidden money to keep the governing body from spending it. This may be done for various reasons. Perhaps it is one-time money and the governing body wishes to spend it for on-going programs which the administrators believe cannot be sustained. Or, the money is being reserved to fund a program that is currently being financed by grant money that will be running out.

3. To Obscure Items from the Governing Body and Public

Some departments will hide controversial items, such as computers or conferences, in obscure places, so that elected officials will be less likely to find them. They were more likely to do so when governing body members had a tendency to use these items to grandstand about frivolous spending.

4. To Protect the Governing Body

If a governing body has had a tendency to raid reserves, the staff may develop creative ways to obscure the total amount in reserves. Administrators who carry out this practice argue very convincingly that if the money is spent unwisely, it is they, and not the elected officials, who are held accountable. Says one city manager, "It's my job that is on the line. I have seen it happen over and over again, they spend all the money and then crucify the staff for failing to control the budget. They need to be protected from themselves. They will sacrifice fiscal stability for one more year of not having to bite the bullet."

Tip No. 105:   ***Budget Padding is a Common***
                        Hiding Technique

Every organization has its own budget culture and this culture may encourage, tolerate or discourage budget padding. Almost three-fourths of the respondents to the budget behaviors survey, conducted by the author, indicated that budget padding is an acceptable practice, and 65 percent indicated that they padded. However, there seems to be a difference of opinion as to what constitutes padding. Some say it means providing a little safety margin for inflation. Others say that providing for inflation is good budgeting — genuine padding begins only after that.

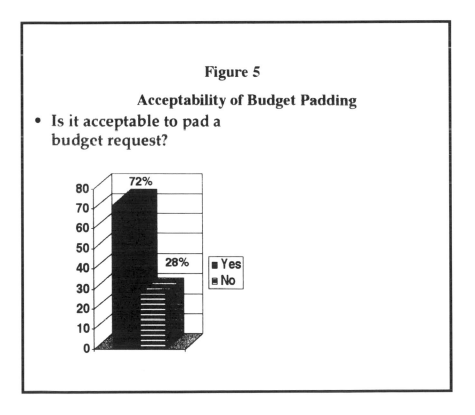

Figure 5

Acceptability of Budget Padding

- **Is it acceptable to pad a budget request?**

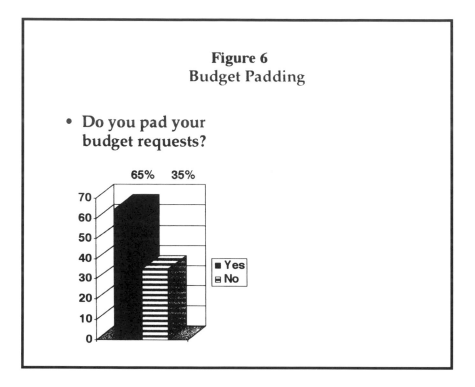

Figure 6
Budget Padding

- **Do you pad your budget requests?**

Another issue relates to which items are padded. Most padders in-dicate that they do not pad everything, only selected items that do not receive close scrutiny. A favorite hiding place used by one police department is the police locker account. The city's administrative lieutenant confides that "we spend 20 times the amount per capita than any other police department on lockers. Police lockers seem so insignificant to the city council, yet with the money they have ap-proved during the last three years, we could have purchased over fifty gold plated lockers for every officer in the department."

The range of responses as to what percentage of the budget gets padded runs from 0 to 40 percent, with the most common response being 5 percent. The two most often mentioned reasons for padding budgets are to offset budget cuts and to be able to respond to the inevitable, unbudgeted priorities that arise after a budget is adopted. As would be expected, the degree of padding goes down during cutback periods.

Tip No. 106:   *Budget Padding can be Minimized*

Padding thrives best in an environment plagued by a lack of certainty and distrust. Participants admit that padding is reduced when budget deciders take positive action to discourage the practice of padding. Often cited steps that can be taken include:

1. Communicating the Criteria Used to Make Budget Decisions

Clarifying how the budget process works and how decisions are made is one of the best antidotes to padding. Uncertainty leads to cushioning one's budget. If program managers don't know how decisions are made, they may assume deciders are arbitrary and the best defense is padding.

2. Giving Program Managers Flexibility to Move Dollars Around in Their Budget

Strict line item control doesn't work. Making departments toe the line with every line item account creates unintended and undesirable consequences. First, it encourages people to add extra dollars to every account to avoid being overdrawn. Second, people will charge items to inappropriate accounts when they run out of money in the proper account. Controlling by the bottom line is the more effective oversight strategy.

3. Providing Supplemental Funding Whenever a Major Unbudgeted Project or Program is Given to a Program Manager

If people are expected to absorb unbudgeted items, they will build in a tolerance for this practice by padding. If a new item comes up that was not anticipated or cut out of the proposed budget, it should be funded from the unappropriated balance and not from the department's budget.

4. Reward Good Budgeting

Acknowledge and reward good budgeting practices, such as not padding budgets, not spending money just because it is available, and implementing cost reductions.

The last point is crucial because it represents a reversal of the entrenched "larger budgets mean higher pay and esteem" operating norm that is prevalent in virtually all governments. From a public manager's standpoint, it does not make good sense to cut your budget. Not only are you risking lowering your salary, you are also undermining your standing with employees. Too often elected officials take conscientious budgeting for granted without reinforcing it. Until good budgeting is rewarded, bad practices will continue.

Tip No. 107:   ***"Giveaways" in the Budget***
Are Common

During the city council budget work session, City of Burbank, California, Parks and Recreation Director, George Izay, made an impassioned plea for the Royal Thespian Deluxe Mobile Puppeteer Stage and Sound System (RTDMPSSS). After dutifully listening, the council politely nodded their heads. To an outsider, it looked like the Parks and Recreation Department should begin scheduling puppet shows throughout the city.

One week later at the public hearing on the budget, the city council wasted little time in focusing on the RTDMPSSS. Several members expressed concern about the rising cost of government. After a prolonged discussion on the benefits and costs of this desirable but somewhat extravagant item, the council took great pride in performing their oversight responsibility. With lots of devotion to duty they swiftly, mercilessly and unceremoniously deleted the Royal Thespian Deluxe Mobile Puppeteer Stage and Sound System from the budget.

After watching this play out of the democratic process, the author was impressed. Government works and the council performed its oversight role. The audience was pleased. George Izay appeared stunned.

However, this was the first time. The very next year, Izay re-submitted the RTDMPSSS as an important Parks and Recreation budget item, and it again was made part of the proposed budget.

Puzzled, the author asked Izay why he was submitting a sure loser that would do nothing but bring him grief. His answer was enlightening and became an important lesson on budgeting. Confided Izay, "There is no way the city council will ever approve the RTDMPSSS. I don't expect them to; but if I don't offer a tasty morsel to cut, they will begin looking for other things. Every one of them told me in private they were sorry for the rough treatment. After telling me to keep up the good work, they also encouraged me to put the RTDMPSSS in the next budget."

Budgeting culture apparently condones the practice of people putting items in the budget, knowing that they will be cut out. In the author's survey of budgeting practices, 81 percent of the respondents indicated that this was an acceptable practice. The purposes of this tactic include giving the budget deciders something to cut out and trying to deflect the focus away from more vulnerable programs.

Tip No. 108:	*Even Governing Bodies Resort to Hiding*

Your governing body has a budget to provide for basic activities such as salaries, benefits, office expenses, travel, lodging, meals and subscriptions. In some cases, your budget will be combined with another such as the administrative budget. When presented this way, the governing body's budget is less obvious to the public. This makes it harder to find, let alone attack. The more common approach, however, is to present the governing body's budget as a completely separate budget. Obviously, when the budget is laid out for all to see, it becomes an inviting target for political opponents and the media — especially if it shows an increase over the previous year.

In an attempt to avoid the heat, some governing bodies will hide some of their expenses in other budgets, such as putting travel in the non-departmental or community events. In other cases, a portion of travel costs may be budgeted in the governing body's budget with the bulk carried elsewhere. Similarly, if the governing body requires capital items, the items may be budgeted in another budget such as non-departmental. While this may be done under the semblance of good budgeting, the result is an obscuring of the total governing body budget.

Five years after he took office, California Governor Pete Wilson proudly pointed to his personal office budget and exclaimed, "The governor's office is being run by the same number of staff as when I took office." This was an important admission since Wilson was a strong advocate of smaller government. What the governor didn't say was that his personal staff was being supplemented by 29 employees who were being budgeted by other departments. Records showed that while Wilson's budget remained flat with no increases, his reliance on staff from other departments increased from 14 to 29.

The departments who paid the employee's salaries rarely saw them. Wilson's press secretary defended the arrangement by noting that it was a time honored practice used by previous governors and that all of Wilson's appointees served at his pleasure no matter what department they worked in. "It's a matter of seating arrangements," he said.

Opponents objected to the practice for two reasons. First, it obscured the total number of people working for the chief executive. "If the governor needs more people, he should ask the legislature for them," complained Senator Byron Sher. Second, Sher believed it was inappropriate since some of the contributing departments, such as the Lottery and the Department of Motor Vehicles, were funded by restricted special funds and user fees.

At the local level, it is not uncommon to see personnel offloaded to other departments, especially if the chief administrator's and governing body's budgets are under scrutiny.

The "shenanigan's list" was born when the California State Assembly, which was controlled by Republicans, presented a budget that sliced $9.5 million from State Controller Kathleen Connell's budget. Connell was a possible Democratic candidate for governor. Connell's outrage spread quickly, "The draconian cuts suggested by Assembly Republicans will cripple the controller's ability to be a tough fiscal watchdog and will limit the aggressive audits that taxpayers deserve." She also convinced the Senate President Pro Tem Bill Lockyear that the Republicans were playing partisan politics with her budget. Lockyear lost no time in directing his colleagues to slice the budgets of Republican governor hopefuls, Attorney General Dan Lungren and State Treasurer Matt Fong. To further make their point, they sliced other Republican state official's budgets, including Governor Pete Wilson's. The Republicans counter punched by slashing the budget of Democratic state schools chief Delaine Eastin, who was also considering a run for governor.

Most of the items were restored by Governor Wilson when things cooled down, but the so-called shenanigans actually identified genuine fat. The only independent in the Senate, Quentin Kopp was amused by the battle. "I believe some of these items are meritorious. Even the controller conceded some of the items deleted in her budget were meritorious. Looking at the items targeted for reductions, I think some belong on the 'M' for meritorious list and not the shenanigans list," reflected Kopp.

Tip No. 109:

Don't Expect Hidden Money
to be a Panacea

Most budgets contain some hidden money, but you will most likely find that it represents a small percentage of the entire budget. In 1993, the Los Angeles County Board of Supervisors conducted a nationwide search for a new county administrative officer. They eventually settled on Sally Reed, who had held the top administrative post with Santa Clara County for 12 years. Reed was known as a fiscal conservative and had earned widespread recognition for her firm leadership in financial matters.

Reed was selected because of her reputation for bringing fiscal discipline to the Santa Clara County Board of Supervisors — a group who, at that time, had a propensity for spending more than it received. She also was selected because several county officials believed that Reed could work magic and find all the secret pots of money in the county budget.

After taking the new position in Los Angeles, Reed began an educational campaign with the board of supervisors. The message was concise and straightforward, "We cannot continue to spend beyond our means." As part of her program to get the government on an even financial keel, Reed convinced the supervisors to publicly state that they would stop borrowing to support current operations. She also got them to adopt five other basic financial policies:

- Match on-going costs with on-going revenues
- Fund one-time costs with one-time revenues
- Fund liabilities when they are first recognized
- Base the budget on realistic estimates
- Establish a reserve for contingencies at 2 percent

While the board agreed to these policies, they were not committed to implementing them. Supervisors were still hopeful that Reed would find hidden money or some other magic to resolve the deepening budget crisis. Reed's idea of magic was spending restraint and good financial practices.

It didn't take long before the reality of the budget balancing goal collided with public demands for service. In 1995, Reed had to close a $1.2 billion budget deficit. The deficit was carried forward from previous failed efforts to balance the county budget. Reed took it head on and recommended severe cuts, including the elimination of 20 percent of the general fund work force and the closing of County-USC Medical Center — the aging, inefficient flagship of the county hospital system.

The board of supervisors balked. It was too much too soon. "I don't mind people being blunt," said Supervisor Dean Dana, "...but this is a political job. We are here to meet the needs of our constituents."

The board opted to gamble on a bailout from the federal government; and, fortunately, their gamble paid off. It was an election year, and the federal government provided a huge grant to keep the hospital open.

After almost three years of head butting with the board, Sally Reed called it quits. She had an enticing job offer from the Governor of California to become Director of the Department of Motor Vehicles. Later, Reed reflected on her experience, "The board wanted me to find all the hidden pots of money that could be tapped, which we did. They were surprised when they found out these hidden funds were too small to close the gap. I don't think they envisioned an outcome that was going to require significant reductions in services we provide."

Supervisor Zev Yaroslavsky summed it all up after Reed left, "She gave the board and the public the stark truth about county finances. The hidden money just was not there."

Just as Linda Sarver of Covina and the Los Angeles Board of Supervisors discovered, the perception of large secret money pots is usually wishful thinking. One should not bank on a hidden cache bailing an agency out of a severe financial problem.

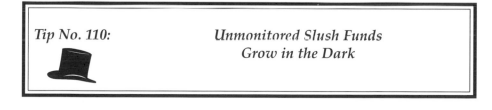

Tip No. 110:   ***Unmonitored Slush Funds***
                              Grow in the Dark

Senator Sam Nunn wanted assurance that the Pentagon would not use expired appropriations to fund $1 billion in repairs for the troubled B-1 bomber. "No sir, absolutely not," Pentagon Comptroller Sean O'Keefe said. Deputy Secretary of Defense Donald Atwood added, "We assure you that we will not do that." Not withstanding the pledges, the repairs were made from expired appropriations that sat in a stealth account known as "M."

All budget appropriations approved by Congress specify how long they last, which is usually from one to three years, or so thought Representative John Dingell of Michigan. "I have always believed that congressional appropriations had to be obligated or spent within the period specified by law. Instead, they are laundered through the U.S. Treasury and returned to Pentagon control." The size and lack of control over the slush fund also stunned the Congressional Budget Committee. It had grown from $30 billion from the year before to $43 billion the next year.

According to the Inspector General, the funds represent only a commitment to spend that has been approved by Congress. However, weak controls made the "M" account vulnerable to misuse, particularly in the payment of old bills for which proper documentation had not been maintained. The Inspector General's report also stated, "We found that at all levels and throughout all organizations the "M" account was one of management's lowest priorities; and, therefore, had weak internal management controls."

"The existence of these accounts seriously diminishes the Congress' control over the appropriations process. With these slush funds, the Congress could virtually kill a weapons program and find out years later that it was still being funded from these accounts," complained Dingell.

This represents a vivid example of how slush funds grow. The Pentagon was authorized to accumulate expired appropriations to spend at its discretion through a long forgotten congressional action in the 1970's. It then grew and grew with little oversight. "No one up here had any idea how big these accounts were," a congressional aide admitted, "and they've never been audited."

Several years ago, the City of Burbank was looking everywhere for monies to help close a budget gap; and an intern found the big prize. Two decades before the city council had established a Cash Basis Fund which was to be used to meet cash needs when expenditures came in before revenues were collected. The Cash Basis Fund had never been used, and successive city councils and city managers were unaware of it. Yet, each year the finance department religiously contributed $25,000 to the mysterious and obviously obscure fund.

Tip No. 111:   ***Don't Plead Inability to Pay***
                              with Unions

During periods of economic stress, local governments will plead poverty in an attempt to dissuade unions from pressing for higher salaries and benefits. In other cases, the agency has the money; but the governing body simply does not want to pay more. So, they plead inability to pay. What seems like safe financial footing at first can turn into quicksand very quickly if the union institutes a search for the hidden money in the budget. Unions love the challenge. Called a "treasure hunt," unions will either take on the search themselves if they have the expertise or call upon the national union for assistance. In many states, if the governing body makes the inability to pay case, they must provide the substantiating information. Unions are very adept at finding the fat and then putting the pressure on the governing body to take the discovered proceeds and use them for increased salaries and benefits. It is very difficult for the governing board to deny increases once the money is known to exist. Bringing community pressure to bear through the use of press conferences and releases alleging that the agency has hidden money is a favorite technique.

The other problem with the inability to pay argument is that once the financial problem subsides, the employee groups will use that argument for more money. "Okay, we suffered with you last year; now that you have the money, it is only fair that you make up for it," they demand.

Establishing a fair and equitable compensation program is one of your most important functions. However, employee compensation should be approached on such factors as wage and benefit comparisons with competing jurisdictions, competing priorities and the actual ability to pay for the on-going costs associated with salaries and benefits.

Many organizations have adopted a strategy of laying out the budget for the unions so that they can see where all the money is budgeted and why. This removes the potential embarrassment of hidden money miraculously appearing and shifts the argument to the use of the money, and no group is better at deciding the priority of programs as the governing body.

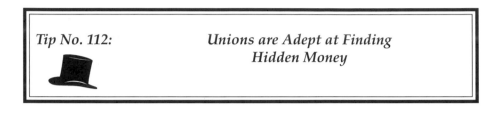

Tip No. 112:   ***Unions are Adept at Finding Hidden Money***

Union search efforts have helped refine the art of finding hidden money. They do a complete analysis to follow the flow of funds to make sure that the balances, revenues and expenditures actually link together. What they look for are the conflicting documents or statements produced by the governing body and management. The starting points include annual budgets and external audit reports for the last three or four years. These documents lay the basis for the search. They then look for:

- Recent Bond Prospectuses. Since organizations must honestly reveal their financial condition to investors, these documents can be a gold mine. While the budget message may highlight a dire fiscal situation, the bond prospectus touts the agency's sterling financial position.

- Analysis of financial condition from bond rating agencies. What is the organization's bond rating and what are its financial strengths.

- The mayor's or chief administrator's state of the agency address. Many of these speeches are full of glowing statements about the organization's hopes and successes.

- Promotional literature on the organization published by the public relations office or economic development unit about the organization.

- Newspaper articles about the agency's financial condition and plans for the future.

- Agreements made with other unions or employee groups.

- Training and travel budgets.

- Insider information from supportive elected officials and staff members.

This same list of items can be very helpful for the new governing board member to determine if the agency's rhetoric is consistent concerning its financial status.

Tip No. 113:   ***How to Look for Hidden Money***

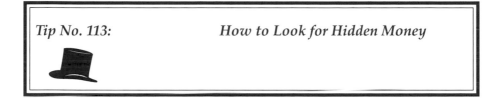

The remainder of this chapter is devoted to some relatively simple checks to determine if money is being hidden in the budget and to what degree. One of the first things to do is to obtain copies of the last four or five proposed budgets. Some agencies will prepare a proposed budget and then a final budget. The proposed budget contains the recommended programs and funding for the year, whereas the final budget contains the programs and funding actually adopted. In some cases the final budget includes revised numbers, so you do not want to wind up comparing proposed budgets to final budgets. An option is to obtain your agency's audit reports for the last four or five years. Recognize that the numbers in the audit report will not be the same as the budget as they are compiled differently.

Tip No. 114:   ***Examine General Fund Revenue***

One of the first things to examine is the revenue side of the budget. A simple comparison between budgeted revenues to actual revenues will indicate whether revenues are estimated conservatively and by how much. If you enjoy doing your own analysis, you can construct your own charts. If not, ask staff to develop them for you. This comparison should be made with the general fund first. Using the entire budget may skew the results especially if capital improvement funds are included. Here is a sample chart that will help in the analysis.

Table 2

General Fund Budgeted Revenues Compared to Actual Revenues

Year	Budgeted Revenue	Revised Revenue	Actual Revenue	Dollar Difference	Percentage Difference
1	$6,000,000	$7,700,000	$7,800,000	$1,800,000	30%
2	$7,800,000	$8,500,000	$8,600,000	$ 800,000	10%
3	$8,600,000	$9,800,000	$9,900,000	$1,300,000	15%

Total three-year revenue difference $3,900,000

The budgeted revenue figures are the revenue estimates when the budget is adopted. Revised revenues are the revenue estimates after mid-year, and other revisions are made. Actual revenue is the final revenue figure after the fiscal year has ended.

This analysis shows that the general fund revenues are being underestimated by significant percentages from 10 to 30 percent per year. After three years, the total difference between budget and actual revenues is $3,900,000. Major differences may be due to an increasing tax base, inaccurate estimating techniques or a deliberate attempt to conceal money.

When doing this analysis, it is critical that the benchmark be the original budgeted amount and not the revised revenue figure. Some agencies will compare the revised revenue figure and not show the original budgeted amount. This effectively hides the fact that revenues are being significantly underestimated. As shown below, if the revised revenues are compared to the actual revenues, the difference is 1 percent per year.

Table 3
Revised General Fund Revenues Compared to Actual Revenues

Year	Budgeted Revenues	Revised Revenues	Actual Revenues	Dollar Difference	Percentage Difference
1		$ 7,700,000	$ 7,800,000	$ 100,000	1%
2		$ 8,500,000	$ 8,600,000	$ 100,000	1%
3		$ 9,800,000	$ 9,900,000	$ <u>100,000</u>	1%
Total three-year revenue difference				$ 300,000	

As a governing board member, you would have no idea that the agency was masking a large surplus each year unless you could see the original budgeted revenues.

Tip No. 115:   *Examine General Fund Expenditures*

A similar chart can also be use for evaluating expenditures. As was the case in the revenue comparison, make sure that the budgeted expenditure column has not been revised, otherwise you will get a distorted picture.

Table 4
**General Fund Budgeted Expenditures Compared to
Actual Expenditures**

Year	Budgeted Expenditures	Revised Expenditures	Actual Expenditures	Dollar Difference	Percentage Difference
1	$ 6,800,000	$ 6,500,000	$ 6,600,000	($ 200,000)	-3%
2	$ 6,900,000	$ 6,700,000	$6,700,000	($ 200,000)	-3%
3	$ 7,000,000	$ 6,800,000	$6,900,000	($ 100,000)	-1%
Total three-year dollar difference				($ 500,000)	

In this example, actual expenditures came in under the original budgeted amount by 1 to 3 percent during this three-year period, and actual expenditures were below budgeted expenditures by $500,000. To complete the fiscal year within 3 percent of the adopted budget probably means that the agency is exercising good budget planning and control.

This $500,000 surplus can be obscured if the original budgeted amount is deleted or changed to the revised expenditure figure.

Table 5
**General Fund Budgeted Expenditures Compared to
Actual Expenditures**

Year	Budgeted Expenditures	Revised Expenditures	Actual Expenditures	Dollar Difference	Percentage Difference
1		$ 6,500,000	$ 6,600,000	$ 100,000	2%
2		$ 6,700,000	$6,700,000	0	-
3		$ 6,800,000	$6,900,000	$ 100,000	1%
Total three-year dollar difference				$ 200,000	

If the revised budgeted expenditure figure is substituted for the budgeted figures, it obscures the fact that over the three-year period, a $500,000 surplus was generated from budgeted expenditures coming in lower than anticipated (see Table 5).

Tip No. 116:	Check Fund Balances First

In the previous examples, a surplus is being realized on both the revenue and expenditure sides of the budget. The extent of surplus is being masked if revised figures are used. But even though the surplus money is masked, it has to be somewhere in the budget. The question becomes — where is the money? The first place to check is the general fund balances.

Table 6
Beginning Balances Compared to Ending Balances

Year	Beginning Balances	Actual Revenues	Actual Expenditures	Ending Balances	Change in Balances
1	$ 2,000,000	$ 7,800,000	$ 6,600,000	$ 3,200,000	$ 1,200.000
2	$ 3,200,000	$ 8,600,000	$ 6,700,000	$ 5,100,000	$ 1,900,000
3	$ 5,100,000	$ 9,900,000	$ 6,900,000	$ 8,100,000	$ 3,000,000

Additions to Fund Balance over three-year period $6,100,000

In Table 6, the entire surplus from both the underestimation of revenues and overestimation of expenditures is recorded in the general fund balance. If your agency generates surpluses, this is the place you want it to be.

Tip No. 117:   ***Favorite Resting Places for***
Surplus Monies

If the surplus money does not show up in the fund balances, it has to be in some other place in the budget. Here are some of the questions to ask:

- Are monies being transferred to the capital projects?
- Are monies being contributed to internal service funds such as vehicle, equipment or building replacement funds?
- Are monies being transferred to other funds such as self-insurance or legal liability?
- Are monies being carried in a contingency for unpaid bills?
- Are monies being used to subsidize enterprise funds?

These are some of the more common uses for surplus funds. In many cases, the money is not hidden, it's just that the trail is not as clear as it could be. In some cases, agency policy will specify how surplus funds are to be handled.

Tip No. 118:   ***Check for Increases in***
Expenditures

The surplus may be used each year to fund increases in departmental budgets. As was the case above, if the adopted expenditure level is revised to take care of supplemental appropriations and overdrafts, you will not be able to determine the extent of the growth. If, however, you use the following chart, growth in a department's budget is very evident.

Table 7
Department Spending Analysis

Year	Adopted Expenditures	Actual Expenditures	Percentage Difference	Agency Difference
1	$1,200,000	$1,400,000	17%	3%
2	$1,500,000	$1,700,000	13%	2%
3	$1,800,000	$2,100,000	17%	4%

In this particular case, the department's spending is increasing from 13 to 17 percent per year — well above the average for the entire agency.

What Is an Adequate Fund Balance?

"Typical fund balance amounts range from 3 to 25 percent for the general fund and around three months' operating expenses for enterprise funds."

Response to James S. Wiggins Internet request on the appropriate size of fund balance from a City of San Diego CPA

From: James Wiggins, a Fort Walton Beach, Florida resident. I am very new on the Internet and am seeking specific information.

To: Government Finance Officers Association.

Regarding: Immediate need for detailed information. The city council meets Tuesday, September 5. If possible, send reply to jsw@fwb.net. Please include either name and title or some other authority I can present to the city council to counter city manger and finance director.

Situation: The Fort Walton Beach City Council is considering $1 million in rate increases for the water, sewer, and sanitation enterprise funds. The city has a total budget of $25 million and a population of 22,000.

I believe the rate increases are unnecessary and have been trying to lead the council to a better solution versus just complaining. I have spent numerous hours going through the budget, preparing spreadsheets, attending all the workshop meetings, and presenting my case to the council. The city manager called and pointed out the fallacies in the data I distributed. (I do not have access to the city's financial computer, the city manager has the knowledge of the details, and knowledge is power over the council).

Issue: The size of the general fund's unreserved fund balance and enterprise fund net income. The city manager is trying to build the general fund unreserved balance to $4.2 million and enterprise accumulated net incomes (retained earnings?) to equal 6 months' operating expenditures. The city manager's budget also includes $495,000 in the various funds for "contingencies." He claims this makes it easier on the council, that is, the technique avoids council action to cover unbudgeted expenses.

Question: What is a reasonable amount for the general fund balance and enterprise net income (and accumulated net income) for a healthy city our size?

My Position: All together, the budget has too much in unreserved funds and contingency funds. I've recommended that all excesses be transferred to the general fund unreserved fund balance, and the council can move monies to an enterprise fund as contingencies require. The city manager told the city council this is not fund accounting. Thank you for your help, James Wiggins.

This was an actual inquiry sent to the Government Finance Officers Association via the Internet. Wiggins indicates that he received a suggestion that he obtain a copy of *"An Elected Official's Guide to Fund Balance,"* authored by Stephen J. Gauthier. He also received a response from a CPA employed by the City of San Diego, California, suggesting that fund balance amounts range from 3 to 25 percent for the general fund and around 3 months' operating expenses for enterprise funds.

What is an adequate fund balance is undoubtedly the most often asked financial question. This chapter deals with issues to consider when establishing a fund balance level.

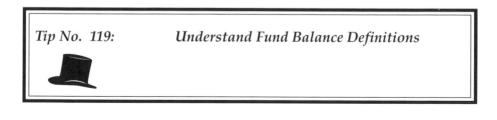

Tip No. 119: ***Understand Fund Balance Definitions***

What is your agency's fund balance? Fund balance is not the same as the cash balance of your agency. Nor is it simply the difference between revenues and expenditures for the year. The Government Finance Officers Association defines fund balance as the cumulative difference of all revenues and expenditures since the government's creation. This definition suggests that your current fund balance results from the cumulative financial decisions made by every governing body since your agency's formation.

When your agency talks about fund balance, what is meant? Positive fund balances are sometimes called reserves. However, the fund balance that is listed in financial statements may not reflect what is available to the governing body to spend. Fund balance may include receivables (accounts receivable or loans to other funds) which cannot be spent, or, the fund balance may be legally restricted to a specific purpose such as to repay a debt.

Specific definitions are, therefore, used to designate assets that are and are not available for spending or for appropriation by the governing body.

- Reserved fund balance is used to designate net financial assets that are set aside for specific purposes. They cannot be spent or appropriated for other uses.

- Unreserved fund balance represents the amount that is available for appropriation or spending.

Unreserved fund balances are sometimes earmarked for specific purposes such as to pay for an unusually high legal bill or for a planning study. This setting aside of funds, called "designations," can only be effected by the agency's governing body or chief administrator.

Designations, however, do not carry the same status as reserved fund balance. Designations are indications or preferences that the money be used in a specified way. There is nothing keeping the governing body from appropriating the money for other purposes. This distinction was lost on a city council who could not understand why the fund balance always seemed to be the same even though the city had generated surpluses for ten years in a row. Not until they discussed it with the auditor did they discover that these surpluses were carried in the financial reports as designations for continuing projects.

When comparing your agency's fund balance with that of other agencies, be sure to compare apples to apples. If your agency uses unreserved fund balances as a benchmark for comparisons, make sure comparative agencies are using the same benchmark and not undesignated, unreserved fund balances.

To back up his argument that his city's 10 percent unreserved fund balance was too high, a councilmember obtained fund balance figures from colleagues in two surrounding cities. The results seemed to confirm his position and provide the ammunition to blast the city manager. The two cities showed fund balances of less than 5 percent, even though the city manager indicated in a report that their balances were in excess of 15 percent. Unfortunately, the councilmember was given the unreserved, undesignated figures by the other cities. Both comparison cities had designated millions of dollars of unreserved fund balances for major civic projects. Fortunately, the councilmember showed his figures to the city manager before going public and thus avoided public embarrassment.

Tip No. 120:　　　　　　*Find the Primary Fund Balance*

With most local governments, the general fund is the most significant operating budget; and this is where the primary fund balance is carried for contingencies or financial problems. It may be carried in an "unreserved, undesignated reserve" account or "unreserved designated for contingencies" account. A few local governments have created "rainy day" funds that are carried as separate accounts outside of the general fund. Ask staff to explain how fund balances work. Bottom line — you want to know where the unrestricted money is carried that provides for contingencies, emergencies and new programs.

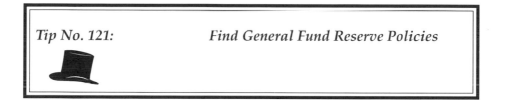

Tip No. 121:   ***Find General Fund Reserve Policies***

Many local governments have formal fund balance policies that have been mandated by state law, established by charter, or fixed by ordinance, resolution or decree. As a governing board member, you should determine what those policies are. Different approaches are used to establish a fund balance level. Approaches include establishing an amount equivalent to a:

*   fixed number of months of operating expenses.
*   percentage of annual operating expenditures.
*   percentage of annual operating revenues.
*   fixed amount such as $25 million.
*   per capita amount such as $150 per capita.

The City of Tempe, Arizona's fund balance policy for the general fund is:

*   The city will continue its healthy financial reserve position. Fund balance for the general fund will be maintained at a level at least 5 percent of the general fund revenue.

The City of Urbandale, Iowa has the following general fund reserve policy:

- The city will establish a contingency reserve at not less than 2 percent of general operating revenues. In addition, the city will maintain a "carryover balance" in an amount necessary to maintain adequate cash flow and to reduce the demand for short-term borrowing. The carryover balance should be a minimum of 4 percent of general operating revenues.

Agencies may also have policies requiring that a portion of any operating surplus be deposited into unreserved fund balance. Some require the dedication of revenues from a specific source such as sales tax to build and maintain an adequate unreserved fund balance.

Tip No. 122:   *Obtain a Historical Trend of Your Agency's Fund Balance*

A starting point in determining the adequacy of your agency's fund balance is to obtain trend information on fund balance for the past ten to twenty years. Compare the current fund balance to the historical level. Is the current fund balance high, low or about the same?

Table 8 compares the actual balance to expenditures over the last 20 years.

Table 8
Fund Balance Trend Information (in $ millions)

Comparison Item	20 Years Ago	10 Years Ago	5 Years Ago	2 Years Ago	1 Year Ago
Actual Balance	$2	$3	$3	$3	$3
Expenditures	$10	$20	$25	$33	$36
Percentage of Expenditures	20%	15%	12%	9%	8%

This trend indicates that beginning sometime between five and ten years ago, the agency quit making contributions to the fund balance. As a result, the fund balance level dropped from 15 to 8 percent. While percentage of operating expenditures is used as the benchmark, other comparisons such as percentage of revenues can be used.

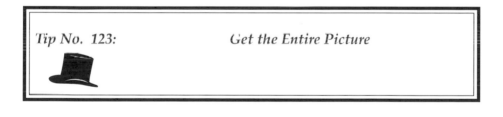

Tip No. 123:   *Get the Entire Picture*

James Wiggins' Internet inquiry recognized that reserve money was located throughout the Fort Walton Beach budget. Here are some questions to ask to get an overall picture of fund balances and reserves.

- How many and where are they?
- How were they accumulated?
- What is the relative size?
- What has been the recent rate of accumulation?
- What are they being used for?
- What are the prospects for continued additions?

- Can they be reestablished if used?
- What are the community attitudes regarding fund balances?

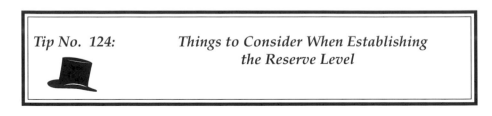

Tip No. 124:   ***Things to Consider When Establishing
the Reserve Level***

Obviously you do not want too much nor too little in reserve. While there are no general rules on what size fund balances should be, the following are key questions that have a bearing on the size of the fund balance:

- **Cash Flow**

    Does your agency have enough money in fund balance to take care of cash flow needs? If balances are not high enough to take care of the gap that usually develops between the time monies are needed and when revenues come in, the agency must borrow money and pay interest on the borrowed funds.

- **Revenue Volatility**

    How volatile are revenues? If the revenue base is vulnerable to major economic fluctuation, enough money must be kept in reserve to take care of the downward swings.

- **Lawsuits**

    What is your agency's possible vulnerability to an adverse legal judgment? Some agencies attract more lawsuits than others. This may be because they operate services that historically get many claims, such as transit services; or the agency may get involved in costly lawsuits defending restrictive zoning practices. While it may not be desirable to stockpile sufficient funds to pay potential adverse judgments, fund balances can be accumulated as a litigation war chest to pay legal fees.

- **Insurance Coverage**

  Does the agency have sufficient insurance coverage? If the agency is self-insured, it should develop sufficient reserves to take care of the open claims the agency faces. If the agency belongs to an insurance pool, it may still need to accumulate reserves for the deductible portion. In some cases the agency may also feel that the upper limit is too low and may wish to provide excess coverage.

- **Natural Disasters**

  For what natural disasters must your agency prepare? Agencies subject to hurricanes, fires, earthquakes, tornados, or floods have a history of dealing with the problems that result and an idea of the costs involved. There are also people produced disasters that fall into this category such as potential problems resulting from a toxic chemical plant located within the agency's boundaries. Sufficient funds should be accumulated to help deal with the next disaster.

- **Other Natural Events**

  The higher latitude local governments face major budget impacts due to snow and ice removal. While an agency may budget sufficient funds for a relatively normal winter, an unusually difficult one can create major hardships. In 1996, the City of New York budgeted $13.5 million for snow removal. But six major snowstorms hit the East Coast that year, forcing the city to spend $100 million. Vernon, Connecticut, a community of 30,000 budgeted $104,000 for snow removal but wound up spending $260,000. While the city received $40,000 in Emergency Management Agency grant funds, it still had to tap its reserves for $115,000. If grant funds and/or snow insurance is not available or is not sufficient, an adequate reserve needs to be established.

- **Grant And Non-Recurring Revenue Source Dependency**

   To what degree is your agency dependent on one-time sources? Some local governments are very dependent on federal and state grants for on-going services. Ideally, sufficient funds should be accumulated in reserves to carry these programs one fiscal year.

- **Ability To Borrow**

   Can your agency borrow money at acceptable rates if disaster strikes or a recession hits? While your agency may be able to borrow, it may be required to pay a premium at that time.

Tip No. 125:   ***Check Reserve Policies of Other Funds***

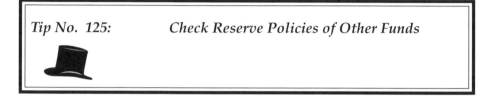

Some agencies have established policies for other funds. For example, the Torrance, California, Water Department uses the following policies devoted to developing and maintaining adequate reserves for the water fund:

- Maintain a working capital (cash flow) reserve equivalent to two months' operating and maintenance expenses.

- Maintain a minimum Disaster Preparedness Reserve equivalent to $1,000,000.

- Maintain a minimum Rate Stabilization Reserve equivalent to 15 percent of the total water operating budget.

- Devote $.07 of every $1 in sales to reserve establishment or replenishment.

The City of Tempe, Arizona, has the following policies for its other funds:

- The city will maintain an unrestricted optimum fund balance level of 25 percent (or 91 days coverage) of anticipated revenues in the Water/Wastewater Fund.

- The city will maintain an unrestricted optimum fund balance level of 10 percent (or 37 days coverage) for the Water/Wastewater, Sanitation and Golf Funds.

Tempe also provides a report in the budget which compares the actual status of reserves to the budgeted policy.

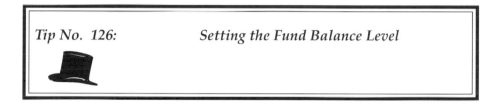

Tip No. 126:   **Setting the Fund Balance Level**

The charts listed in Appendix G depict fund balance levels by percentage of expenditures and per capita for cities, counties and school districts of varying population sizes. The charts are based upon figures from Comprehensive Annual Financial Reports submitted to the Government Finance Officers Association. The charts indicate that the larger the agency, the smaller the fund balance as a percentage of the operating budget. The charts also indicate that the larger the agency, the smaller the amount reserved per capita.

Table 9 summarizes some of the information from these charts for selected local governments of varying population sizes.

Table 9

General Fund Balance as a Percentage of Expenditures for Selected Governments

Government	Population Range	Fund Balance		
		Low	Median	High
Cities	25 - 50,000	-17%	14%	215%
Cities	100 - 200,000	-37%	7%	89%
Counties	<100,000	-5%	23%	127%
Counties	100 - 250,000	-0%	15%	52%
School Districts	25 - 50,000	-11%	4%	23%
School Districts	100 - 200,000	-6%	12%	38%

Treasure Your Treasurer

"The moral of the Orange County story is that track records, past earnings, and ancient history are just that. Together, they still do not provide an excuse for not reviewing basic policies, for not examining assumptions, and for not asking questions."

Marian Bergeson,
Orange County Board of Supervisors

The Dress Rehearsal

The news reverberated throughout the nation during May 1984. The eleventh largest city in America, San Jose, California, had just announced a multi-million dollar investment debacle. The city treasurer had invested in repurchase and reverse repurchase agreements and used leverage to increase the yield. The treasurer's strategy was based upon the assumption that interest rates would drop. This strategy worked fine until the market changed and interest rates began to rise. At that point the underlying value of the city's portfolio disintegrated at an alarming rate. In response, the city sold what remained of its investments. When the smoke finally cleared, San Jose had lost over $60 million dollars and its top seven administrators were gone. Mayor Tom McEnery put the loss into perspective, "We lost enough money to pay for 100 cops for 10 years."

Through an aggressive litigation effort, the city was eventually able to recover 25 percent of the $60 million lost. State law was also changed to require local agencies to prepare investment reports for their governing bodies. At the time it was believed that other local governments would take notice of what happen in San Jose and be able to avoid similar investment mistakes.

Act One
It only took three years to prove this prediction erroneous. In 1987, the investment officer of the City of Camarillo, California (population 52,000) adopted an aggressive strategy to earn more interest income. Long-term securities were purchased with the expectation of generating short-term gains resulting from anticipated declines in interest rates (sound familiar?). By March 1987, the investment officer had committed to or purchased at least $273 million in government securities. This was at least ten times the amount of city funds that were actually available for investment. Had long-term interest rates decreased, the city would have benefitted handsomely. However, interest rates increased during the months of March, April and May 1987.

When interest rates increased, the value of the entire investment declined and the city was at risk and responsible for losses on the entire $273 million, not just the $27 million actually advanced to finance the purchases. When the market value of the portfolio declined, the investment officer was required to transfer additional collateral to securities dealers. This collateral came in the form of long-term certificates of deposit. These certificates were eventually cashed in, and the city incurred additional losses through penalties for early withdrawal of funds.

When the hemorrhaging stopped, the city had lost $30 million, exhausting the general fund reserves and the city employee's deferred compensation funds. Surely, every local government had taken notice of what occurred in Camarillo.

Act Two
The new Rancho Palos Verdes, California, city treasurer was aghast. The previous city treasurer had invested approximately $1 million with E.F. Hutton on what turned out to be a leveraged investment.

After the investment dropped 50 percent of its value, Rancho Palos Verdes threatened to sue. The city was fortunate. Hutton settled by restoring the original principle plus interest.

Others were not as lucky. In his October 1987 memo to the Three Valley's Board of Directors, District Manager Richard Hansen, recommended that the district begin using investment firms to increase the district's interest income. At the time the average yield was 6 percent from the district's approximate $16 million reserve fund, and investments were confined to certificates of deposits, U.S. Treasury bonds, passbook savings accounts and investments in the state's investment pool. Hansen suggested that reserves be invested in high-yield portfolios, which would increase the district's interest income by more than $35,000 for each $1 million invested. By a 4 to 1 vote, the board voted to invest $1.5 million each with E. F. Hutton, Prudential-Bache and the Dover Group.

In September 1988, learning that the district had a margin account with E.F. Hutton and had lost close to a million dollars, the board of directors voted to close the account "at the most propitious time."

The City of Lawndale, California used a contract finance director who entered into a brokerage arrangement with E. F. Hutton. The finance director did not advise the city about the use of leverage. In fact, no one within the city knew about the margin account until the accounting supervisor received a call from a brokerage company instructing the city to wire $253,646 to meet a margin call. Fearing the loss of the city's original investment, the finance director authorized the payment. Five more wire transfers were made before the finance director advised the city manager who advised the city council and city attorney. At this point the city attorney contacted E. F. Hutton, closed the account, and demanded that all city funds be returned. In total the city lost $1.67 million, which represented a little over half of its general fund reserve.

Several other governments, including the cities of Bellflower, San Marino, Palmdale, and Maywood were talked into similar programs. The broker, who moved from E.F. Hutton to First Investment Company, (and took many clients with him) was very convincing. Sure there was some risk, but it was minimal. Besides, the window of opportunity would not remain open long.

In several of the cases, the investment was in zero-coupon treasury notes paying an 8.25 percent yield over 25 years. Zero-coupon bonds pay all their accumulated interest at maturity instead of regular intervals, such as every six months. That makes their prices sensitive to interest rates. Because of this provision, zero-coupon bonds are considered one of the more volatile types of bond issues.

The biggest problem though was that the bonds were purchased on margin. When the bond market went through a steep decline in 1987, the governments were confronted with margin calls — send more money or lose the entire investment. All of these governments scrambled to get out of the investments, but not before losing a combined total in excess of $10 million. Later E.F. Hutton sent refunds to each of the cities for brokerage fees during the time the company handled their accounts. The lost principal, however, is still under dispute.

Several articles were written about these disasters, and safeguarding investments was the hot conference topic. It is hard to believe that anyone with investment or oversight responsibility could have missed the lessons.

Act Three
In 1992, the City of Torrance had a $77 million investment portfolio administered by a fiscally conservative city treasurer. Tom Rupert, was a savvy, 28-year veteran treasurer who served as president of and legislative analyst for the Municipal Treasurers Association. Most of the City of Torrance's portfolio was invested in relatively safe certificates of deposit. A portion of the portfolio, $6.2 million, was being managed by investment advisor Steve Wymer. An agreement with Wymer's investment company, Denman Company, specified that the city's money could only be invested in the safest of investments, such as high grade U.S. Government securities.

For three years the arrangement appeared to work. The city received above market yields, and interest checks were forwarded on a regular basis. Reports were also being prepared and presented to the city council monthly. These reports showed the total investment with the Denman Company and the generous rate of return. The fact that the Denman Company investment produced 10 percent returns, while other investments were averaging around 6.5 percent, did not cause any raised eyebrows nor did the one report which showed the investment yielding an unbelievable 17.7 percent. Councilmembers admitted that they gave these reports little more than cursory reviews, especially since the reports were provided as information only and did not have to be formally adopted by the city council.

Wymer finally caught the city council's attention when he was arrested on 30 counts of securities fraud. Trusts in Iowa and Colorado and ten California cities had also utilized Wymer as their investment advisor, and over $120 million of their funds was found missing after an audit by the Securities and Exchange Commission. The Commission advised Torrance officials that they had less than one hundred dollars left of their $6.2 million. The City of Orange lost all except $4000 of its $7.2 million investment with Wymer. The big loser was the Iowa Trust which lost $65 million. Other big losers were the City of Palm Desert, $12.1 million and the Coachella Valley Joint Powers Authority, $8.1 million.

At the height of his success, Wymer managed a portfolio of $1.2 billion for 64 customers and enjoyed the millionaire's life. He acquired several properties in four different states, expensive art, power boats and ten luxury cars. The millionaire lifestyle was financed by diverting over $12 million from investors.

Part of Wymer's success was that he used respected local government officials to get his foot into the door. These local government officials were practitioners and had many contacts who trusted them. He also used a profit sharing approach. Instead of charging the customary commission, Wymer's contracts with local governments specified that his firm would split net trading gains, with local governments getting 70 percent and his firm 30 percent.

Wymer confessed that while he began as a legitimate business person, he lost millions in bad investments and had to cover up the losses with fake reports. "The false statements I made to clients were not planned from the beginning. The situation got out of hand and snowballed. I lost $66 millon in bad securities deals and paid $75 million in bogus profits." To survive, Wymer wound up using the classic Ponzi scheme, taking money from the most recent clients to pay interest earnings to earlier clients.

Wymer received a 14-year prison term after pleading guilty to racketeering and securities fraud. He was also ordered to pay

$209 million in restitution and forfeited his personal wealth. Great damage was done to many unsuspecting public officials who found their careers in ruin. Federal prosecutors termed the case "one of the most significant and financially devastating cases of securities fraud ever perpetrated on governments."

Was there any public official in the United States who did not know about the pitfalls inherent in public investments?

Curtain Call

All of the previous debacles paled in comparison to the news announced on December 6, 1994. The board of supervisors of the wealthiest county in the United States, unsure of the bond market, afraid that its portfolio would continue to decline, and unable to meet more calls for collateral, voted to declare bankruptcy. Shockwaves reverberated across the nation. Invincible Orange County, California had filed for bankruptcy. A wave of disbelief riptided from the west coast to the east coast in a matter of minutes.

The public and private sectors were shocked. While the massive $21 billion dollar investment pool had only experienced an unrealized loss of about 8 percent, the ship was abandoned.

Robert Citron became Orange County treasurer in 1973; and over the years, he performed satisfactorily in that role. It wasn't until the 1990's, that Citron began borrowing heavily to boost interest earnings. By that time, over 200 cities, school districts and special districts were investors in the Orange County Investment Pool. At that time, Citron also started investing heavily in derivatives. For the next four years, Citron produced returns that were 2 to 5 percent above those being generated by other treasurers and investment pools. Several cities, pleased with the returns being generated, actually borrowed money to invest in the pool. What you had was a city borrowing money to invest in a pool that was heavily leveraged itself by over 300 percent. Unknown to the pool participants, the treasurer's office was also skimming interest off the pool, so that pool participants would not become alarmed at the excessively high returns.

In February 1994, the Federal Reserve began raising interest rates. Citron's strategy was based upon the assumption that interest rates would decline, not increase. With each increase in the interest rates, the pool took another big hit. During this period, Citron convinced an unknowing board of supervisors to issue more debt to cover the collateral calls being made by lenders. He also transferred millions from the county accounts to the other local government accounts. This act, which eventually led to felony charges, saddled unsuspecting investors with a $271 million loss, but it was not enough to forestall the inevitable raid on the pool by both lenders and investors.

Orange County Treasurer Robert Citron's flawed investment strategy resulted in the largest municipal bankruptcy in history.

When a lender foreclosed on $2 billion on securities, the county board of supervisors panicked and filed two bankruptcies, one for the pool and one for the county. The county also began liquidating the pools, resulting in a loss of $1.64 billion. Shortly thereafter, Citron was pressured into a hasty retirement.

In 1995, Robert Citron pled guilty to six felony counts of falsifying documents and misappropriating public funds. He was given a one-year jail sentence and fined $100,000. The once renown financial genius, who juggled billions of public dollars, capped his career by sorting inmate requests for candy bars, cigarettes, and tabloid magazines at the jail commissary.

However, the ultimate blame for the financial calamity was laid at the board of supervisors' doorstep. The Orange County District Attorney, Michael Capizzi, presented the issue to the Orange County Grand Jury, who issued a 60-page report, searing the board for not exercising their oversight responsibility. Among the board failings identified by the grand jury were:

1.   Failure to properly develop and exercise effective oversight of the treasurer and his investment operations.

2.   Failure to take steps to participate in the development of rational treasury investment guidelines and operating strategy.

3.   Failure to gain an effective understanding of the risks inherent in the treasurer's investment strategy and take effective actions to manage the risk.

4.   Failure to develop, in conjunction with the county's auditor-controller, an effective audit strategy of the treasurer's office.

District Attorney Michael R. Capizzi filed criminal and civil complaints against Orange County Supervisors for failing to provide proper oversight over Robert Citron's investment practices.

District Attorney Capizzi armed with the grand jury results pursued willful misconduct charges against two of the supervisors who remained in office. Capizzi was determined to hold the supervisors accountable for their laxity by having them removed from office. The issue was not resolved until March 21, 1997, when the

California Supreme Court ultimately refused to review an appeals court dismissal of the misconduct case. Even though the court did not pursue the case, the message to all elected officials was unmistakable — you can no longer be complacent when it comes to financial oversight.

Tip No. 127:　　　*Treasury Oversight Deserves
More Attention Today*

Historically, oversight of the treasury function was not as complex as it is today. In the past, the treasurer could not get into too much trouble because of the restrictive laws and a lack of attention from investment brokers. Four factors changed the rules of the game:

1.　　A growth in the dollars available for investment.

　　　Today, state and local governments have close to $750 bil lion in financial assets under their control, not including public employee retirement funds.

2.　　An increase in the number and complexity of investment products.

　　　Complex investment instruments are now available that can produce breathtaking returns. These same instruments are also capable of producing heartbreaking losses.

3.　　A loosening of the restrictions on the types of investments.

　　　No longer is the bulk of the public's money stashed in bank checking or savings accounts. Over the years both public and private lobbying efforts at the state and national levels have resulted in liberalizing restrictions and an increasing number of permitted investments. This has increased the potential for higher yield but also has resulted in greater risk.

4.   Added pressure to produce interest income to fill gaps between expenditures and revenues.

With local governments needing revenues and unable to increase taxes, the temptation to increase monies through investments is seductively luring. At the height of the Orange County investment success, one out of every three dollars of general fund revenue came from investment income.

These factors have raised this subject to the top rung of vulnerability for elected officials.

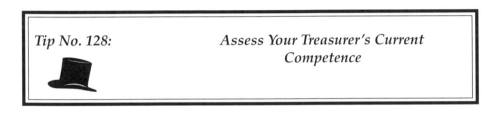

Tip No. 128:   *Assess Your Treasurer's Current*
                              Competence

Returning a higher percentage of interest than other treasurers for several years, Treasurer Robert Citron had earned a deserved respect from the county's board of supervisors. Warnings of dangerous financial management practices by the county's own internal auditor and an outside CPA, went unheeded. Citron had produced over the years, and there was no reason to question his approach or methods.

So how do you assess your treasurer's current competence? First, don't let a treasurer's external image cloud your assessment of their overall investment ability. The individual's reputation may have developed from active participation in local treasury groups. These groups do not evaluate a treasurer's abilities nor certify that a treasurer is competent. Second, don't rely solely upon past performance. It may be that the treasurer gained the reputation during a favorable market period.

Orange County Treasurer Robert Citron had an almost godlike image within and outside the county. He had over 25 years of success as a county employee and was named the Treasurer of the Year by *Governing* magazine. Contrast that to his statement in front of the

California State Banking Committee investigating the Orange County financial calamity, "I believed at the time that I was (an expert). Since this situation has happened...I must humbly state that I was not as sophisticated as I thought I was."

An audit, conducted by the Arthur Anderson Company after the Orange County bankruptcy announcement, discovered the following problems within the department:

1.   The department did not have any written investment guidelines.
2.   Internal controls were weak or nonexistent.
3. ' No one provided oversight of Citron's purchases and sales.

Here are some questions to ask of your treasurer or investor to get to know more about their investment approach:

•   What is your underlying investment strategy?
•   What needs to happen in order for the investment strategy to work?
•   What is the risk to the portfolio if interest rates go up one percent from where they are now? Two percent?
•   What is your investment background and experience?
•   What are the biggest portfolio mistakes you have made in your career?
•   What are the riskiest investment instruments in the portfolio?

You are entitled to clear, understandable responses; and most treasurers will be happy for the opportunity to explain their investment background and strategies.

Tip No. 129:   ***Train and Compensate Your Treasurer***
Adequately

Managing a public agency's portfolio is an extremely important and complicated task. The ability to obtain competitive prices, exploit opportunities and avoid extreme risks requires current professional experience. It also requires the latest in technology to track investments and trends.

The complexity has risen geometrically recently, and compensation rates have not followed. Competent investing requires highly specialized knowledge and constant involvement with a sophisticated, temperamental market. The Municipal Treasurers Association of the United States and Canada provides several treasurer educational courses. Many state associations also provide treasurer certification courses. The cost of these workshops and training sessions are minimal compared to the benefits.

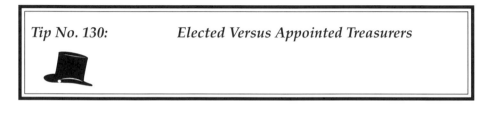

Tip No. 130:   *Elected Versus Appointed Treasurers*

What is the difference between elected and appointed treasurers? Thomas Rupert and Robert Citron were elected treasurers. Many of the other government agencies that had investment problems had appointed treasurers. Appointed treasurers like to emphasize their professional training and investment expertise. Elected treasurers point to their independence from administrative staff and freedom to act as watch dogs over agency finances.

Neither professional expertise nor the watch dog ability is the province of the elected or appointed treasurer. The issue really relates to the treasurer's investment savvy and ability. What type of education, training and experience does the treasurer have? In many cases, the elected treasurer is a figurehead who defers to the finance officer when it comes to investments. According to the survey conducted by the Government Finance Officers Association, the substantial majority of governments (81 percent) indicate that the ultimate responsibility for investment management lies with appointed officials. Interestingly, after the Orange County Investment Pool collapse, the Orange County cities of Brea, Orange, San Clemente and Huntington Beach all put the question of replacing their elected treasurer with an appointed treasurer on the ballot; and in each case, the voters rejected the measure.

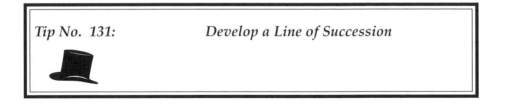

Tip No. 131:   ***Develop a Line of Succession***

The City of Orange, California didn't know how important developing a line of succession for the city treasurer's office was until it incurred a huge loss. The city had $28 million invested in the Orange County Investment Pool when the county declared bankruptcy on December 6, 1994. Eight months earlier, the city's investment committee had decided to reduce investments in the pool to $20 million. City Treasurer, Mark Weiss, should have implemented this change by withdrawing property taxes that automatically went into the county pool. This didn't happen because Weiss incurred an extended illness that kept him away from his duties for most of the year. Weiss said that city officials knew he was sick and should have removed the funds from the county pool. The City Manager, David Dixon, argued that the elected city treasurer was the only person authorized to withdraw funds from the county pool. The manager also said he had a memo from Weiss dated May 20, 1994, which noted the investment committee decision and that Weiss would continue to withdraw funds. After the finger pointing was over, the city council decided to adopt a process delegating investment and treasurer authority to various city officials should the city treasurer or finance director be absent for an extended period of time.

Tip No. 132:   ***Don't Press too Hard for Yield***

In most of the investment disasters, the public agency treasurers and investment officers did not gain financially and most had honorable intentions. They got into trouble by acquiescing to increased pressure to produce more income. In the Orange County case, Robert Citron was producing 36 percent of the general fund revenues from investment income before the collapse. Conny Jamison, San Diego City Treasurer, puts it this way, "Don't put pressure on your investment officials to increase yield unless you have a thorough discussion of the risks involved."

While treasurers and financial officers may not benefit financially, they may respond to the ego satisfaction and accolades that come from obtaining higher than market returns.

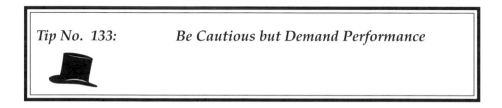

Tip No. 133:   *Be Cautious but Demand Performance*

Can the treasurer be too cautious? Yes. Four-term treasurer Christina Dabis was criticized by the Nevada County, California, Grand Jury for being too cautious and overly worried about risk. In its report to the Nevada County Board of Supervisors, the grand jury accused Dabis of not securing high enough returns. The report suggested that the treasurer should have earned an additional $1 million dollars in interest income had she used the State of California Local Agency Investment Fund during the period from 1987-95. The treasurer admits that she is risk adverse and opted to invest in safe U.S. Treasury Bills, high-rated securities and a passbook savings account at a community bank. Says Dabis, "I do have a conservative portfolio, and I'm proud of it."

Any time you have funds on hand you take a risk. If money is put under the mattress, it earns no interest; and inflation eats away at its value. According to Arthur Levitt, Jr. Chairman of the Securities and Exchange Commission, the guiding principle should be — take as much risk as you can comfortably absorb. Permitting dollars to sit idle with no return is not only too conservative, it's poor cash management.

Newly-elected Redondo Beach City Treasurer Ernie O'Dell presented what he thought was a win-win proposal to the city council — one which would result in an additional $59,000 in interest earnings for the fiscal year. O'Dell's reasoning was straightforward and logical.

1.   For the last five years, the city needed approximately $5 million to finance an operating budget cash shortfall.

2.   Each year, the city would borrow internal funds to meet the cash deficit. Until needed, these funds were invested at market rates in the state investment pool which produced an average yield of 5.6 percent.

3.   The state offered an alternative for local governments which allowed them to "borrow funds" and issue short-term notes to fund projected operational cash flow deficits. Called Tax and Revenue Anticipation Notes (TRANs), these notes could be issued at tax-exempt interest rates of approximately 3.75 percent.

4.   By issuing TRANs at 3.75 percent and leaving the city's investments in the pool earning 5.6 percent, the city would net an additional 1.85 percent in interest earnings. The net fiscal advantage would be an additional $59,000 after issuance costs were deducted.

When O'Dell took the proposal to the city council, he was caught by surprise. The city council was not buying. Councilmember Greg Hill's motion to approve the sale of Tax Revenue Anticipation Notes died a lonely death, without even a perfunctory second.

Three factors were working against O'Dell. First, Orange County, which was less than fifty miles away, had just filed the United States' largest local government bankruptcy. The Orange County crisis was caused in part by borrowing large sums of money to increase yield. Second, the city council had never had to deal with such a transaction and were concerned about its legality and safety. Third, O'Dell had just unseated an incumbent who had spent approximately 20 years in the position. She produced an analysis which cast doubt on the proposal.

O'Dell could have decided to forget about the proposal; however, he embarked on an education program. In a workshop with the city council, he addressed all of their concerns about legality, safety and yield. O'Dell's efforts were successful. In his efforts to familiarize the city council on the merits of using TRANs, he also increased their confidence in his abilities. The vote was 4-1 to follow the program outlined by O'Dell.

Tip No. 134:   ***Insist Upon an Adequate Cash Management Program***

Some treasurers tout their performance of obtaining so much return on invested funds. Such an approach does not measure if the treasurer is investing all the funds available. The real test of the cash management system is to compare the percentage of funds that are available to invest to those actually invested. A treasurer could show a high return on invested funds, but be losing interest income because a high percent of the funds available for investing sits idle in the checking account. This usually occurs because the treasurer, lacking an adequate cash forecasting system, leaves unnecessarily large amounts of money idle to avoid overdrafts.

The single most important element of a cash management program is a schedule of cash flow requirements. You have to know how much money you have, how much money you need to pay the bills and when you're going to pay them. Effective investment of funds cannot be done until the cash flow of the agency is clearly determined.

Tip No. 135:   ***Make Sure Safety is the Top Priority***

The SLY principal is a snappy investment anagram that stands for safety, liquidity and yield. These steps are stated in priority order: safety first, liquidity second, and yield third. Unfortunately, some agencies pay little more than lip service to the concept and recklessly pursue yield. "The three fundamental priorities of every investment policy are safety of principal first, liquidity second, and yield third. For Robert Citron, it was yield first, second and third," said John Moorlach, the CPA who was one of the first to publicly challenge Citron's investment strategy. Moorlach, was appointed Orange County Treasurer after Citron resigned.

Safety means that the entire amount invested will be intact when you want it. If you put $10,000 in an investment, are you assured that you will get $10,000 out when you need it? A key element of safety is getting it when you want it. In the Orange County and most of the other local government treasury collapses, the entire principle would have been returned had these agencies held on to their investments until maturity. The problem was they could not wait the many years until maturity for the price to rise again. They needed the cash.

Liquidity means you can get your money in a usable fashion when you want it. Can you get it without notice or must you give a specified number of days advanced notice before money will be made available?

Yield represents the profit obtained from an investment. Governing body members should become very inquisitive when their agency is getting a much higher or lower return than other agencies are getting.

To achieve a balance between the three standards, governments will typically choose to:

• Invest in instruments which are short-term in nature and insured or guaranteed in some way, such as certificates of deposit and U.S. Government (treasury or agency) obligations.

• An investment strategy which involves purchasing securities and holding them in the portfolio until their maturity, matching maturities to cash flow needs.

Ask your treasurer or investment officer how he/she complies to the SLY principle and more importantly, how the safety aspect is achieved.

Tip No. 136:   ***Let Independent Third Party Custodians***
Hold Your Securities

There was no way you could have convinced the Torrance City Council that disaster would strike their city. They had a well-respected, seasoned city treasurer who helped write many of the laws governing municipal investments.

Torrance City Treasurer Thomas Rupert retired a year after the scandal surfaced. He later lamented, "The moral is, you can never beat a crook. There was nothing anyone could have done. We had audits year after year and were always given AAA ratings." Unfortunately, observers indicate that there was something to be done. Rupert relied upon Wymer to hold the purchased securities instead of using a third party trustee.

An independent third party custodian holds the securities that the agency receives when an investment is made. These are negotiable instruments, so it is vital that they be safeguarded. A third party custodian holds investment documents in trust, and they cannot be commingled or used in any manner.

Everyone who lost money with Steve Wymer lost it because they were not using an independent third party custodian. Instead, they used one who worked for Wymer. Many other public agencies did business with Wymer but used independent third party custodians. The County of San Diego Retirement System had over $50 million with Wymer but did not lose a cent because they made him deliver all securities to the third party custodian. They also demanded to see custodian reports, monitored all transactions and got explanations.

Tip No. 137:   *Have an Independent Auditor*
Evaluate Internal Controls

Internal controls are necessary to protect the people's assets against misuse or loss and to make sure that all financial transactions are legal and authorized. The key is to divide duties and to have more than one person review investment decisions. Checks and balances can be in place, but they also must be followed.

Four decades ago the city council of San Fernando, California, decided to combine the part-time city treasurer position with an accounting technician position. The city treasurer would thus wear two hats and receive two salaries, a nominal one for city treasurer and a regular salary as a city employee. The idea was to provide a reward by increasing the compensation for the elected city treasurer.

This arrangement, like many decisions, became permanent and was passed on to the next three city treasurers. It was in effect until the city's independent auditor raised a red flag. The auditor recommended that the two positions be separated to improve internal control. By permitting one person to perform both functions, the city had violated one of the basic rules of internal control — do not let one person be in a position to handle an entire transaction. In this case the treasurer was in a position to make investments but also to account for and to report upon the investments. Auditors consider this a material internal control weakness.

Failure to divide duties and other internal control lapses led to the problem in Camarillo:

1.   The functions of making investments, accounting for the investments and reporting of investment activity were all performed by one individual — the investment officer / treasurer.

2.   Bank wire transfers which were used for securities trading were not reported to anyone outside the finance department.

3.   With one exception, the investment officer did not receive

any professional investment advice other than from individuals who had a direct financial interest in the types of investments made by the city. In the one case where outside legal advice was obtained with respect to a transaction, the advice was ignored.

4.   The investments of the city and its related entities were all commingled in a common investment pool. Once commingled, the limitations on the types of investment that a municipality could make were effectively overridden.

There are horror stories about people having the ability to wire transfer money to their private bank accounts. Make sure there are controls prohibiting this. There is also the case of an Illinois finance officer who went off the deep end. He managed to convert some of his agency's investment cash into gold coins, got into a car and literally made an unsuccessful run for the Canadian border. While rare, this behavior happens; and the best way to contain it is through the adoption of adequate internal controls.

Tip No. 138:   ***Follow-Up on Requested Evaluation Reports***

When the Three Valleys Municipal Water District decided to liberalize its investment program and begin using investment firms to increase yields, the board requested an evaluation. The board's specific motion to authorize the investments called for performance evaluation of the three firms to be presented to the directors after six months.

William Koch, the dissenting director, asked about the evaluation report after six months had expired but was told that the board had agreed to extend the review period from six to twelve months. Koch, not remembering that the board had taken such an action, checked with the board minute taker who advised him that no such action had been recorded. Koch had a right to be upset. "If staff had brought the performance evaluation back to the board within six months like we had voted, we could have closed our portfolio and avoided a large part of this $900,000 loss," argued Koch.

Tip No. 139:   *Make Sure Your Treasurer is Not Enamored by Brokers*

After dealing with an investment broker for a period of time, treasurers may develop a friendship bond and begin to rely too much on the salesperson's advice. The treasurer may overlook the fact that the broker makes a commission on brokerage transactions. Many brokers and salespeople work in both the private and public markets, so they, too, may not distinguish the difference in approach between the two sectors. They also view public officials as knowledgeable investors who should know the risks of what they are buying.

In the Orange County situation, Robert Citron relied upon a securities salesperson who was also a key advisor in the San Jose debacle. In a State Senate hearing, a company representative stated that the brokerage was "never a financial advisor to Orange County Treasurer Robert Citron. We were a purveyor of products."

In 1995, Cuyahoga County, Ohio was forced to close down an investment fund known by the acronym SAFE (Secured Assets Fund Earnings) after reported losses of an estimated $115 million. The *Cleveland Plain Dealer* blew the lid off with articles accusing the fund managers of using various risky investment strategies. The lawsuit filed by the county commissioners alleged that six brokerage houses and a bank took advantage of fund managers' lack of investment sophistication. The lawsuit also charged the brokers with churning the investment account to increase commissions.

Public agencies are also finding that brokers are not, in many cases, the knowledgeable professionals they are assumed to be. "The brokers are sales people with very little training and no particular expertise in these flashy new securities that are coming out," says Frances F. Goins, a Cleveland attorney who sued two brokerages that sold highly volatile, risky securities to Ohio counties. "What you have," she says, "is an arrangement where customers think they have a knowledgeable and expert investment advisor — and what they've got is a refrigerator salesman."

Ask your treasurer to divulge the people and companies he/she has dealt with (and frequency) during the previous year.

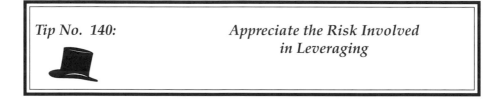

Tip No. 140:   ***Appreciate the Risk Involved***
                              in Leveraging

Leverage is the use of credit to enhance an investor's ability to purchase securities. In virtually all of the instances of investment crises, improper use of leverage is a factor.

Dealers will not lend investors the full purchase price of a security, so the investor is usually required to put some cash into the transaction (referred to as margin). In the case of Camarillo, the investment officer used $24 million to purchase $273 billion in securities.

In a leveraged transaction the upside is very attractive. Assuming $5 million in margin, a local government could finance the purchase of $100 million in securities. If the market is favorable, the government reaps the increase on the entire $100 million portfolio.

Unfortunately, the downside works the same way. If the $100,000,000 drops 1 percent, the value of the securities drops to $99 million. Not much, but this $1 million loss eats up 20 percent of the investor's $5 million investment. When the market declines, it does not take very long to consume the entire investment.

In the Orange County crisis, Treasurer Robert Citron leveraged $7.6 billion into a portfolio worth more than $20.5 billion. In this case, a county treasurer was not prohibited from leveraging public money by nearly 300 percent. In comparison, private sector individual margin purchasing is limited to 50 percent of the value of the stock in their portfolio. Unrestricted leveraging enabled Mr. Citron to achieve above-market returns that he publicly touted for many years. It was the same leverage, however, that exacerbated the downward spiral and caused the financial crash when the Federal Reserve raised interest rates six times in nine months during 1994. When interest rates rose, the value of the underlying securities plummeted; and the use of leverage magnified the loss. Although securities were sold at an average loss of only 8 percent, the leveraged loss amounted to approximately 23 percent of the portfolio.

The actual losses resulted because the investment fund was liquidated prematurely at the time of the county's bankruptcy filing. Had the securities been held to maturity, which was Mr. Citron's investment strategy, the portfolio would not have incurred a loss of principal. However, he was so heavily leveraged, he could not meet the cash withdrawal demands the pool participants and creditors were making.

Tip No. 141: *Make Sure Your Investment Policy is Followed*

Most agencies now have investment policies that define investment guidelines and procedures. The investment policy, at a minimum, must be clear about the investments permitted, maturity limits, liquidity requirements, internal controls, reporting requirements, and portfolio diversity requirements. It should also be very clear on who has the authority to make purchases.

The Municipal Treasurers Association of the United States and Canada (MTAUS&C) provides local governments with a model that contains the basic issues that should be covered in an investment policy. Once your agency develops an investment policy, it can be submitted to the MTAUS&C for a certificate of excellence if it meets the established criteria.

Kay Mirabelli, City of Ventura, California, Treasurer says: "Your investment policies are only good if you follow them. Cities and counties are required by law to have investment policies, but a lot of times they are not being followed."

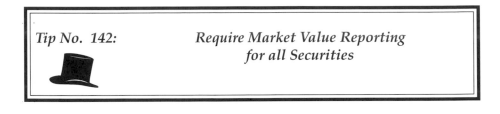

Tip No. 142:   *Require Market Value Reporting*
for all Securities

If Orange County had been required to disclose on a timely basis the decline in the market values of its securities, investors would have learned months earlier than they did that the county's investment strategy was not working and that losses were accumulating. Paul Brady, Irvine City Manager stated: "The sad part of all this is in May of 1994 (eighteen months before), this problem was identified; but nobody at the county level did anything about it — at a tune of $400 million. That problem was solvable. It could have been handled very comfortably instead of having a $1.7 billion crisis. Nobody provided the oversight."

By not having to disclose the problem, the underlying Orange County portfolio was permitted to continue to erode. No corrective action was taken until losses were publicly disclosed in December 1994. The Orange County Treasurer filed reports with the county board of supervisors just once a year. While elected officials and the public cannot be expected to understand and assess complex investment strategies, they can understand losses. Financial condition can be disclosed promptly and regularly by a process called "marking to market." This involves a comparison of the original purchase prices of securities compared to their current market values.

Annual reporting is too infrequent in today's fast moving financial markets. Only regular reporting concerning market values of securities is likely to provide timely information for adequate protection of invested funds.

Tip No. 143:   ***Nurture an Effective Investment***
Committee

Each legislative body needs to determine whether or not it needs an investment oversight committee. In making this determination, legislators need to decide if they have sufficient financial and investment expertise to be able to properly evaluate reports and strategies. The size and complexity of the agency's portfolio is an important factor to consider.

Investment oversight committees perform a variety of tasks, including review of the investment policy and procedures, oversight and/ or development of the investment strategy, and designation of permissible investments. Some issues to consider when establishing an investment committee include:

1.   **Purpose.** Generally, investment committees do not approve individual investments. However, they do monitor results by reviewing the treasurer's investment report. An agency should make sure that the investment committee's work program does not evolve into approving every investment. When this occurs, the lines of responsibility become blurred between the treasurer and the committee. Good management requires that investment responsibility remains with the treasurer.

2.   **Potential Conflicts of Interest**. In many cases, the chief administrative officer appoints members of the investment committee and makes sure that no member is in the position of benefitting financially from inside information.

3.   **Membership**. Unlike many other committees, appointments should be made on the basis of expertise and not representation of a particular group or interest. Members are expected to have a knowledge of municipal investments and practices. Typical membership might include staff members, such as the treasurer and finance officer, and community members with professional investment experience. The Town of Normal,

Illinois uses the following make-up: the finance director who is also the treasurer, two bankers, and a professor from the finance and law department of Illinois State University. This make-up provides the committee with a balance between the theoretical, as well as practical viewpoints.

Some agencies have found their investment committees to be ineffective and/or politically contentious. This is especially true if the elected body appoints too many members and/or political allies who have limited investment experience. When establishing an investment committee, lay out their mission, responsibilities, and authorities. The type of reporting the governing body desires should also be clarified. It is not a bad idea to meet periodically with the investment oversight committee.

Tip No. 144:   *Make Sure Investment Reports are*
                            Timely and Adequate

A major failing in many of the financial crises is that investment reports were not prepared or distributed on a regular and timely basis even though state or local law may specify reporting requirements such as monthly or quarterly. The elected body should insist that reports be presented on a timely basis. Late reports may indicate poor record keeping or investment losses.

Too often, investment reports are ignored or reviewed briefly and filed. Investment reports should be put on the governing body's agenda and not on the consent calendar. Since investments put elected officials at high risk, these reports should be discussed so that elected officials are reasonably comfortable with the state of investments.

Mike Uberuaga, City Manager of Huntington Beach and a participant in the Orange County Investment Pool, gives an insight into the type of reporting the Orange County Treasurer was permitted to make. "I don't think he [Citron] had adequate reporting. If you look at his report in September 1994, it's a five-page report to the board of supervisors that talks about philosophy; it does not talk about leveraging; it does not talk specifically about his investments, where they were, what was happening with those investments, how liquid they were, or the specific kind of information that you would need to make a determination on the status of your portfolio."

Thomas Hayes, former California State Finance Director brought in to help resolve the Orange County fiscal crisis observed, "The general public, the press, everyone thinks the financial side of government is boring. This will not be the last time that you have a major financial problem with a government." The author believes that financial matters need not be boring. It is a matter of insisting that staff focus their presentations and written reports on the important policy items and not all the boring detail. If you permit them to bore you, they will do so. Administrative staffs can be trained to focus on the important items and to keep the elected body interested and informed. Here are some of the issues an investment report should address:

- What is the rate of return? Is it higher or lower than the previous month?
- What is the average maturity of the portfolio?
- How many transactions were conducted during the month and what were their volumes?
- What is the market value as compared to the adjusted purchase price?
- Do investments comply to the investment policy?
- Were any sales made prior to maturity?
- What was the interest earnings accrual for the month?
- What is the makeup of the portfolio and what percent accounts for each type of instrument?

Reports are improving. Some treasurer reports address all of these questions with snazzy graphics presented on a single summary page. The back-up matter is then attached.

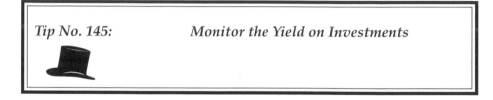

Tip No. 145:   *Monitor the Yield on Investments*

Before anyone had even caught the problem, San Jose had reported in their monthly investment report, a total return of zero percent. It did not get the city council's attention. Someone in the finance department had caught it, but accepted the treasurer's explanation. In fact, the return was negative; but they didn't want to show that on the investment report, so they showed zero.

When Orange County was receiving 9 percent on its invested money, other agencies were earning 5 to 6 percent. It is always tempting when someone says you can get 3 to 4 percent more on your investment than you are already getting. When something seems too good to be true, it generally is. "We had an opportunity to place money with the Orange County Investment Pool, but I didn't have a lot of interest. We knew Orange County could not guess right forever," said Beverly Hills Finance Director Don Oblander.

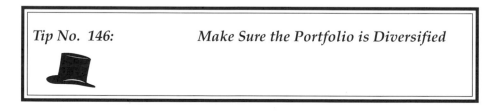

Tip No. 146:   *Make Sure the Portfolio is Diversified*

One of the best ways to hedge against risk is to diversify. This includes not putting all investments into Treasury bills or even putting the entire portfolio in an investment pool. Diversity also includes using more that one investment broker. If your agency is only using one or two, you may not be getting the best competitive bid.

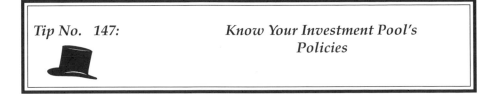

Tip No. 147:   *Know Your Investment Pool's*
Policies

If your agency invests through a county or state investment pool, make sure that the types of investments the pool is utilizing, are permitted by your own policy. Ken Hansen, a local resident and investment advisor, took the City of Irvine, California to task for violating its own policy of putting over $200 million in the Orange County Investment Pool. According to Hansen, the pool regularly used foreign investments and commingled funds. Both these practices were specifically prohibited by the City of Irvine investment policy. Hansen was quoted in the *Orange County Register,* "The question is, did the city know the county investment policy was less stringent than its own? If not, it's just bad management."

Many cities and special districts found themselves in a similar situation. While they were permitted to invest in the Orange County Investment Pool, their own policies specifically prohibited them from directly making the same type of investments the Orange County Investment Pool was permitted to make.

Requiring a statement of compliance with your agency's investment policy from your administrative staff will help you determine whether on-going investment practices are in conformity with your agency's written investment policy. A statement of nonconformity is an obvious red flag. Letting people know that these reports are available to the public will improve accountability of local officials to taxpayers.

Tip No. 148:   *Thoroughly Examine an Investment Pool*
Before Joining

Approximately ten months before the Orange County Investment Pool went bust, the City of Laguna Hills considered a staff recommendation to become a participant in the pool. At the city council meeting, councilmember Randal Bressette pled for a one week delay before joining. Bressette had concerns about the safety of the pool and wanted a higher level of comfort. Bressette raised the issue with the county treasurer and was promised background material, but it had not arrived before the meeting. Believing that there was no reason to delay, the city council voted 4 to 1 to move forward with its investment.

It's impossible to judge had the material been delivered whether the outcome would have been different. The lesson is clear. At a minimum, the agency must know how the money is being invested. When asked whether he wanted to say "I told you so," Bressette replied, "I don't take any particular pleasure in being right. I just thought we should have asked more questions."

Over 60 Minnesota local governments brought suit against the Piper Jaffry securities firm for misleading advice they received regarding the safety of a mutual fund marketed by Piper. The fund performed spectacularly during the early 1990's and at one point it boasted of a 21.7 percent rate of return. While the mutual fund originally contained only U.S. Government and agency securities, the company changed its strategy and began using leverage and investing in mortgage-backed derivatives. In 1994, the balloon burst when the fund's derivatives became illiquid, creating a cash crisis. In total the fund lost over $100 million. Ultimately the localities received a $1.25 million settlement when the National Association of Securities Dealers found that facts about the riskiness of the investment were not adequately disclosed to the investors.

Generally speaking, investment pools are not regulated by the Securities and Exchange Commission. There is a general governmental exemption to a whole body of regulations that apply to private sector funds. This means that there is an element of risk potential. Before joining an investment pool, you may wish to ask if the pool is following the same rules as the private sector pools. If not, why? Here are some questions to ask of the pool manager:

1.   What is the average portfolio maturity? This single item alone would have alerted participants to the Orange County Investment Pool. When you go beyond 180 days, you run into the inviolable rule that when interest rates go up, the price

goes down.

2.   What are the permissible investments? How risky are they?

3.   What are the professional fees? Some investment pools can be extremely complicated when you try to get to the bottom line on what is the cost. In one section they may have a custodial fee and in another an investment advisory fee. Ask for a summary of the comprehensive fee structure.

4.   What is the custodial arrangement for holding purchased securities? Many of the investment scandals involved the failure to deliver securities to an independent third party trustee.

The California Society of Municipal Finance Officers (CSMFO) publishes a pamphlet titled *"Before Entering a Government Pool,"* that outlines items to examine.

Tip No. 149:   ***Don't Let the Treasurer Buy if It Can't be***
                        Explained to You

The majority of cities, counties and districts do not use so called exotic instruments, such as inverse floaters and derivatives or use leverage to increase revenues. Nor do the majority put all of their funds into public or private investment pools. Some highly skilled treasurers, however, argue that leveraging and exotic instruments, when used properly, increase yield at a manageable risk.

A 1995 survey of 1300 governments across the U.S. and Canada by the Government Finance Officers Association and the MBIA Insurance Corporation was conducted to determine how states, counties, cities, and districts invest their funds. This extensive survey, completed just after the Orange County fiscal disaster was revealed, found that most governments use a conservative approach when investing public funds. The most common investment instruments used are certificates of deposit, Treasury bills, and Treasury notes. Survey findings included:

- Less than 5 percent of the governments had any investments in inverse floaters, reverse repurchase agreements, or flexible repurchase agreements.

- Investment policies in 43 percent of the governments prohibited any investments in derivatives.

- In fact, 46 percent of the respondents believed that derivatives should never be used.

Irwin Bornstein, President of the California Municipal Treasurers Association, has a guiding principal, "I don't invest in anything that I don't understand."

1994 Ballot Statement of Robert L. Citron:

In an era when taxes are rising and service quality is failing, my performance in office has been the exact opposite. Because of my record of achievement, last year more than 185 public agencies throughout California, including cities, school districts, and county government, asked Bob Citron to manage your tax dollars. Being Treasurer requires financial expertise and integrity. Managing your tax money is an awesome responsibility that I take very seriously. As your Treasurer, I have annually reduced taxes by diligently seeking the highest return on tax monies in the treasury. Last year, compared to bank passbook rates of 2.5 percent, I received an 8.5 percent return which earned county taxpayers $364 million of tax savings.

But there are powerful people who want to play politics with your tax dollars. They want to inject their politics into money management decisions. I will never play politics with your tax dollars. Never.

I invite you to contact your city finance director or the county auditor and inquire about my reputation for integrity and good money management. A reputation absolutely free from politics. I have worked hard to earn your trust.

Thank you for your support and I respectfully ask for your vote.

Robert L. Citron

Performance Measurement: What's the Fear?

"It is not enough to be industrious, so are the ants. What are you industrious about?"

Henry David Thoreau

Crisis

The Long Beach, California, City Council had just received the community survey results; and they were elated. Crime was declining in Long Beach, and people felt safer about living and working in the community. What really struck them was that 64 percent of the respondents indicated that they felt safe in their neighborhoods.

In many communities across the country, only 64 percent would be disappointing and a cause for great concern. It could be translated to mean that more than one-third of the community did not feel safe. However, local government issues are relative, and Long Beach was on the upside of a terrible crime problem. The percentages had progressively improved over the previous five years from 50 percent in 1993 and 54 percent in 1995.

In 1990, the City of Long Beach Police Department was in shambles. Over a period of five years, violent crime had more than doubled, and gang and drug activity had gotten out of hand. During this period the town changed dramatically; the population had increased by 15 percent, and the community had become more dense and ethnically diverse. The police chief had recently been fired, and the department was preoccupied with internal strife. As a result, the police department didn't keep up with the dramatic changes taking place in the community.

The quality of service was spiraling downward. Calls for service had grown by 35 percent during the past five years, yet sworn officers per 1000 population had been reduced by 10 percent. Officers had no time to patrol or to interact with neighborhoods, as they were totally consumed by requests for service. Response time continued to drop; and more troubling, in some cases, there was not a response at all.

In 1991, the city informally declared a state of emergency. Substantial action was required to bring crime under control and improve the level of safety. Jim Hankla, City Manager, floated the idea to contract with the Los Angeles County Sheriff to provide police services to over 100,000 Long Beach residents. This would allow the city to immediately infuse additional police resources into the town, while buying the city time to reengineer the police department. Hankla was able to convince the Long Beach City Council to sign a contract with the sheriff. While contracting for sheriff's services was not unusual, it was unheard of for a city of Long Beach's size to do so. It didn't take long for the Long Beach Police Department to feel the competition brought about by the contract.

The quality of service provided by the sheriff's department was much better than that provided by the police department. The sheriff wanted to make an impact, and did so by providing personal service and higher visibility. Deputies took time to interact with the community and build trust. This resulted in a groundswell of support from residents and some councilmembers to get the sheriff to police the entire city.

While Long Beach sometimes gets lost in the shadow of Los Angeles, it is a major city. It has a population of 430,000 and is the fifth largest city in California and the thirty-second largest in the United States. "For a major city like Long Beach to say we failed at providing police services, and we need the sheriff to come in and do it, was a bitter pill to swallow," relates Scott Bryant, Long Beach Director of Strategic Management.

The city went through eight months of spirited public debate about contracting with the Los Angeles County Sheriff and eliminating the Long Beach Police Department. Finally it came to the showdown, and on a close 5 to 4 vote, the city council decided to keep its own police department.

Strategic Plan Preparation
The message was not lost on the police department. One more vote and the Long Beach Police Department would have ceased to exist. Said Bryant, "There is nothing like the threat of going out of business to wake you up. The police department recognized that change was not only desirable, it was necessary for the organization's actual survival."

Up until that point, the department was very inwardly focused and had built walls around itself. It was necessary to gather data to help understand what was really happening. This was done in three different ways. First, the department developed a statistically valid community survey which was printed in the three primary languages spoken in the community — English, Spanish and Khmer. Survey questionnaires were mailed to 1800 randomly selected addresses in the community and they were also printed in the local newspapers and placed at public offices.

Second, 14 separate focus groups were conducted. Residents were asked to express their fears on crime and concerns about their police department. They were also asked to complete the survey questionnaire. The surveys and focus groups provided further insights about what things concerned residents.

Third, the department surveyed ten comparable police agencies, comparing approximately 100 different factors such as response times, calls per capita, and crime clearance rates. This provided information on what the department was doing well and what it was not doing well.

Fourth, a departmental survey and internal focus groups were used to identify employee attitudes and opinions about their job, the department and the community. The survey asked tough questions about management support and fairness, level of motivation, and suggested changes.

The Strategic Plan

A profile of current and future issues facing the police department and the community emerged from these efforts. It was clear that both the level of public safety and the perception of public safety had to be improved within Long Beach.

A strategic plan was developed which had 14 major goals and over 400 implementation strategies. The Police Strategic Plan had two primary focuses: (1) to improve the level of public safety in the community and (2) to enhance the public's perception of safety. In addition, performance measures were developed for each of the goals. The focus of the measures was on outcomes or results. The department did not settle for counting the number of police officers but instead subjected itself to being gauged on such things as how violent crime changed.

The Results

The results have been nothing less than outstanding. Between the period of 1993 and 1996, the city recorded the following changes in crime and perception of safety:

Actual Crime Statistics:

- Violent crime decreased by 38 percent.
- Property crime decreased by 19 percent.
- Gang-related incidents have decreased by 38 percent.

Perception of Level of Safety Statistics:

- Percentage of those who feel safe in neighborhoods increased from 50 to 64 percent.
- Percentage of those who feel likely to be crime victims within the years deceased from 38 to 23 percent.

- Percentage of people frequently observing gang activity decreased from 58 to 35 percent.

The department's goals and performance measures have proven very beneficial to the city council. They have been useful in communicating with the community on the progress being made in the public safety area. The *Long Beach Press Telegram*, the city's major newspaper regularly reports on the progress being made and uses the graphics and tables provided by the city. The *Press Telegram* has also conducted its own community polls regarding public safety, and the results parallel those of the city.

The strategic planning process enabled the Long Beach Police Department to concentrate resources and apply them on its most important problems. Measurable targets and outcome measurements, critical components of strategic planning, led to improvements in both service efficiency and effectiveness. By comparing actual performance to intended outcome, the department was able to determine which strategies worked and which ones did not.

City Manager Jim Hankla, summed it up with the following statement, "The experience of the Long Beach Police Department clearly illustrates the importance of understanding the needs of the community. Not understanding the community it served, nearly led to the demise of the police department. Targeting the community's priorities, establishing goals and performance measures has led to the department's recent success."

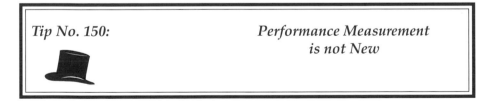

| Tip No. 150: | *Performance Measurement is not New* |

A few local governments have been using performance measurement for several decades. Lakewood, Colorado; Palo Alto, California; and Savannah, Georgia instituted quality standards during the 1960s. Savannah used such performance standards as two weeks to trim a tree after the request, a 90 percent efficiency level for water wells, meeting water quality standards 90 percent of the time, and a promised vendor's payment within ten days. The performance measurement concept, however, did not catch on with the majority of local governments.

Recently, the popularity of performance measurement has been rekindled. Much of this results from elected official and staff dissatisfaction with the traditional input approach to budgets. The input approach focuses on what goes into the budget, not what results. For many years, the typical local government would argue over how many people were needed to carry out a function. Public Works would ask for so many maintenance personnel, schools would ask for a certain number of teachers, and fire departments would ask for so many firefighters. This is what we need the governing body was told. The discussion very rarely got into what these new personnel promised to accomplish or what results the community could expect. During the past few years, the community has been asking questions like "What results can we expect if we fund three more police officers?" The demand to know has pushed local governments to respond with performance results.

Measurement practices have also improved considerably because of advances in technology. A personal computer has more computing power than a room full of 1960's mainframes. This additional capability enables governments to collect and manage data undreamed of before. The proliferation of personal computers has also spurred creative approaches to performance reporting. There are numerous examples of user friendly reports that rely heavily on simple, understandable graphs and tables.

The media can also take some credit for the renewed interest in performance measurement. The extensive coverage of the federal Government Performance and Results Act of 1993 (GPRA) has exposed the entire country to measurable goals and outcomes. Residents of local communities are putting pressure on their local officials to talk about measurable targets and program results. Local newspapers have increasingly resorted to their own community surveys to determine citizen satisfaction of community services.

Some of the benefits of performance measurement include:

1.   Evaluation of how a program is working.

2.   A method to compare contracted to in-house services.

3.   Empowerment of employees because they can operate within the framework of goals and not be forced to always wait for direction from supervisors.

4.   Improved communications with the public.

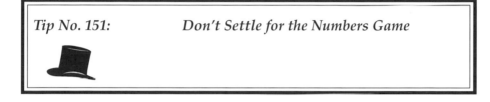

Tip No. 151:   ***Don't Settle for the Numbers Game***

A community activist from Long Beach had one issue — to increase the number of sworn police officers per 1000 population. At one point, he even qualified a measure on the ballot to set the number of officers per 1000 population in the city charter. Fortunately, the proposal was rejected by the voters. The problem was there was no incentive to effectively use those resources. In fact, there was absolutely no evidence to suggest that the number of officers per 1000 had any correlation with how safe a community was. The community with the most police officers per 1000 is Washington D.C., and it is not considered a safe community.

The focus on inputs is deeply embedded in government culture. President Clinton led the charge to focus on outcomes at the federal government level with the Government Performance and Results Act of 1993 (GPRA). Yet, when he rolled out his initiative to fight crime on the streets of America, he couched it in terms of inputs. His COPS program promised to put 100,000 police officers on the street — not reduce crime. Unfortunately, the 30-second sound bite of "100,000 more cops on the street" obscured the real question regarding the effectiveness of the program in reducing crime.

Tip No. 152:

**Have Staff Develop
Outcome-Oriented Objectives**

The key to a useful performance measurement system is to develop outcome-oriented objectives. While this is the most critical step, it is also the most difficult. Outcome-oriented objectives go to the reason of why a service is provided.

By focusing on outcomes, the Coast Guard's Office of Marine Safety, Security and Environmental Protection was able to significantly reduce deaths on the high seas and inland water ways. Its mission is to protect the public, the environment, and U.S. economic interests through the prevention and mitigation of marine incidents.

Traditionally, the Coast Guard based its marine safety efforts on inspections and certifications of vessels. It measured its performance by counting outputs, such as the number of inspections conducted and the number of mechanical problems rectified. Outcome performance measurement brought a new insight. After assessing performance data, the Coast Guard found that equipment and material failure had a relatively minor role in marine deaths. Only 18 percent led to casualties; the other 82 percent were caused by human and environmental factors. As a result, the Office of Marine Safety switched efforts from inspection to addressing human error and environmental factors. It also redefined its mission from doing more and better inspections to saving lives. The Coast Guard and the towing industry jointly developed training and voluntary guidelines to reduce the causes of fatalities. This joint effort contributed to a significant decline in the reported fatality rate — from 91 per 100,000 people to 27 per 100,000. According to the Coast Guard, the program achieved its results by giving field commanders greater authority and by investing in activities and processes that went most directly to the goal of reducing risks on the water. "We defined what our real mission was and then devoted resources to achieving it."

Tip No. 153:   ***Be Ready to Focus on Results***

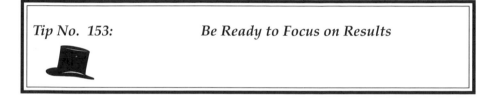

Countless studies by the General Accounting Office have concluded that federal agencies often fail to appropriately manage their finances, to identify clearly what they intend to accomplish, or to get the job done effectively with a minimum of waste. After decades of seeing these problems recur in agency after agency, Congress finally moved to address this endemic situation on a government-wide basis through the Government Performance and Results Act of 1993 (GPRA).

In an effort to have government run in a more businesslike manner, every major federal agency must now address these basic questions:

1.   What is our mission?
2.   What are our goals and how will we achieve them?
3.   How can we measure our performance?
4.   How will we use that information to make improvements?

The intent is to force a shift in the focus of federal agencies — away from traditional input concerns, such as staffing and activity levels, and toward a single overriding issue — results. GPRA requires agencies to set goals, measure performance, and report on their accomplishment.

As federal government agencies become more proficient in performance measurement, they will undoubtedly require local governments to submit outcome type objectives and measurements with grant and other program proposals.

Tip No. 154:   ***Performance Measurement Works with Contract Services***

When Rancho Palos Verdes, California, incorporated as a city of 41,000 in 1973, it had only one practical option in terms of providing police services — to contract with Los Angeles County.

The sheriff's department submitted a budget proposal that would have taken 65 percent of the new city's general fund revenues, leaving relatively little for other community services, such as road maintenance, parks, recreation and engineering. The sheriff's department insisted that the proposed service level was minimal and was the same level as existed prior to incorporation. City officials believed that the community had not received adequate service before incorporation and that the proposed service level cost too much. To prove their point, they requested and received data from the sheriff's office which showed that Rancho Palos Verdes' response times were approximately double those of neighboring cities, burglary was the major problem, constituting 70 percent of all felonies and traffic accident rates were two times greater than neighboring cities.

Faced with this information, the sheriff's officials agreed to reduce the first year's cost and establish measurable objectives. The objectives agreed upon between the city and sheriff's office included:

- To reduce burglaries by 10 percent over the previous year.
- To reduce traffic accidents by 15 percent over the previous year.
- To achieve an average emergency response time of four minutes, 90 percent of the time.

In 1973, establishing law enforcement objectives under a contract was a unique experience for the sheriff's department and additional resources were provided to implement the program. The city council established a subcommittee of two members, who along with the city manager, met quarterly to review progress on the objectives.

By the end of the fiscal year, the response time and traffic objectives were exceeded but the burglary objective was not. However, by evaluating the performance information, the department was able to reallocate existing resources to focus on the burglary problem. The council was pleased with the results as they had data to show the improvement in police services.

The unfortunate sequel of the story was that after the council and city manger had left office a new group, not recognizing the importance, let the program lapse. This is not unusual in local government. Programs are implemented and once the originators leave, the programs are forgotten and abandoned.

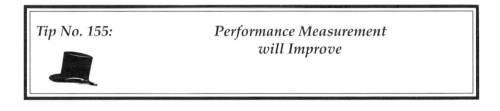

> **Tip No. 155:**   *Performance Measurement*
>   *will Improve*

For the last six decades, the financial people have been refining their craft and the results are apparent. A person can visit various governments across the country — Salem, Oregon; Houston, Texas; and Portland, Maine and find the same high quality financial reporting. They follow standard rules on how data is gathered, categorized, summarized and reported. As a result, the techniques used for local government financial reporting are considered to be of high quality and reliability.

Performance measurement, on the other hand, is still in its infancy. Its quality when compared to financial reporting, is still very low. Putting a system of objectives and performance measures in place takes time. The process evolves through trial and error. However, each year, organizations learn more about performance measurement and reap greater benefits.

Chief Administrative Officer Sally Reed, when she was instituting performance measurement in Los Angles County, had this to say, "I am somewhat cynical about performance measures. They are not a perfect guide to allocating dollars, but they are a means to an end. The county has zilch now. The system is so aggregated and politicized that the board of supervisors benefits from the muddiness. I know that performance measures are subject to manipulation — your imperfect data against mine; but as we get better at performance measurement, it will take us to a new level of understanding about the services we provide." Reed recognized that it would take the county a number of years to develop a viable system.

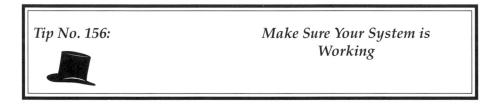

Tip No. 156:   *Make Sure Your System is*
                                                Working

A number of years ago, a county jumped headlong into performance measurement. The staff heralded the new management system with promises of improved productivity, better planning, and increased communications with the public and elected officials. Six years after the system was put in, the board of supervisors, hearing complaints, requested that an outside auditor evaluate the system.

The auditor's results were revealing. The new system had not improved planning or productivity. Instead, a insatiable bureaucratic paper mill was created. Departments went through the motions of creating objectives and measures, but the ones selected were trite and meaningless. No one seemed to pay much attention to them once they were compiled. This was brought out when the auditors discovered that some departments kept submitting the same results year after year with no variance at all.

As a follow-up, confidential interviews with employees and management were conducted. The results surprised everyone. The most often mentioned complaints were:

1.   **No Review.** Management and the board of supervisors had gotten into the habit of filing the results without examining their significance. Employees felt that no one was really paying attention to them. One public works supervisor bragged about submitting year end reports four years in a row that showed tree trimmers cutting three times the number of street trees the county actually maintained.

2.　　**Imposed Objectives.** The objectives were developed by the department heads, who did not confer with the people who were responsible for carrying them out. Because employees did not participate in their development, there was no buy-in.

3.　　**No Training.** Even when the system was first implemented there was no training on how to develop or use objectives and performance measures. As a result, the quality was very low.

After identifying these problems the county reengineered the system. It also made some changes:

• 　　Employees were provided an orientation and training on how to develop and use performance measures.

• 　　Technical assistance was provided to departments that requested help.

• 　　The focus was on a few significant objectives and measures with a greater emphasis on outcomes and results.

• 　　A participatory process was developed whereby employees contributed to the establishment of objectives and measures.

When the system was set up, the county did not devote sufficient resources to do an adequate job. After the initial failure, the board of supervisors realized that a good performance measurement system takes resources just as any other program.

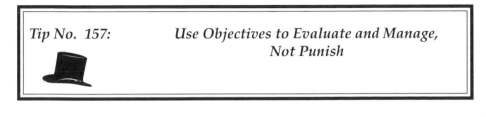

Tip No. 157:	*Use Objectives to Evaluate and Manage, Not Punish*

The biggest problem resulted from the board's lack of understanding on how to use objectives and performance measures. The board would publicly berate departments if they did not achieve their objectives. To avoid the public embarrassment, department heads started submitting vague and/or easily achieved objectives.

After being castigated for failing to hit her target on reducing injuries, the personnel director changed her objective of "Reduce on-the-job injury accidents by 10 percent" to "Provide the highest level of accident prevention training for employees." The tactic worked. There was no way the board of supervisors could nail her on whether she achieved the objective or not. Unfortunately, both the personnel director and the governing body lost the benefits of a valuable management tool.

Performance measurement is an imperfect tool. It works best when it is used to evaluate results and make adjustments. The administrative staff owes elected officials worthy objectives and performance measures. Elected officials owe staff the proper use of objectives. If measures are misused, the system will not work.

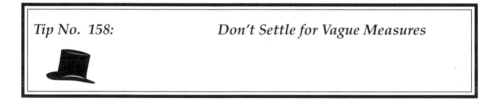

Tip No. 158:   ***Don't Settle for Vague Measures***

Here are some examples of vague objectives that were taken out of various local government budgets.

- Continue efforts to cut red tape and streamline various processes and procedures.

- To maintain high professional and ethical standards in all financial practices and procedures.

- Plan, direct and coordinate the affairs of the agency in accordance with objectives and established legal and professional standards.

- Process candidates, including background investigations, polygraph, physical fitness, etc., in a timely fashion.

- Ensure that 100 percent of LP 236 and SCSP 115 participants complete mandated training during the fiscal year.

When one looks at each of these, it is apparent that there is no way to really measure the accomplishment of these so called objectives. How does one know if the task was completed, let alone if it was done well. Note also that the last example is so infested with office jargon that it is not understandable to anyone outside the department. Don't encourage poorly written objectives. Send them back and request that they be rewritten.

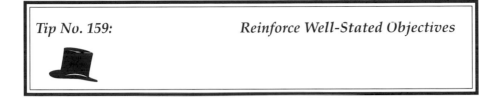

Tip No. 159:   *Reinforce Well-Stated Objectives*

It is surprising the differences you will find between departments or programs within the same agency. These well stated objectives were gleaned from the same budgets as the vague ones.

- Resolve 80 percent of complaints within five days of receipt of the call.

- Reduce traffic accidents by 5 percent during the fiscal year.

- Respond to all sewer system breakages within two hours of the call.

- Achieve a 85 percent literacy rate for children.

- Achieve a good to excellent service rating of 80 percent from residents for street sweeping.

A well-stated objective is simply stated, concise, meaningful, and measurable. It is written so that you can determine whether it has been achieved. The street sweeping objective is directed at assessing residents' perception of the quality of street sweeping. The best way to do this is to use a survey.

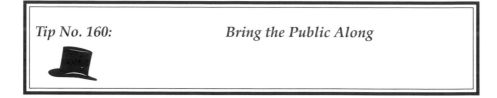

Tip No. 160:   ***Bring the Public Along***

On the one hand you want staff to develop meaningful outcome type measures. On the other hand you want to be very careful on the ones you select. An important outcome for a water agency relates to the quality of the water it delivers. One water district submitted the following objective to the board of directors: Meet or exceed all state and federal water quality standards 98 percent of the time.

The 98 percent was selected by staff because there had been minor, non-life threatening water quality problems in the past.

The board went ballistic. "You mean my water will not meet standard 2 percent of the time? Why don't you and your family come over and drink it first?" In some cases, anything less than perfect is not acceptable to the public.

You may wish to forgo the politically sensitive measures until the public becomes more attuned to the uses and limitations of performance measures. Someone will take these objectives and use them to create political hay. It can become a distraction that hinders progress.

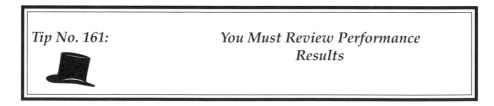

Tip No. 161:   ***You Must Review Performance***
                                    Results

One of the shortcomings of many performance measurement programs is the failure of the governing body to spend time evaluating results. When elected officials ask questions about results, it signals the importance to staff members. On the other hand, when objectives and performance measures are given cursory attention, staff tends to degrade their importance. One city council gave its staff the following feedback regarding the new objectives that were adopted 12 months before:

1. Reliance on an achievement date, while measurable, does not emphasize the qualitative aspects of a project. A street reconstruction project may be completed on time, but what was the quality of the work?

2. Due to the large number of problems and challenges facing the community, objectives need to be prioritized.

3. While the city council may agree to priorities at the beginning of the year, things change so quickly that staff should realize today's top priorities may change within a few months.

4. The regular reporting system of the city emphasized day-to-day activities and ignored objectives. The reporting system must reflect performance information or attention is diverted to crisis and routine items.

5. Objectives should be adequately defined. The city council found a difference between their and staff's interpretation of the objectives.

Tip No. 162:   ***Look for Unintended Consequences***

Sears began a program of paying commissions to auto-repair service employees who achieved sales objectives. The objectives were focused on selling parts and services. The program quickly turned into a nightmare. Service personnel were accused of selling unneeded parts and repair services. After the states of New Jersey and California accused Sears personnel of bilking customers, the company discontinued the incentive program. Sears Chairman Edward Brennem acknowledged that, "The policies for compensation and goal setting created by management for our service advisers in the auto centers were a mistake."

Sears' mistake resulted from not thinking through the consequences of the sales objective. Perhaps a more appropriate objective would have been to achieve a 90 percent customer service satisfaction rate.

Public agencies must also make sure the objectives they establish don't create unintended consequences. The county that sets a numerical goal for number of burglary convictions by the district attorney may find that more serious cases, such as assault and armed robbery, are being slighted. A probation department that sets an objective to increase the percentage of restitution collected by probation officers may find that the crooks are committing more crime in order to meet their restitution payments.

It doesn't mean that the objectives are bad and should be rejected. In some cases, the objective can be rewritten or a companion objective that deals with the problem should be developed.

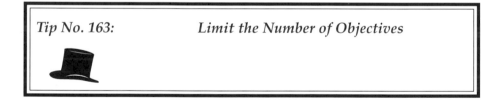

Tip No. 163:	*Limit the Number of Objectives*

Some agencies have gotten carried away by the number of objectives. My suggestion is to develop as few as possible. One to four per program may be enough. Focus on quality rather than quantity.

Tip No. 164:	*Modify Objectives When the Situation Changes*

For objectives to work, they must be linked to the budget. Objectives are created based upon the budgeted dollars. These dollars purchase the personnel and equipment needed to achieve the objective. If the budget is cut, the staff should be able to adjust the objective to reflect the new situation. One city, facing severe financial problems, had to cut back considerably; but they did not want to admit to the community that police services also were being reduced. So they kept the authorized strength at 300 officers but refused to let the department fill vacancies. As a result, the department had the worst of all worlds; it was operating with 30 less officers and being held to the old response time standards. Local governments need to educate the public and keep them apprised of the actual situation.

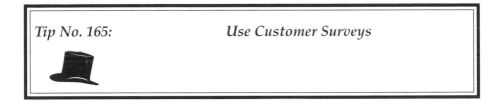

Tip No. 165:   ***Use Customer Surveys***

Some of the most important information on quality of services is subjective. How do your customers feel about the condition of the streets or how safe do they feel. One of the best ways to get this data is to use surveys. The County of Santa Clara Planning and Building Division uses a report card format to provide employees feedback on customer service.

All visitors to the Santa Clara Planning and Building Division are given a customer service form to immediately fill out or to mail back later. The issues rated include visitor perceptions on:

• How long the person waited until being served
• The courtesy of the staff member
• The technical knowledge of the staff member
• The efficiency of the process
• The customer's general satisfaction with the process

Responses are compiled into a simulated report card and distributed to employees monthly. The county believes that the customer responses have contributed to improving customer service. Figure 8 is a sample of the Public Service Report Card.

Figure 8

County of Santa Clara Planning and Building Division Customer Service Report Card

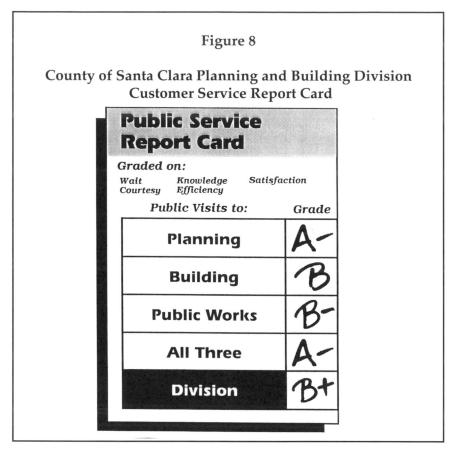

Culver City, California is a city of 40,000 in Los Angeles County. During the day, its population swells to around 300,000. This influx results in traffic congestion and accidents. Culver City traffic officers issue approximately 18,000 traffic citations annually, and they do receive occasional complaints. During a two-month period, the police department decided to conduct research to determine motorist reactions to how moving violations were issued. A survey form was developed and mailed to 100 randomly selected traffic ticket recipients. The questionnaire asked for opinions on the officer's courtesy, professionalism, and willingness to listen to the motorist. Respondents were assured that their answers would be anonymous.

One would assume that someone who just received a citation might not be too willing to respond, let alone to do so objectively. Surprisingly, both assumptions proved wrong. Thinking that a 15 to 20 percent return would be good, the department actually received 36 percent and the results were predominately positive.

Table 10
City of Culver City Police Department
Traffic Enforcement Attitude Survey

♦ **The officer took the time to explain the violation to me.**

Strongly Agree			Agree		Strongly Disagree
1	2	**2.7** 3	4	5	

♦ **I was given the opportunity to explain my side of the story.**

Strongly Agree			Agree		Strongly Disagree
1	2	3 **3.4** 4	5		

♦ **The officer was courteous.**

Strongly Agree			Agree		Strongly Disagree
1	2 **2.4**	3	4	5	

♦ **I felt comfortable/non-threatened while speaking with the officer.**

Strongly Agree			Agree		Strongly Disagree
1	2	**2.5** 3	4	5	

♦ **The officer acted professionally.**

Strongly Agree			Agree		Strongly Disagree
1	2 **2.2**	3	4	5	

The question regarding motorists not having enough time to explain their side of the violation resulted in the department changing its approach. Drivers were given additional time to provide an explanation as long as the situation remained under control. Culver City's experience provides an excellent example of using performance information to improve practices based upon customer responses.

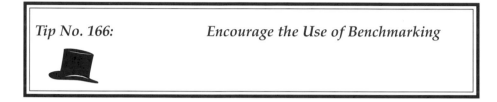

Tip No. 166:   *Encourage the Use of Benchmarking*

The University of North Carolina at Charlotte released a study in 1996, that ranked 120 transit systems in the nation. It was the first study to compare and rank transportation systems by examining resources used and results obtained. The best ranked system was in Champaign-Urbana, Illinois, and the lowest ranked system was West Palm Beach County Transit in Florida. The study concluded that the efficient operators were in medium-sized cities. Larger cities tended to be the least cost efficient.

Such a comparison offers valuable benchmarking information. For example, the San Francisco Municipal Railway (Muni) ranked 104 out of the 120. Some specific rankings for Muni included:

- Cost per vehicle mile was $9.19 compared to a national average of $4.58.

- Operating cost per hour was $84.90 compared to a national average of $59.00.

- Vehicle collisions at 4.0 collisions per 100,000 miles was four times the national average.

- The system ranked among the highest on ridership per capita, service frequency, and number of vehicles on the street.

"The Muni is a good deal for riders — fares are low, and the service provided is high. But it is not a good deal for the taxpayers. The bottom line when the smoke clears is that the system's negatives outweigh the positives, which is why San Francisco is ranked 104," said David Hartgen, the study director at the university. "A major factor for the high cost is labor. Labor costs represent 72 percent of the budget; and under the San Francisco charter, the municipal railroad must pay its operators the average of the first and second highest paying operators in the nation."

Benchmarking provides a new level of information for elected officials and can be invaluable when evaluating budgets.

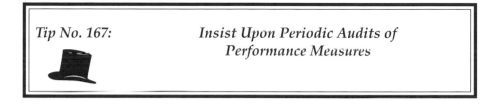

Tip No. 167:   ***Insist Upon Periodic Audits of
                              Performance Measures***

In many cases, departments may be responsible for not only developing performance measures, they may also be responsible for collecting data and reporting results. This leads some to feel that the information is not reliable and can be manipulated. You're at their mercy in terms of the reliability of the data.

Prince William County, Virginia, uses independent audits to assess the validity of data. Craig Gerhart, County Executive says, "We found that police and libraries have been at the 98 percent accuracy rate for their measures, and they have been able to demonstrate an audit trail satisfactory to our auditors. On the other hand, we have seen social services and public works down around 52 percent and 54 percent accuracy. Those are only half right. Just by going through the audit process and reporting results publicly, I think a lot of the other agencies are taking this process a lot more seriously."

Where Do We Get the Money?

"We determined that our taxpayers would be better served by declining the grant."

New Britain Township Manager Robert Bender

While grants represent a desirable method for funding new projects, they can create significant new burdens. Witness what happened to New Britain Township in Pennsylvania. Officials discovered that the Township's planned bikeway qualified for federal assistance. Preliminary estimates were that the three-mile bikeway would cost $80,000 to construct and that federal funds would provide up to 75 percent of the money.

New Britain officials soon discovered that federal assistance came with a myriad of strings. All told the burdensome federal regulations and specifications significantly increased the cost of this seemingly simple project to close to $300,000. The feds required the township to pay union scale wages and hire new inspection personnel.

The deal killer, however, resulted from the requirement that the planned four-foot- wide bikeway be doubled in width and provided with banked raceway curves. In a memo recommending against federal participation, Township Manager Robert Bender summed it all up with this comment, "The multitude of rules, regulations, accounting and auditing procedures, bidding procedures, specifications, engineering and inspection requirements, prevailing wages, and other requirements have made, indeed, a federal case of this project." The township declined the federal funds and built the bikeway themselves at considerable less expense and fewer headaches.

Public agencies need money to operate; and as expenses go up, revenues must also increase if cutbacks are to be avoided. This chapter addresses issues related to raising and administering revenues through grants, taxes and other fees and charges.

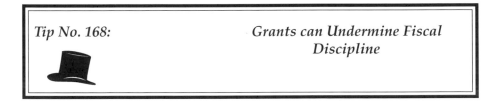

Tip No. 168:   ***Grants can Undermine Fiscal Discipline***

In 1994, the federal government offered cities and counties a deal that couldn't be refused — one hundred thousand federally-funded police officers to fight crime through the COPS (Community-Oriented Policing Program). Since there were an approximate 650,000 police officers employed by local governments at that time, this represented a substantial boost.

Local governments are always happy to get any money the federal government passes their way, but this money came with a huge balloon payment. Recipient agencies were expected to participate in the funding of these officers by increasing their contribution each year until they paid the entire bill. The formula was:

Year	Federal Government Contribution	Local Agency Contribution
1	75%	25%
2	50%	50%
3	25%	75%
4	0	100%

By the third year of the program, the City of Los Angeles accepted approximately $50 million to hire 643 new officers. A larger grant for $55 million scheduled to fund an additional 710 officers was reluctantly turned down because of the matching requirement and the negative impact on other city services. When you add so many additional personnel in one department, you put demands on other departments that provide support services.

Two grants for a combined total of $9 million were approved for the City of San Francisco. This would have enabled the city to hire an additional 120 police officers. After the hype was over, however, the city scaled its request and opted for $3.15 million, which would add 42 new officers. This was done after they were advised by the feds that the grants had to be used to increase the total number of police officers and not for replacements.

The program allowed St. Louis, Missouri, to hire an additional 23 police officers. However, St. Louis, like thousands of other local governments, did not provide for the future. "I truly don't believe that many cities, including ours, thought about how we were ever going to be able to afford it when the grants ran out," lamented Sergeant Robert Heimberger, city coordinator for federal grants.

Dan Rosenblatt, Executive Director of the International Association of Police Chiefs admitted. "We knew future funding was going to be a big problem. I think many departments felt that it would be hard for city councils to trim back once the officers were on board. Now when I talk to police chiefs, they are hoping some money comes along to save them."

This is not to denigrate these grants, but an agency must make some hard choices before accepting these windfalls. True financial accountability involves a public airing of these issues:

- The degree to which the level of service is being increased.
- The plan to pay for the program at inception and after the agency is required to provide full funding.
- The ability to pay for the impacts in other departments created by the grant.
- The ability to pay for housing and other uncovered grant expenses.
- The degree to which the grant program will divert money from other needy programs.

Continuation of the program after funding runs out is rarely a public discussion topic at the time of grant application and acceptance. Attention seems to always be focused on not losing the grant and getting the agency's fair share. If the political risk is too high to turn a grant down outright, lay out the facts to your community and get their input. Is the community willing to assume the increased cost once the grant funds run out?

Tip No. 169: *Don't Blame the Feds*

To become eligible for COPS funding, cities and counties had to agree to plan in good faith to retain the new officers with local funding at the end of the grant period. Application forms also required cities and counties to show how they were going to pay for the additional officers. One police chief laid it out, "Sure we knew the requirement was there, but three years was a long time away and besides we just knew the community would bail us out."

"If cities and counties had no intention of following through on their commitments, they would have had to be damn creative on their applications," said Charles Miller, Justice Department spokesman.

Tip No. 170:   ***Avoid the Grant Pitfalls***

Grants have to be worth the effort. Obtain answers to these questions before approving new grant requests:

Acquisition:

- Will it require significant lobbying and political effort?
- Will waiting for grant approval delay a critical project?
- Must your agency's funds be advanced before grant funds are received?
- Will matching fund requirements reduce money for other projects?

Administration:

- Will the accounting, reporting and auditing requirements require additional staff?
- Will a new clientele be built that must be dealt with?

Long-Term Impacts:

- Will it change the scope, size or character of a planned project?
- Will it create a new service that your agency would not have started without outside funding?
- Is it a one-time or is it an on-going project?
- Will the grant require a significant local contribution?
- What other contributions must your agency make?
- Where will the money come from?

Tip No. 171:   ***When to Apply for a Grant***

So when do you apply for grants? The following are some guidelines:

- When the grant purpose ties to one of your goals.
- When the strings are not too burdensome.
- When you have the money to meet required matching funds.
- When you have the time to go through the process.
- When there is a good possibility that you will receive the grant.
- When you are convinced that staff can handle the additional administrative burden.
- If you can truly handle the demands of the new clientele which will be created.

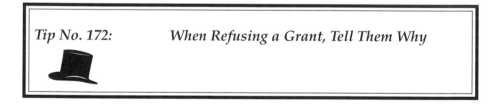

Tip No. 172:   ***When Refusing a Grant, Tell Them Why***

Pressure can be brought to bear against an agency for refusing to apply for grants for which they are eligible. A number of eligible cities refused to apply for homeless grants due to the small dollar amount and the burdensome requirements. The press characterized the failure of these cities to apply for the monies as insensitive and uncaring about a segment of the community. When turning down grants or refusing to apply an agency should aggressively publicize the reasons why.

Tip No. 173:   ***The Property Tax is Still the***
                             Most Despised Tax

In its latest annual survey, the U.S. Advisory Commission on Inter-governmental Relations (ACIR) included its long-term trend question on taxes:

- Which do you think is the worst tax — that is, the least fair: federal income tax, federal Social Security tax, state income tax, state sales tax, or local property tax?

This was the 23rd annual public opinion survey conducted by ACIR, and the negative attitudes about the property tax have not subsided. The Gallup Organization conducted their poll with a sample of 1003 adults.

Twenty-eight percent of Americans chose the local property tax as the worst tax or the least fair. The feeling for the federal income tax was also negative with 27 percent viewing it as the worst. The state sales tax was third with 14 percent of Americans viewing it as worst, followed by the Social Security tax with 12 percent. The tax with the lowest least fair percentage was the state income tax.

Regarding the property tax:

- Americans over age 45 and retirees gave it the highest negative ratings (36 percent and 38 percent).

- Homeowners were more negative than renters (33 to 18 percent).

- Those employed gave it a higher negative than those not employed (34 to 26 percent).

- Regionally, those living in the Northeast and the North like the property tax least (33 percent) compared to Westerners (21 percent).

- The property tax got the fewest negative responses among professionals (24 percent), sales and clerical (23 percent), and those under age 35 (22 percent).

- There was a substantial difference in the percentage of Americans in rural areas (35 percent) and those living in central cities (23 percent), citing the property tax as worst.

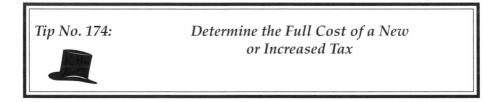

Tip No. 174:   *Determine the Full Cost of a New*
or Increased Tax

While there are costs associated with the levying of a new or increased tax, governing bodies sometimes discount them. When considering the impact, the amount of revenue raised is not the full measure of the cost of the tax. The true cost of a tax must include the lost revenue resulting from businesses and residences relocating to another area. Washington, D.C. found that, as taxes were increased, businesses moved out of the city. Other issues that must be considered before taking action on a new or increased tax include:

1.   How much revenue will be raised?
2.   What is the cost of collecting the tax?
3.   Does it increase the cost of doing business?

The cost of doing business within a community can vary widely, and these costs are now being compiled and compared. For instance, a survey conducted in 1996, by Kosmont & Associates, a real estate consulting firm, found that Los Angeles was the most expensive place in California to operate a business. The study used various comparisons to make the point. A hypothetical law firm would pay combined yearly taxes of $13,300 in San Francisco, $70,650 in Oakland and $116,650 in Los Angeles. In Santa Clarita, a city less than 40 miles from downtown Los Angeles, the firm would not pay any taxes.

President Larry Kosmont says that, "Companies use what are called first-tier factors such as quality of work force, transportation proximity of distributors and clients when making a decision as to where to locate a business." Taxes are a second-tier factor and are usually used as tie-breakers for companies looking at several competitive locations, according to Kosmont.

Tip No. 175:   *Avoid the Static Analysis Pitfall*

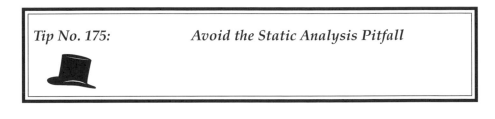

In 1990, the federal government instituted a 10 percent luxury tax on boats and planes. Congress believed that the new tax would result in more revenue, but just the opposite occurred. Revenues declined appreciably because people stopped purchasing the items. Only after thousands of private boat and plane building jobs disappeared did Congress repeal the tax.

In New York, the state government allowed local governments to suspend the 8.25 percent sales tax for a week. The results exceeded the wildest expectations. Sales doubled for the week as compared to the same week in the previous year. While the 8.25 percent did not seem to be that significant to government officials, it was to consumers.

A library district attempted to close a budget gap by instituting new fees and raising several user fees. A new $5 fee for audio tapes was instituted, and the estimated increased income was based upon previous usage. The fee for borrowing items from other libraries was increased from $1 to $5 per request. Again the expected income was based upon previous usage figures. In both cases, the revenues collected were less than 40 percent of projections. The district eventually realized their mistake and reduced the fees to $1 per audio tape and $2 per borrowed item.

In all these examples, a "static analysis" mistake was made. This error occurs when governmental officials fail to factor in how people might change their behavior when a fee or tax is implemented or changed. They assume the usage will remain the same, yet it rarely happens. So, before you raise a fee or institute a new tax, request an analysis on how consumer behavior will change.

Tip No. 176: 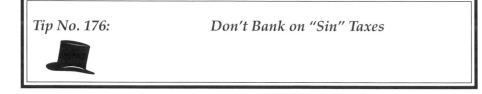   ***Don't Bank on "Sin" Taxes***

Because they are so visible and affect so many people, broad based taxes, such as personal income, sales, business and property taxes, are difficult to raise. As a result, some local governments opt for raising the less visible and less intrusive taxes. Raising revenues by taxing the excesses or addictions of the electorate is sometimes selected as an alternative. Cigarettes and alcoholic beverages, two of the so-called "sin" taxes are the most popular. These type of taxes, the thinking goes, offer a "twofer." They not only offer the benefit of increased revenue, they also discourage the consumption of these undesirable products.

Maryland's Governor had a goal of lowering the personal income tax. To make up for the gap in revenues, he proposed that the cigarette tax of 36 cents per pack be increased to 72 cents. There are problems with this approach. If the personal income tax is lowered, it will probably be difficult to increase in the future. On the other hand, if the government is serious about discouraging smoking, the cigarette tax will not increase and will undoubtedly shrink. To offset this decline, the state must continue to raise the cigarette tax or promote cigarette consumption. Neither alterative is desirable. Moreover, at some point, consumers will go to other sources, especially since the neighboring state of Virginia only has a 2-1/2 cent per pack tax. This actually occurred in New Hampshire. After several surrounding states increased cigarette taxes, its cigarette sales went up significantly. The opposite happened in those states that raised taxes.

A good way to avoid the sin tax dilemma is to use proceeds from the tax for medical and educational programs on the dangers of these products. This is the approach used by Massachusetts and California, and they don't count on "sin" taxes as a recurring revenue source.

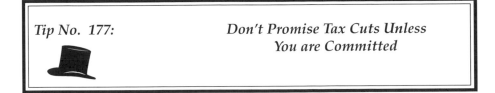

Tip No. 177:   ***Don't Promise Tax Cuts Unless***
                          You are Committed

During recessionary times, some local governments are forced to implement new or increased taxes. A common approach is to make a promise to the community that the tax will be phased downward or eliminated after a period of time or when economic conditions improve. For example, one city council passed a 10 percent utility tax, but promised to phase it out over the next four years. The phase-out schedule was:

Year	Tax Rate
1	10%
2	8%
3	5%
4	0%

The promise looked good on paper, and it was tendered in good faith. However, after the first year, the city manger prepared a budget report outlining the programs that would have to be cut in order to reduce the utility tax.

Unfortunately, the city manager was not consulted on the original promise, and while she tried to make good on it, the economic situation had worsened. The city council took considerable heat from the community when they decided to forgo their promise to reduce the tax.

Tip No. 178:   ***Don't Overreact to Tax Limitation***
                          Measures

Proposition 13, sponsored by Howard Jarvis, hit California local governments, counties, cities, school districts and special districts with a slam in 1978. It not only rolled property taxes back to their 1975-76 tax year level, it also limited assessed valuation increases to no more than 2 percent. Moreover, the proposition prohibited these governments from imposing any new taxes without a two-thirds approval from voters.

Up until the passage of Proposition 13, local governments had used the property tax to close their budget gaps. It was convenient and relatively easy to do. When the proposition passed, this method of balancing budgets was eliminated. Many local governments had been predicting doom; and when the proposition passed, they implemented their doomsday plans. One city turned off every third street light, and a school district sent out layoff notices to 20 percent of their employees. These were blatant overreactions which tended to further infuriate the public.

Perhaps the worst were the agencies which printed up lapel buttons for their employees that contained a simple message: "Go See Howard."

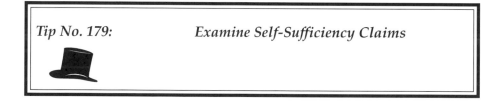

Tip No. 179:   *Examine Self-Sufficiency Claims*

For several decades, the United States Forest Service claimed that the department's logging operation not only paid for itself, it made a profit. The Forest Service's annual report for 1995, showed a modest $59 million profit. For many years, environmental groups contested this claim, saying the Forest Service accounting practices hid overall logging costs.

In 1997, a report, prepared by the Council of Economic Advisors, showed a $234 million subsidy. This report concluded that the Forest Service collected $616 million in timber receipts but spent more than $850 million. To the environmentalists' glee, the report revealed, "Generally, Forest Service subsidizes timber extraction from public lands by collecting less in timber sales revenues than it spends on timber program costs." As it turned out, the Forest Service excluded the cost of building timber roads and the 25 percent share of timber revenues it is required to give to states.

It is not unusual to find that a public program thought to be self-sufficient is actually being subsidized. For many years the City of Claremont, California, Parks and Recreation program claimed to be self-sufficient. An inquiry by a city councilmember revealed that the parks and recreation department excluded indirect costs such as building, utilities, custodial services and supplies. Self-sufficiency to the department meant off-setting the cost of the instructors' salary and class materials. So, what was touted as a self-sufficient program, in fact, was being subsidized by approximately 25 percent.

In another city, the Kids Camp program was loved by the elected officials and community. The program was instituted as a day care program for children. While everyone knew that it was drawing children from outside the community, the city council was not alarmed since the program was said to pay for itself. However, after an audit, they changed their minds. The program was a magnet and continued to grow because fees were lower than the local private day care providers. It also drew over two-thirds of the program participants from outside of town. The kicker was that while the program was suppose to pay for itself, only direct salary costs were being recaptured. As a result, the city was providing a 50 percent subsidy.

Tip No. 180:   ***Make Departments Responsible***
for Revenues

An audit by the Government Accounting Office found that the Forest Service was losing millions of dollars per year because the Service failed to charge market rate fees for special use permits. The GAO audit recommended that permit fees for oil and gas pipelines, power lines, and communication lines be raised to more competitive rates. Overall, the Forest Service charged about a dime for every $1 that other governments and private owners charged. The most blatant example cited was the case of an owner of a natural gas pipeline who paid the State of California $130,726 an acre for access to state-owned land but received similar access to national forest land for $814 per acre.

This is not unusual for local government operating departments. Historically, they have been held responsible for expenditures but not revenues. While building departments estimate building fees, public works departments estimate construction permit fees, and police agencies estimate citation fees, they have not been held accountable for inflated estimates. This can play havoc with the general fund budget because an inflated estimate of expected receipts has the same impact as overspending. With budgets getting tighter, the governing body should hold staff more accountable for accuracy of revenue estimates. Departments should also be held accountable for:

- Reporting projected revenue shortfalls early.
- Requesting grant reimbursements promptly.
- Collecting outstanding bills on a timely basis.
- Implementing fee increases in a timely manner once they are adopted.

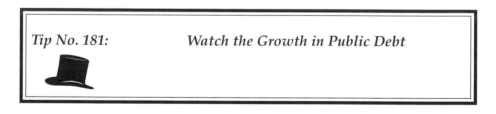

Tip No. 181:   *Watch the Growth in Public Debt*

Bond financing has grown in popularity in recent years as a relatively painless way to pay for public improvements while postponing cost to taxpayers. "It seems that everything under the sun is being financed by municipal bonds, including aquariums and baseball stadiums," complains Zann Mann, publisher of the *California Municipal Bond Report*. "It's this sort of excessive use of municipal, or tax-exempt bonds, for these unessential purposes that's causing a semi-rebellion among some taxpayers."

Several debt instruments, such as certificates of participation, can be issued without voter approval. When issuing these instruments, the governing body pledges to make annual lease payments out of the general fund. As debt grows, however, a greater portion of the operating budget must be used to service the debt.

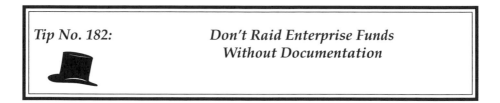

Tip No. 182:   ***Don't Raid Enterprise Funds***
Without Documentation

Enterprise funds are set up for functions which are suppose to operate like a business. Electric utilities, water reclamation plants, airports, harbors and refuse collection are all examples of enterprise operations. The accounting method used is more like business accounting than governmental accounting, and enterprise functions are expected to operate without a deficit. Historically, your enterprise funds may have been subsidized by the general fund, or they may have been used as a cash cow by the general fund.

There are legitimate charges that should be made to enterprise funds, such as the general fund providing fire protection, police, accounting, data processing, and financial reporting services; but there needs to be a rational and defendable basis for the assessment.

In 1996, Mayor Richard Riordan transferred $31 million from the Los Angeles Airport to the city general fund saying the money was owed for past services provided by the city to the airport. Fire services alone, the city claimed, amounted to $25 million for services rendered from 1925-1970, before the airport had its own fire protection services. The remainder of the money was for miscellaneous services, such as police, investigations and rescue.

Acting under a policy that prohibits unauthorized transfers from airports that receive federal grant funds, the FAA demanded the money back. "It is longstanding FAA policy that when you transfer funds from an airport, you have to have adequate documentation in order to get approval," said Steve Okum, FAA special counsel. "The City of Los Angeles could only document $1 million. To add teeth to their demand, the FAA froze $60 million in federal grants for airport capital improvements. "These funds will be frozen until the city repays the money it took," declared Okum.

Fearing a challenge, the city had the foresight to place the money in an interest generating escrow account. Later, after the FAA refused to back down, the Los Angeles City Council restored the "raided" funds.

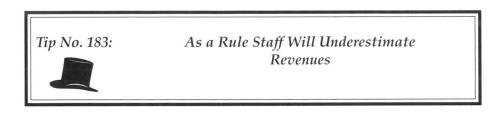

Tip No. 183:   ***As a Rule Staff Will Underestimate Revenues***

When Los Angeles City Treasurer J. Paul Brownridge publicly admitted that he had overestimated city revenues by $21 million, he expected flack. His office predicted close to $40 million in investment income in the current budget. Brownridge knew that there would be repercussions, but he was not prepared for Councilmember Zev Yaroslavsky's tirade, "This was a horrendous act of incompetence and a horrendous act of unprofessional behavior."

Talking about a clear message to every administrator and finance officer of a local government who heard about it — Never, never, never, overestimate revenues.

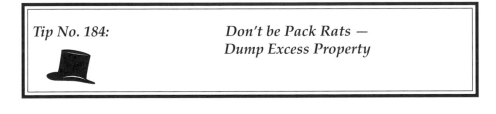

Tip No. 184:   ***Don't be Pack Rats — Dump Excess Property***

Over the years, public agencies can accumulate a considerable amount of land and buildings. This property comes from slivers of land left over from public works projects such as street construction, from land seizures for non-payment of taxes, or from agency projects that never materialized. While there can be strong sentiment to keep the land, it costs money to bank land. Costs can include:

•   Lost property taxes

- Property maintenance such as litter and weed control
- Security costs
- Potential legal liabilities from accidents

There is also the lost opportunity that results from failure to develop the property. This may occur when the parcel may be integral to any development of surrounding parcels.

Some agencies bank land for future projects or to keep development from occurring in a sensitive environmental area. Some developers try to reduce their costs by offering to donate unbuildable land to public agencies. Whatever the reason, the public agency should compute the holding cost of the land and assess the cost of lost opportunities. Is it really less expensive to acquire the land now? What are the accumulated costs for holding the land for a number of years?

While disposing of public property can involve a laborious process, involving a number of steps, excess land should be disposed of regularly by the public agency rather than waiting every 15 or 20 years.

Sewers and Classrooms Don't Vote . . . Right Away

"You can pay me now, or you can pay me later."

Fram Oil Filter Commercial

Butte County is a rural Northern California county with a population of 204,000 and 1640 square miles. Its population density of 111 persons per square mile is sparse when compared to San Francisco County's 15,502 persons per square mile. Butte has a relatively low crime rate and very few violent crimes each year. In the late 1980's, Butte County suffered severely from the recession, costly mandates, and state revenue takebacks. The county was on the verge of bankruptcy. A now infamous photo showed Butte County employees standing impatiently in crowded lines at a local bank to cash their payroll checks before the county literally closed down.

One cost saving effort implemented by the county was to require that sheriff's patrol vehicles be driven 180,000 miles, 80 percent more than the California State Highway Patrol, before replacing them. Even though maintenance costs increased with the age and condition of the vehicle, county officials believed that they were saving money by not having to purchase new vehicles as often as in the past. This strategy appeared to work until one day when the sheriff's department received an emergency call from an outlying area. A patrol unit was immediately dispatched; but before getting half way to the destination, the unit broke down and could not complete the call. Not to worry, another unit was dispatched. Unfortunately, this unit also broke down about half way to the destination. A third unit was dispatched, and it made it to the scene and dealt with the problem.

The assistant county administrator summed up the situation as follows, "Our savings were artificial at best. Sure we saved the outlay of dollars for new units, but look at what happened. We had two units out of operation that had to be towed back. Our department has less than 80 sworn deputies, so the loss was significant. We also faced a potential lawsuit for failure to respond in a timely manner."

Your agency has spent millions and perhaps billions of dollars acquiring and developing capital assets. Guarding the public checkbook also means keeping this valuable investment in satisfactory operating condition. This chapter deals with the importance of maintaining capital assets and major equipment.

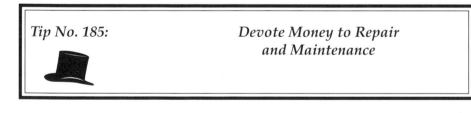

Tip No. 185:   ***Devote Money to Repair and Maintenance***

Your infrastructure consists of the basic buildings, facilities, grounds, equipment, utilities and installations your government needs to function. In most public agencies, millions of dollars have been devoted to constructing the infrastructure. Governmental Accounting Standards require your agency to keep track of your investment in fixed assets. Unfortunately, during periods of fiscal stress, infrastructure maintenance dollars are diverted to other things, such as salaries, benefits and current operating expenses. A federal study conducted by the Government Accounting Office in 1996, found that one-third of the United States' public elementary and secondary schools needed major repairs; and 60 percent of these needed work on a major feature, such as a roof, floor or wall. In many cases, governing boards and administrators have consciously decided to reduce expenditures for these capital items in order to pay for salaries and related expenses. The result of this diversion is not seen immediately. In some cases, it takes years before the problems begin to appear; but eventually they show up in very grotesque ways.

For example, here are some comments from students in the Los Angeles School District concerning the condition of their schools:

- Narbonne High School Senior: The plumbing on our campus needs to be taken care of. No one drinks the water, because it is yellow. It's kind of pointless when we wash our hands. You look at the urinals, and they're yellow even after they have been cleaned."

- Venice High School Junior: "Three times this year the girls' bathroom has overflowed, and there was sewage everywhere. We have cockroaches and little mice all over the place. The sinks are horrible."

- John Marshall High School Senior: "There are a lot of defects in the classroom ceilings. It's hard to concentrate when raindrops are falling inside a classroom. Your papers get wet."

- University High School Senior: "The environment is ugly and you can't really concentrate when you feel unsafe because there's asbestos in the floor tiles that are coming up. Why do we have to work in these conditions?"

These defects were undoubtedly caused by many factors — ordinary wear and tear, vandalism, aging and collateral damage from the Northridge earthquake. The bottom line, however is that these problems did not occur overnight. Administrators, teachers and board members permitted problems to fester and feed on themselves.

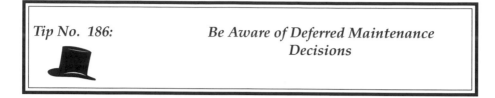

Tip No. 186:   ***Be Aware of Deferred Maintenance***
Decisions

The Torrance Unified School District in Southern California made a conscious decision after the passage of a tax limitation measure to put a lower priority on maintenance. Complaints about cracks in the blacktop, failed plumbing, gas main leaks, electrical problems, and structural problems were accumulated in a file titled "deferred maintenance." Over the years, these neglected problems built up to the point that in 1997, the district had tallied a $135 million repair bill with no way to pay for it.

How did the problem develop? Robert Koeser, Associate Dean of the School of Management at California State University, Dominguez Hills offered this explanation, "You have to spend on what is more critical at the moment. Then you look at postponable items. In the short term, maintenance and modernization can be postponed. You can't put the faculty on a two-year furlough. If you lose the faculty, you lose the programs. If you can't serve students, it doesn't matter how well the buildings are maintained." The Torrance school administration and board decided over the years that salaries and benefits, which comprise 85 percent of the budget, were more important.

Not all school districts follow this approach. El Segundo, California, School Superintendent Bill Manaham revealed, "Some school districts are resourceful. For example, the Saddleback Valley School District in Orange County, California, set aside money for roof and carpet replacements. Prudent districts set aside a dollar amount for maintenance. We had sound management principles."

Professor Richard Chase, USC Business Professor is very critical of the decision to divert maintenance money. "If schools were a business, they would be ripe for a takeover. The competition would swoop down. The CEO would be out. Stockholders would be screaming. That's why vouchers are becoming a more popular idea. We lack a unified vision of the critical nature of training kids."

Arnold Plank, Superintendent of the Torrance Unified School District disagreed. "Management has nothing to do with it at all. Our school board and administrative leadership has been prudent and wise in its expenditures. There are simply not enough funds." Shortly thereafter, Plank recommended that a bond issue be placed on the ballot to pay for all the accumulated deferred maintenance items.

The voters did not agree with Superintendent Plank's analysis. They rejected the bond issue. Janice Perichine made one of the most angry, yet telling, post election statements: "Who do they think they are? What gives them the right to let our children's schools fall apart? Why did they let things get to the state they are in now? Have their eyes been closed for all these years? They pay lip service to our children but they really care about their salaries and benefits. Shame."

The governing body should be aware when staff makes a decision to defer maintenance of the agency's assets. The issue for the governing board member is to determine why money for maintenance is being diverted. Good budgeting requires that a percentage of current revenues be carved out of the budget for repair and maintenance of assets. Regardless of cuts, maintenance and repair should keep its proportionate share of the budget. Ask for an analysis from staff showing the percentage of your agency's budget that has been used for maintenance and repair during the past 20 or more years. What does the trend show? Has maintenance remained the same, gone up, or gone down as a percentage of the total operating budget?

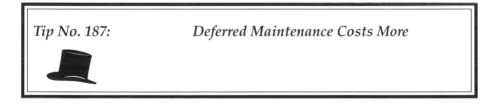

Tip No. 187:   *Deferred Maintenance Costs More*

Nothing seems to draw a response to a public problem like a public outcry. In 1994, the City of San Diego put $12 million in its budget to replace 180 miles of leaky, obsolete, cast-iron water mains. No one complained when the budget was pared by $2 million the next year, until a pipe burst spontaneously causing a mammoth traffic jam. When a city council committee requested a report on the problem, they found that while the cast-iron pipes only comprised 7 percent of the entire water distribution system, they were responsible for 80 percent of all water main failures. The report summarized the situation. "Repeated failure in these cast iron pipes continues to plague the older areas of San Diego with water service and traffic disruptions and damage to both public and private property, resulting in costly repairs and claims. The last three water main breaks cost $74,000, $143,000 and $99,481 respectively."

The council committee also found out that water officials had intended to cut the budget to zero for the new fiscal year "because the water department has too many other infrastructure needs that are more critical." The committee, however, instructed the water staff to revise its proposed budget to include a reasonable replacement schedule. "We don't want to see any zero's down there," admonished committee chairperson, Councilman Harry Mathis. "We very clearly have a serious problem here that we have to address in an aggressive way, and it's something we're going to have to find the resources to do."

Governing bodies across the nation have learned the one unchangeable truth. Pretty soon you can no longer defer asset maintenance, and you must rebuild or replace ignored assets at a much greater cost.

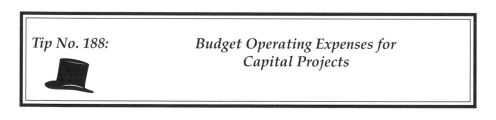

Tip No. 188:   ***Budget Operating Expenses for Capital Projects***

Too often, organizations fail to recognize the operating expenses that accompany new capital projects. One city built a beautiful new cultural center but neglected to budget the cost of maintenance, utilities, supplies and staffing. Since this was a community showpiece, the affected departments had to rob other deserving programs to provide upkeep for the highly visible new facility. When confronted by this seeming oversight, the administrator sheepishly admitted that had she divulged the actual operating expenses, the project would not have been built.

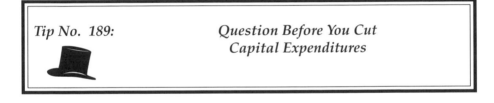

Tip No. 189:   ***Question Before You Cut***
Capital Expenditures

Regardless of financial problems, a percentage of the budget should always be devoted to preserving an agency's investment in its capital assets. Not to do so acerbates community deterioration. The crumbling nationwide infrastructure is due to the failure to devote the money necessary to maintaining the original investment. Some questions to address before cutting back capital expenditures are:

1.   Will the action result in property value reductions?
2.   Will the reduction require a higher cost to bring the asset back to acceptable standards?
3.   Will the reduction create a hazard or safety problem?
4.   Will this particular reduction impact the preservation of other capital assets? (The roadway is not maintained; so water seeps in and undermines the foundation of a bridge.)

Tip No. 190:   ***Make Sure Proper Security Measures***
are Implemented

During a three-year period the Los Angeles City School District suffered over 3000 classroom break-ins and lost over $16 million in computer equipment. To make matters worse, much of the equipment was not replaced since the school district stopped insuring itself against vandalism and theft. When asked about security for class rooms, district officials responded that they could not afford to wire additional rooms with alarms or put more school police on night patrol.

Of course, the students are the ultimate victims of this short-sighted financial philosophy. Just as capital expenditures require new operating expenses to be budgeted; security costs must be factored into

the cost of equipping class rooms with computers and other elec-
tronic equipment.

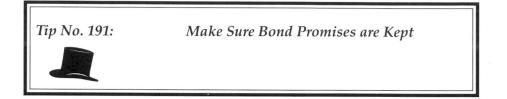

Tip No. 191:   *Make Sure Bond Promises are Kept*

The Los Angeles Police Department made an urgent plea to residents to approve a $200 million bond issue to upgrade the city's 911
emergency system. The system, which was originally installed in
1984, was considered antiquated within months of its original in-
stallation; and the number of incoming calls had increased considerably with no staffing increases. During the "night stalker" killing
spree, peak-time callers had to wait up to 30 seconds to get an operator. Many calls were abandoned by callers. Two attempts, in 1990
and 1991, were made to obtain voter approval to improve the system. Both attempts failed, even though the number of incoming calls
had increased 79 percent since the system was built. The problem
peaked in 1992 during the Los Angeles riots, when callers could not
even reach an emergency operator. Sensing the urgency, voters finally approved a bond issue that raised $235 million from property
taxes to build the new dispatch facilities.

The city promised to build two state-of-the-art dispatch centers in
different community locations. An additional center was considered
necessary to provide back-up. While the bond issue did not include
a specific timetable, immediate improvements were promised by
proponents. Yet, more than five years after the measure was passed,
the project was stalemated. The city had not decided on one of the
dispatch center sites, and the critical computer contract had not been
signed. Cumbersome regulations and lack of management follow-
through were blamed. During this time, the 911 emergency system
continued to deteriorate with 40 percent of non-life threatening calls
abandoned by callers due to the long delays. The city's communication consultant said it was the worst situation he had seen and that
it was a very serious public safety problem that should be addressed
immediately. Voters were perplexed. If this was such a serious problem, why was there so much foot dragging? Councilmember Michael

Feuer declared, "There is a lack of leadership. If we are ever going to get another bond issue passed by city voters, we have to get this done immediately."

This is not an unusual situation. Many public organizations will make promises during the bond campaign and fail to follow through. It's as if the end goal was to get the money and not to complete the project. This failure to follow through, however, is not missed by the voters.

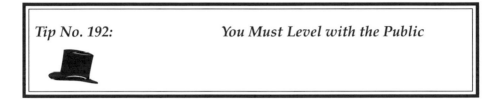

Tip No. 192:   ***You Must Level with the Public***

The Palos Verdes Library District was the crown jewel of the four hillside communities that are situated on a scenic peninsula 30 miles south of the City of Los Angeles. The district serves approximately 68,000 residents from all four cities with a main library and two branches. The district had a low tax rate, an excellent service ethic, and unanimous support from virtually all the residents it served. While the cities on the hill periodically engaged in fights, the library district stood tall, the stabilizing institution that united all peninsula residents. When city councils of neighboring cities engaged in conflict, they were admonished to be more like the library trustees. The library board was so in tune with its public that only the friends and supporters of the library showed up at meetings.

All that changed. Desiring to expand and partially justifying its actions on the need to meet ADA requirements, the library district board of trustees placed a bond issue on the ballot to pay for a major expansion of the main library.

The proposed expansion, however, was placed before the electorate just when the region and state were headed into a deep recession. Besides poor timing, the library board and staff grossly exaggerated:

1.   Expected population growth.

2.   Existing and projected library use.

These inflated statistics were provided to the project architects, enabling them to design a much larger and more grandiose library than the district needed. More troubling was the failure of the Library Director, Linda Elliott, to reveal the projected operating and maintenance expenses of the expanded library.

The library district had so much goodwill that the few protests about cost and timing were cast aside in a momentous campaign wake. The bond issue was approved overwhelmingly, and the expansion plans proceeded despite clear warning signs of a deepening recession.

Months later, when the State of California grabbed a big chunk out of the library operating revenue budget, the district was forced to bare parts of its precarious financial condition to the community. Details were also revealed as to what it would cost to open and operate the new expanded library. But once again, Elliott and the board of trustees decided to not disclose critical information such as:

*   Only 75 percent of available operating money was being spent on operations.

*   The other 25 percent of available operating revenues were being diverted to the building fund to purchase new furniture and equipment.

The board's solution to the loss of income was to cut back operations, lay off 30 employees and close the branches.

Poorly timed expansion of the main Palos Verdes Library almost resulted in the closing of two branch libraries.

At this point the proverbial roof fell in. The community was furious. How could the district be so irresponsible to let the situation get to the point of closing the beloved branches? Library board members claimed they did not know that the economy was going to go sour. During a heated meeting, Trustee Chris Tara declared, "I can tell you that when the bond issue was put on the ballot, nobody could have predicted the economic difficulties which were ahead of us." The facts showed, however, that the board was cautioned in an insightful letter urging restraint because of the recession. Moreover, even after the fiscal problems became apparent, the board refused to reduce the scope of the project.

The board's failings led to the formation of a watch dog group called Save Our Libraries (SOL). The group had the goal of stabilizing the district's finances and saving the branches. To do so, they set about analyzing the district budget in detail and effected a million dollar reduction in furniture and equipment purchases.

Finally acknowledging the community outrage, the Palos Verdes Peninsula Library Board of Trustees established the Creative Solutions Committee to obtain community feedback on revenue enhancement. Not satisfied with being limited to revenues, the committee expanded its mission to include expenditure control, operations and community involvement. The committee came up with 79 recommendations. The board eventually adopted the majority of the recommendations, but rejected a recommended cutback in finished space that would have reduced operating and maintenance expenses.

Although the original building project envisioned adding 30,000 square feet to the existing 35,000 square foot building, the size was incrementally increased to 91,000 square feet after the bond election. Most of the added space was stone decked corridors and a 16,000 square foot staff area. These changes increased the cost of the project from $14.5 million to $19.5 million. Later, a library watcher summed it all up: "I seriously doubt the people of our community 'dreamed' about the prestigious awards this structure might win while the budget was being approved. I believed what started out as a project to better our community has turned into a multi-million dollar boondoggle to personal vanity. What we wanted was a library; what we got was a shrine."

The problem was more profound. Here was a board that was so focused on building a larger and better central library that they lost sight of the bigger picture which was the overall fiscal viability of the library system. Trustees should have asked questions about the relationship between the massive library expansion and the impact on the rest of the library district's programs. If we undertake an expansion program, what will be the effect on the branches? Can we afford an expanded library and the branches?

The story is sad. Community trust which had been built up over many decades was squandered over a poorly planned and timed expansion of the main library. Library managers and trustees spent so much of their time on the building expansion that library operations suffered.

Shortly afterward, a majority of the board members quit or lost their reelection bid. New board members came in, and felt they had to get into the minute administrative details in order to put the library back on track. The perceived micro-management only exacerbated the mistrust. Employee morale dropped, and key staff members that had been involved in the project left the district. While there was much finger pointing, the roots of the problem go back to the failure of the board and top management to level with the community regarding the expansion project — about its implications and true costs. Unfortunately, the story has not ended. The district is now involved in a multi-million dollar lawsuit over construction design and defects.

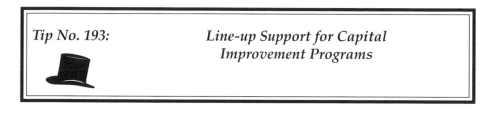

Tip No. 193: *Line-up Support for Capital Improvement Programs*

The County of Monterey, California, put together a countywide list of projects to be funded through a proposed half-cent sales tax increase; and the City of Seaside diligently put together a capital improvements list totalling $16 million for inclusion. Having too many projects, the county staff prioritized projects based upon what they considered regional qualities. When the list was released, every city within the county, except Seaside and one other, had projects within their boundaries. Distressed, councilmembers from Seaside met with county supervisors to get Seaside projects on the list. Councilmember Ira Lively pointed out that Seaside residents would contribute over $35 million over the life of the bond issue. "Yet in no place do I see the word: S-E-A-S-I-D-E." The county held firm, pointing out that four public hearings were held and that the city would indirectly benefit from all the projects.

Miffed, the Seaside City Council unanimously voted to encourage residents to oppose the countywide tax increase, and they did. The failure of the county to bend contributed to the bond issue's failure.

Tip No. 194: *Be Especially Cautious Before and After a Bond Issue Election*

The immediate months before a vote on a public improvement bond are critical. You campaign very hard to convince voters that the cause is important and that you need the dollars. While some voters listen to what you say, most form their opinions based upon what you do or attempt to do. This is your best behavior period.

Right after the Oakland, California School Board pushed the ebonics discussion to the forefront nationally with the help of the media, governing board members of other districts across the nation jumped on the band wagon. Programs were proposed in Detroit, Chicago, New York, and several other districts across the nation. In Los Angeles, school board member Barbara Boudreaux pressed for a language development program for African-American students, two months before a critical bond election. The voters were being asked to pass $2.4 billion in bonds to provide for the repair and renovation of schools that were in a very depressed state, and a two-thirds approval was needed.

The school board rejected Boudreaux's motion for a new program in favor of a compromise motion by Member Mark Slavkin who moved that the district staff document "the achievement levels of African-American students, especially in the area of English proficiency." The staff was directed to provide this report at a date that happened to be three weeks after the bond election.

The *Los Angeles Times*, in an editorial, observed correctly that the whole issue was divisive; and "no program should be expanded before a thorough evaluation determines which works best to improve the language development of children who do not speak standard English." The *Times* noted that the issue needed thorough debate since there was a division between some African-Americans and some Latinos who feared that extra help for black students would come at the expense of bilingual education." Then the *Times* provided great advice to elected officials: "This [the study] is a necessary first step. . .Wouldn't it have been more logical to have done that before the fractious debate began?"

Tip No. 195:   ***Consider Using an Oversight Panel for Capital Projects***

The Los Angeles Unified School District placed a bond issue on the ballot to pay for the repair and renovation of more than 800 schools. Recognizing that many voters were reluctant to vote for the measure for fear of the money being used for administration and salaries, the school board created an oversight committee. The issue, needing a two-thirds affirmative vote for passage, received a heartbreaking 65.5 percent.

After the issue failed by such a slim margin, the school board restructured the oversight board. A new Blue Ribbon Citizen's Oversight Committee was proposed as an independent, nine-member panel with representation from the areas of finance, engineering, architecture and local government.

The specific charge of the panel was to make sure:

- Bond funds were used solely for improvements, such as roofing, wiring, plumbing, plastering and earthquake retrofitting.
- Work was completed on schedule.
- Improvements were made within the $2.4 billion budget.

"The committee's main job is to protect the interest of the taxpayers and to ensure the money is spent where the bond says it should be spent," said Richard Katz, Chairman of the Panel. "What we have here is a strong group of people looking over the school board's shoulder of bureaucracy, making sure the money is spent where it's suppose to be spent."

The oversight panel, that was suggested during the first bond issue, was not truly independent of the board. The new one was independent and reported to the public. Board member David Tokofsky, who originally suggested the idea of a watchdog panel, said, "This goes back to the issue of what the public is most concerned about with school district accountability and effectiveness."

If you want the panel to exercise effective oversight, make sure they are empowered and truly independent. When setting up an oversight commission, clarify its role. Under what circumstances will the staff or the governing board overrule the committee? What authority does the oversight panel have? What authority has been withheld or restricted?

Support Your Local Auditor

"I wish elected officials knew more about what it is we do. I also wish they would make themselves more available to us. We could provide them more service."

Auditor Michael C. Moreland,
Partner, Moreland & Associates

The Population Explosion
Once the site of citrus groves and chicken farms, the City of Fontana had long been considered a company town associated with the Kaiser Steel plant that was located adjacent to its boundaries. Beginning around 1980, the Southern California community began experiencing unprecedented growth in its residential population. According to a 1985 projection, the city would triple its population to over 200,000 by the year 2000. As the community grew, the city organization also grew in the number of employees and activities it carried out.

During this period, problems were beginning to surface. The city organization was experiencing continuous turnover in key staff positions and rumors began circulating in the community about poor city management and financial practices at the Fontana City Hall. While an in depth independent management audit was being called for by citizens, it was not at the top of the city council's list of priorities. Councilmembers rebuffed the request arguing that it was unnecessary, too expensive and that the staff could do an audit; but the pressure continued and an audit was the only way to mollify the residents.

Finally, on a 3 to 2 vote, the city council decided to hire Arthur Young and Company to conduct what was called a performance audit. A performance audit focuses on operational efficiency, including resource utilization and control. The auditors were charged with examining the practices of all city departments. These reviews involved document reviews, on-site observations, interviews, and a survey that was sent to all city officials and employees. Once the analysis was completed, the auditors briefed the city's management to brace them for the public reaction.

Audit Findings

The results of the audit hit the community like a body slam. The audit report delivered to the city council was a 300 page document which included 200 separate recommendations. The overall conclusion was that the city faced bankruptcy if it did not immediately improve city hall's efficiency and encourage development that generated taxes. The analyses indicated that the growth had taken its toll, and the city was not adequately prepared to efficiently and effectively manage its future growth. Some of the specific findings were:

Policy and Administration

- No established mission statement, goals, and objectives adopted by city council.
- City staff played an inordinately large role in the development of city policies and was insufficiently held accountable.
- Councilmembers were too involved in administration of the city.

Personnel Practices

- Labor-intensive and inefficient work methods.

- Absence of accountability of city employees.
- Generous employee salary and compensation.
- Inappropriate and inconsistent personnel policies and procedures.

Development Policies

- Flawed development strategy focusing on single and multi-family affordable housing rather than balancing growth with commercial and industrial projects.

Financial Practices

- Consistent overestimation of revenue.
- Consistent underestimation of expenditures.
- Inadequate or nonexistent financial reports.
- General breakdown or lack of internal controls throughout the city.
- Poor bookkeeping caused officials to make decisions based on inaccurate or incomplete information.

Conclusions

The Arthur Young and Company audit concluded, "The city's general fund is in a rapidly declining position, but the exact figure is unknown since previous financial audits were incomplete." While no one was sure of the true deficit, it was estimated at $4.5 million.

Perhaps the biggest lapse on the part of the city council was allowing itself to be sucked into the administrative detail. In doing so, they spent significant amounts of time working with staff on low priority administrative items at the expense of policy formulation efforts. Conversely, city staff played an inordinately large role in the development of city policies at the expense of carrying out legislative programs and managing administrative matters effectively.

While conducting the performance audit for Fontana, Arthur Young and Company found that the city's financial auditor had not completed the financial audits for the previous two fiscal years. The lateness itself should have been a red flag for both the management and governing body. Auditors warn that failure to receive timely audits is one of the first signs of fiscal problems.

The performance audit was not at the top of the council's agenda; but after it was completed, it became one of Fontana's most important documents. It not only identified current problems, it also provided an invaluable tool for establishing policies and procedures for the city's financial stability.

The audit also identified irregularities that ultimately resulted in management casualties. Shortly after it was completed, the city manager of 15 years was fired amid allegations of mismanagement; and several department heads were removed or reassigned, and the finance director was convicted of embezzlement and sentenced to three years in prison.

Since its near fiscal catastrophe, the City of Fontana has done an admirable job in righting its management and financial systems. It was only after the city council consented to bring in outside auditors, that the city was able to begin rehabilitation. A reluctance to bring in outside auditors when an obvious problem exists can only raise suspicions about the governing board's motives and involvement.

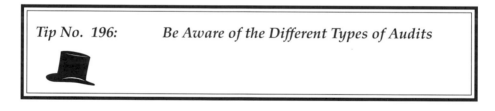

Tip No. 196: *Be Aware of the Different Types of Audits*

The two most common type of audits performed for public agencies are:

1. Traditional Financial Statement Audits

When one thinks of an audit, it is often the financial statement audit. These audits determine whether financial statements of an audited local government present fairly the financial position and the results of financial operations in accordance with generally accepted accounting principles. It also determines whether the government has complied with laws and regulations that may have a material effect upon the financial statements. These are usually performed by independent auditors for local governments and are conducted annually.

2. Performance Audits

Performance audits also go by other names such as management, operations, and program results audits. These types of audits determine whether the public entity is managing and using its resources such as personnel, property and space economically and efficiently. The emphasis is on managerial aspects, including such things as duplication of effort, utilization of resources and mismanagement of equipment. Performance audits also identify the causes of the inefficiencies or uneconomical practices and whether the entity has complied with laws and regulations concerning matters of economy and efficiency. The focus is more concerned with waste, rather than theft of resources. Another variation of performance audits determines whether the desired results or benefits established by the governing body are being achieved and whether the agency has considered alternatives that might yield desired results at a lower cost. Due to the cost and time involved, performance audits are usually not conducted on an annual basis, but rather when a problem is suspected as was the case with Fontana.

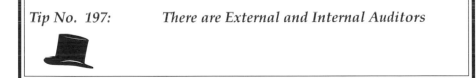

Tip No. 197:   ***There are External and Internal Auditors***

There are two categories of auditors, internal and external. Internal auditors are employees of the organization and they may be appointed or elected. They conduct both types of audits of the various departments and programs in their organization. Internal auditors are less independent than external auditors but they are still given a considerable amount of autonomy. The work program of what is to be audited is usually determined by management or the governing body. Smaller governmental agencies usually do not have internal audit units due to the cost.

External auditors do not work for the engaging organization and are drawn from the public and private sectors. They conduct the annual audit of local government financial statements as well as performance audits. Some states, such as Washington, have government auditors who are responsible for auditing local governments. They are state employees who are totally independent of the entities they audit. Other states such as California, use private auditing firms to conduct the financial compliance audits. Management of these firms are certified public accountants (CPAs).

Tip No. 198 :   *Auditors Must be Independent*

Generally Accepted Government Auditing Standards (GAGAS) require that in all matters relating to the audit work, the audit organization and the individual auditors must be free from personal or external impairments to independence. This means the auditor must be organizationally independent in fact, attitude, and appearance.

A CPA firm hired to audit a Pennsylvania Head Start grant hired the Head Start bookkeeper to assist in the audit. The bookkeeper convinced the audit firm that since she personally designed and implemented the system of internal control, for the program, there was no need to question or test the internal control system. A subsequent examination of the program determined that over $15,000 had been diverted by the bookkeeper to her own bank account.

An auditor is externally impaired if the auditor does not have unrestricted access to a government's records and reports. Impairment occurred in a school district when the accountant literally intimidated the new auditor from insisting upon examining cashed payroll checks. A later audit revealed that the accountant had created a phantom payroll — issuing checks for nonexistent employees. Had the auditor been able to compare the cashed checks with the employee roster, the accountant's ruse would have been discovered right away.

Auditors must also be free of personal impairment. In one Wisconsin case, the external auditor's contract with a city was terminated once it was discovered that the firm had concealed the fact that a partner in the firm was the spouse of the city treasurer.

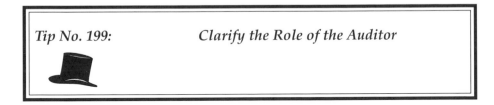

Tip No. 199:	Clarify the Role of the Auditor

What is it that auditors do? Auditors will tell you that the terms of the engagement are spelled out in the audit contract. The contract may indicate that the auditor is responsible for reporting non-compliance with statutes, policies and rules, identifying weaknesses in internal controls and providing an opinion as to whether the financial statements are presented fairly. What about detecting fraud? What about exposing poor financial practices that can lead to fiscal collapse? The differences in perceptions as to what the public believes auditors do and what auditors believe they are responsible for has resulted in an "expectation gap." Fraud and poor financial practices are key issues, and governing board members should have a discussion with their auditing firm to determine if their expectations match. The failure to address the "expectation gap" has led to litigation by government agencies and third parties trying to hold auditors liable for failing to identify problems.

Many governing board members have a strong belief that the auditor is the public watchdog, the one who protects them from fraud and theft. Auditors, however have a different view about being a firewall against indiscretion and dishonesty. "There are no guarantees in auditing. We are evaluating internal controls; and testing transactions, for compliance," says Auditor Gary Caporicci of Caporicci and Larson. "Your best guarantee is quality management and financial staff."

"Many elected officials don't understand the purpose of an audit," says Auditor Mike Moreland. "It is not an insurance policy. Government officials have a great deal of misplaced confidence in what it is that we do. The word 'auditor' comes from the latin word 'audire' meaning 'to hear.' What we are doing is telling the world from an independent viewpoint that the financial statements are fairly presented. And that is all we are doing. We are not guaranteeing that there were no mistakes; we are not guaranteeing that every investment that was made was legal. We do tests of legal compliance, but we don't test everything; and there are transactions that don't get looked at. We are not there everyday; and therefore, there must be systems of internal control established and monitored by the local government. That is the agency's front line of defense."

Don't forget that it is management and not the auditor who is responsible for the accuracy of books and records and that assets are properly safeguarded. As mentioned by Moreland, the auditor is not with your agency all the time. They only inspect a sample of the numerous transactions conducted by the agency, and they could miss the one transaction that could lead to discovering embezzlement or fraud.

That being said, a good auditor is probably the best person to identify financial irregularities. They have access to your organization and its records, and if technically qualified, know how to detect fraud, theft and poor fiscal practices.

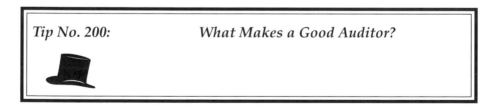

Tip No. 200:   ***What Makes a Good Auditor?***

Mike Moreland says a good auditor is inquisitive and doesn't accept what people tell them necessarily at face value. "It's a kind of show me attitude; professional skepticism is what we like to call it. We are friendly; we make the staff feel comfortable; but at the same time there is a reserve situation where they know that we are there to work. We are not preparing their report card though. We are there as a representative of the governing body. It is an interesting situation. You cannot get too close to staff nor can you stay too far. It is a very unusual situation."

Tip No. 201: **Auditor Red Flags**

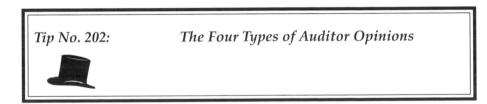

What are some of the things auditors look at? Gary Caporicci indicates, "First, we begin by examining prior reports. We look statistically for a financial picture. Anything that seems unusual or different we focus on. Second, we meet the people. the finance director, staff and the clerks; talk to them, look at their background — just get to know them. That gives you a comfort feeling or uneasy feeling very quickly. A third thing is just walking around and reviewing operations to determine the level of concern about internal controls." Caporicci adds, "We find that problems usually do not result from one item, but rather a number of things that start aggregating."

The same things that alert the auditor should be alerts to the chief administrator and the elected body, says Mike Moreland. "Lateness of reports or the absence of reports and bank statements that have not been reconciled for months are red flags. From an auditors point of view we rely very heavily upon the environment. If we find a finance department that monitors financial activities, a chief administrator who continually asks questions, and a governing board that shows interest, I, as an auditor, feel comfortable in that environment."

Auditor concern rises when cutbacks reduce the accounting staff to the degree that the remaining employees are consumed with preparing data and no one is reviewing it. This weakening of internal controls makes mistakes harder to find and increases the chances for fraud going undetected.

Tip No. 202: **The Four Types of Auditor Opinions**

There are four levels of opinions prepared by auditors:

1.   Unqualified: This is the opinion the agency expects. In it, the auditor states without reservation, that the financial statements are fairly presented in conformity with generally accepted accounting principles (GAAP). These are also called clean opinions.

2.   Qualified: When the auditor submits a qualified opinion, something in the financial statements is not in conformity with GAAP. Most typically, the local government hasn't kept property and equipment records current, or supporting documents have not been maintained.

3.   Adverse Opinion: An adverse opinion says that the financial statements are not fairly presented in conformance with GAAP. Not depreciating fixed assets for enterprise funds or using cash basis reporting instead of accruing for receivables and payables will result in an adverse opinion. Materiality is the difference between a qualified and an adverse opinion and the later usually results from management failures to address a known misstatement or misapplication of accounting principles. Adverse opinions are not issued that often for public agencies.

4.   Disclaimer: When an auditor issues a disclaimer opinion, it says that your records and internal controls are so bad we are unable to render an opinion. The problems are usually outlined in a supplemental letter. Disclaimers are very rare for public sector agencies; and when issued, signify an extremely critical situation.

Tip No. 203:   ***An Unqualified Opinion Does not Mean Everything is in Order***

In 1995, while the Congressional Committee charged with oversight of the District of Columbia's finances was questioning the auditor, a

Senator asked how could the District receive a clean opinion when it had a massive deficit. The auditor replied, "The District received an unqualified opinion even though they carried a deficit in excess of $700 million. The opinion letter says the financial statements are in accordance with generally accepted accounting principles. The audit numbers are fair; but Senator, they must be read in conjunction with the financial statements."

"You're telling me that a government can be on the verge of bankruptcy and still get an unqualified opinion as long as the records reflect that condition?" asked the Senator incredulously. "That's correct, Senator," answered the auditor. Later, the Senator admitted that he had not examined the audit report and that his staff had advised him that the District had received a clean opinion.

This committee discussion was broadcast by C-SPAN and undoubtedly, gave thousands of viewers a new insight into the purpose of audits.

Tip No. 204: **The Audit Report is not the Same Thing as the CAFR**

By now, you have probably heard of the "CAFR," which translates into the Comprehensive Annual Financial Report. The purpose of the CAFR is to provide the governing body and the public an overview of the agency's entire financial condition. The independent auditor's report is usually one page and it expresses an opinion as to the adequacy of the financial statements. When a CAFR is prepared, the independent auditor's report is included with the auditor's letterhead and signature. Except for the auditor's letter, all of the financial statements presented in the CAFR are the responsibility of the agency's management. Some agencies ask the auditor to prepare the CAFR by compiling the information and printing it. However, the financial statements are still the responsibility of the agency's management. The CAFR is divided into three sections:

1.   The Introductory Section includes the letter of transmittal which presents the financial information and how the agency is doing in narrative form. This transmittal is prepared by the finance officer and chief administrative officer. Auditor Gary Caporicci says this is the most important part of the CAFR. "If you don't read anything else, read this letter. It summarizes how the government entity is doing." If the government has received the *Government Finance Officers Association Certificate of Achievement for Excellence In Financial Reporting*, it is also placed in the introductory section.

2.   The Financial Section includes the actual financial statements, such as the Combined Balance Sheet. The independent auditor's report is presented at the beginning of this section. Don't overlook the notes to the financial statements. They provide helpful explanations.

3.   The Statistical Section contains statistical information that relates to physical, economic, social and political characteristics of the agency. It is intended to provide users with a broader and more complete understanding of the agency and its financial affairs. This information does not come from the accounting records and is usually not audited.

While some agencies may add additional information or sections, all cities, counties, school districts and special districts follow the same format. Therefore, a CAFR prepared by Juneau, Alaska will be the same as ones prepared in Nogales, New Mexico, Fort Lauderdale, Florida and Portland, Maine. This is in contrast to their budgets, which will have varying sizes, formats and content.

The CAFR is an intimidating document; and when it is presented at a formal meeting, governing board members are hesitant to ask questions for fear of looking uninformed. Auditor Moreland, suggests that questions can be asked and answered more comfortably in an informal meeting with the auditor. Have staff arrange one if you would like an overall briefing on the CAFR.

Tip No. 205:   ***Your Agency may not Prepare***
a CAFR

Not every local government prepares a CAFR. Larger agencies usually prepare this document, whereas the smaller ones may not. Caporicci says that preparing an agency's first CAFR requires a considerable amount of time and research. "The statistical section contains at least 15 separate tables, and several of these require ten-year histories. Gathering this information takes a ton of staff time that may not be available." Once the ten-year history required for a CAFR is compiled, the job becomes more manageable since management needs only to add the current year's data.

An agency can provide an adequate job of presenting financial information in a financial report, without producing an actual CAFR. "You can do a wonderful job of presenting financial information and giving the chief administrators outlook without preparing a CAFR," says Caporicci.

An agency wishing to issue bonds finds a CAFR very beneficial. Rating agencies look favorably on local governments that have well-prepared CAFRs. It is especially impressive if the Government Finance Officers Association (GFOA) has awarded a *Certificate of Achievement for Excellence in Financial Reporting* for the CAFR. Some officials believe that being able to include a copy of the award in the CAFR will result in a more favorable bond interest rate.

Tip No. 206:   ***The Budget Does not tie into the CAFR***

The adopted budget figures usually do not tie directly to the actual results presented in the CAFR. This is because the figures in the CAFR includes the original budget plus all supplemental appropriations made by the governing body. The major difference between the two documents is the supplemental appropriations. Your staff should be able to reconcile the two documents and show you the difference.

Tip No. 207:   *Obtain Copies of Management Letters*

The management letter is intended to point out operational efficiencies or improvements that the auditor recommends. Management letters are also used to communicate the lack of compliance or reportable conditions (significant deficiencies in internal controls) found during the audit to management. Caporicci says, "In most cases, once management is apprised of the problem, action is taken to rectify it. In those cases, we note the steps taken in the management letter." In other cases, the management staff appends its own letter or memo to indicate what actions have or will be taken to rectify the problems noted.

The management letter will give you a feeling for the types of problems the auditor considers significant. If you do not receive a copy of the management letter, ask whether one has been issued and obtain a copy. You will also want to obtain a copy of the management response. New governing board members may want to obtain copies for the previous three or four years.

The management letter should not be confused with the management representation letter. This latter document is a letter prepared by management for the auditor, acknowledging management's responsibility for the financial statements and affirming that the information in them is complete.

Tip No. 208:   ***Use a Competitive Process to Obtain an
Independent Auditor***

The U.S. General Accounting Office (GAO) recommends that a competitive process be used to obtain an audit firm and that multi-year agreements be used. A Request For Proposal (RFP) should be developed, and the auditing firms technical qualifications evaluated. While cost should be considered, it should not be the determining factor.

Multi-year contracts provide an incentive for an audit firm to devote time to submitting a well-developed proposal and to establishing its learning curve in the early years of the engagement. According to experts, the audit firm usually does not recover its costs until the later years of the contract. Further, firms make the greatest contribution to improving a government's program and financial operations in the later years of the multi-year agreements. This is due to the knowledge the firm acquires after performing a few audits. "I am worth more to a client in the second year of the contract than the first year and more in third year than the second," says Caporicci.

The typical multi-year agreement normally provides for annual contract renewal at the government entity's option — usually contingent upon the audit firm performing acceptable quality work. Although there is some disagreement as to the ideal length of a multi-year agreement, most suggest a period of five to ten years.

GSA also asked experts to discuss the advantages and disadvantages of rotating audit firms once the contract period expires. Opinions vary as to whether the current audit firm should be allowed to submit a proposal. Those experts who favored rotation stated that they believed it was advantageous for the entity to obtain a "new perspective" from a different audit firm.

Others argue that firms commonly assign different staff to these audit engagements; and this rotation of staff is sufficient to provide a new perspective, thus eliminating the need to ban the current auditor from rebidding. The City of La Palma, California, recently rebid its audit services and permitted the current auditor to bid. The competition spurred the current auditor to submit a bid that was 10 percent below its current contract, which turned out to be the lowest bid. Finance Director Olly Silverio said, "The competitive process enabled us to lower the cost and to get the auditor to assign senior staff to our city. I doubt we would have gotten such a good deal had we not solicited proposals from several auditing firms."

Tip No. 209:   *Make Sure Audit Firms are Technically Qualified to Perform Public Agency Audits*

The Single Audit Act of 1984, generally requires all entities receiving $100,000 or more in federal funds to obtain an organization-wide audit of these funds. The act requires these entities to obtain service of independent auditors who are largely CPAs.

A small housing authority in Georgia notified five CPA firms about an upcoming audit and asked them to submit proposals by signing a model proposal and inserting a bid. The standard form did not require proposing firms to include any information on their technical qualifications. Instead, the firm's cost proposal was the only factor in selecting the audit firm. Two firms responded to the solicitation, and the contract was awarded to the firm with the lowest bid. The audit was subsequently given a quality control examination by HUD and was deemed unacceptable in several areas. The CPA who performed the audit admitted to GSA that had consideration been given to the firm's past governmental experience, he would not have been awarded the contract for lack of governmental experience.

A state human services department in Denver procured its organization-wide single audit using a bid proposal that required bidders to divulge their technical qualifications. Unfortunately, even though the human services department had the technical qualification information, they based their decision to award solely on cost. Again, the audit failed to meet quality control standards and was rejected. In this particular case, the agency should have been skeptical since the bid was one-fourth the cost of the other bidders. As it turned out, the winning firm failed to include enough hours to produce a satisfactory audit.

Tip No. 210:   ***Be Sure to Enter Into a Written Agreement***

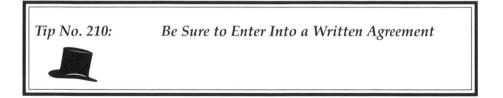

A Florida university was required to obtain an organization-wide audit of its federal assistance programs in accordance with federal law. The entity contracted with the same firm which had prepared the institution's financial statements for the past 17 years. A contractual document was not prepared setting forth the terms and conditions for the audit. Understandings were verbal, and there was disagreement as to whether the auditor would review internal controls. There was no understanding on the recourse in the event of substandard work or contract termination. After the audit was examined and rejected by the Department of Education, the university was stuck with reissuing the audit at additional cost.

Tip No. 211:   ***Auditors Should use Performance Measurement***

An important measure of success of the internal auditor is the extent to which audits result in positive change in the organization. The Portland, Oregon, City Auditor evaluates success by maintaining performance measures on budget size, cost per audit hour, reports completed and recommendations addressed.

Table 11
City of Portland
City Auditor Performance Measures

Fiscal Year	Budget Size	Cost Per Audit Hour	Reports Completed	Recommendations Addressed
1998-99	$763,824	$74	12	81%
1999-00	$851,767	$69	8	87%
2000-01	$823,272	$79	8	84%
2001-02	$757,090	$73	7	97%
2002-03	$778,000	$82	9	74%

Perhaps the most telling performance indicator is the percentage of recommendations addressed. It doesn't do any good if the results of the audit sit on a bookshelf in the audited department.

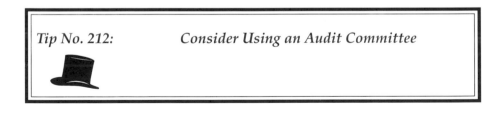

Tip No. 212:   *Consider Using an Audit Committee*

The use of audit committees is well established in the private sector. In fact, the National Commission on Fraudulent Financial Reporting states that an "informed, diligent audit committee represents the single most potentially effective influence for minimizing fraudulent financial reporting." The General Accounting Office believes that an audit committee can serve an equally effective purpose with public organizations. An audit committee for a local government might serve the following purposes:

1.   Participate in the auditor selection process.

2.   Identify and evaluate potential bidders for the audit contract.

3.   Provide on-going monitoring of the audit contract.

4.   Review audit results and assist in post-audit quality evalua-
        tion.

Audit committees, should be advisory to the governing body and
should have members who possess technical skills in accounting
and auditing. Specialized training should also be provided. Committee members must also be independent and have no ties to the
audit firm during the local government's audit.

Audit committees can be ineffective or add real value to a local government. The key is how the governing body and management view
the committee. Has the committee been empowered to carry out
significant tasks such as interviewing auditors and reviewing audit
reports? Are members technically competent and not just political
appointments?

Public-Private Ventures are not for the Timid

"The threat of an initiative will always produce a better deal for the city. The voters drive a tougher deal. You can imagine how good the deal will be if the arena actually goes to the ballot."

Los Angeles Councilmember Joel Wachs commenting on the Kings' owners belated decision to guarantee the repayment of public bonds for the proposed arena amid Wachs' campaign for a ballot initiative

In 1993, the citizens of San Diego were elated to hear NFL Commissioner Paul Tagliabue on national television announce that their city had been awarded the 1998 Super Bowl. The business community could hardly contain their joy about the anticipated $300 million the event promised to inject into the local economy. The NFL Commissioner said he favored the site because it would encourage the city to renovate the stadium. The only written contingency was that temporary seats were to be installed to increase San Diego Jack Murphy Stadium's capacity to 72,000. Very few San Diegans understood the implicit NFL expectation — the city had to refurbish the stadium.

In 1995, the city council struck a deal with San Diego Charger owner, Alex Spanos to renovate the stadium in time for the 1998 Super Bowl. Spanos had intimated that he might be forced to leave town if the stadium was not rebuilt. This comment was made right after his team won the American Conference Championship and played in the 1994 Super Bowl. To many fans, Spanos should not only be granted his wish, he should have been anointed mayor. Many other residents, however, were outraged by an agreement they felt was pushed through with little public comment and gave away the store to Spanos. The deal required the city to issue $60 million in lease revenue bonds to pay for the renovation. While these bonds would be repaid by the users, objectional parts of the deal included:

- The city's guarantee that the Chargers would sell at least 60,000 of 62,000 general admission seats for every regular and exhibition home game for ten years. Unsold tickets would be paid for by the city.

- The Chargers had the right to renegotiate the deal with the city every four years.

Mark Rosentraub, a professor and sports economist, decried the Charger lease as "corporate welfare." This outrage manifested itself in a lawsuit against the city, alleging that lease-revenue bonds required a public vote. Eighteen months later, the suit was adjudicated in favor of the city by the California State Supreme Court. Flushed with victory, the city council completed negotiations and approved the deal in early December 1996; but the cost was now $78 million, an $18 million increase due to the delay and some extras that were added.

Stadium expansion opponents, upon hearing about the new figure of $78 million, immediately began circulating petitions calling for a referendum on the entire deal. The city council, fearing additional delays, took the stand that the original $60 million had been approved and that the referendum only applied to the additional $18 million. After declaring its decision, the city issued $60 million in lease revenue bonds and began demolition of the existing stadium.

The protest could not be stopped. The opponents collected over 50,000 valid signatures, which were sufficient to qualify the issue for the ballot. This put the completion of the stadium reconstruction in doubt. San Diego was then hit with a bomb from NFL Commissioner Paul Tagliabue, who said he might be forced to move the Super Bowl to Los Angeles if the judge ruled against the city, and the stadium reconstruction was delayed. The City of Pasadena was chomping at the bit to help the NFL out by hosting the Super Bowl. In fact, a contingency agreement was signed with the NFL to play the Super Bowl in the Rose Bowl just in case construction was halted.

For two months, while waiting for a judge to rule on the issue, the City of San Diego faced economic ruin. Not only might the city be deprived of the infusion of $300 million for the Super Bowl, it also faced the possibility of defaulting on the $60 million in revenue bonds since no revenues would be forthcoming

A citizen group's legal challenge to the financing plan for the reconstruction of San Diego's Jack Murphy football stadium could have resulted in a $60 million revenue bond default.

So how did San Diego get into this jam? While the stakes were high in San Diego, the situation is by no means unique. Sports teams, major retailers, auto malls and other major tax generators know their value to a community and exploit it by threatening to relocate; and there are always willing accomplices, such as Pasadena, which will promise a little more to land a major tax generator. As a result, governing boards are forced to give in and promise taxpayer support to placate these businesses for fear of losing them. Fortunately for San Diego, the judge ruled in favor of the city, thus avoiding a fiscal disaster.

The blackmail can be very blatant. In San Francisco, the 49ers' football team president, Carmen Policy, jumped into the public campaign over a proposed $100 million stadium renovation initiative by proclaiming, "The 49ers love San Francisco and will never, ever leave under any circumstances, except if you don't give us a new stadium."

Tip No. 213:   *Keep the Electorate Informed*

The San Diego Stadium "deal" was elevated in the public eye by former councilmember, Bruce Henderson, who used Roger Hedgecock's radio program to broadcast a spirited public forum on the issue. While city officials did a credible job in defending the agreement they made, they could not adequately defend the fact that they did a poor job of keeping the public informed. Opponents accused the city council of conducting negotiations as if there were only two important parties, the city government and the San Diego Chargers. Resident Mike Nelson complained, "Who do they think they are? I am a rabid Charger fan, but their decision to cut the public out offends me deeply. I intend to vote against the referendum and these tin gods." Juanita Holland added, "What you're telling us is, lie back, take your medicine, and don't ask any questions. This is frustrating and sickening to us."

It took the San Diego City Council too long to understand that the public needs to be brought along on major issues. While Bruce Henderson was vilified by many proponents, political scientist Mike Andrews felt that Bruce Henderson had saved taxpayers several millions of dollars. "Because of his bulldog objection to the $18 million amendment, the city council backed off. This forced the Chargers to find private money to fill the gap. Hurrah for Henderson."

Tip No. 214:   ***Negotiate Hard and Don't Leave Anything on the Table***

Once the San Diego City Council took action to rescind their motion to amend the stadium reconstruction contract by $18 million, this sent the expansion proponents looking for other alternatives to close the gap. It didn't take long for San Diego Charger Owner, Alex Spanos, and city officials to find another benefactor. Qualcomm, a communications company, promised the city the $18 million if they would change the name of San Diego Jack Murphy Stadium to Qualcomm Stadium.

During the public forum about the stadium deal, Mayor Susan Golding admitted she had "heard the public" and called upon Charger owner, Alex Spanos, to "renegotiate the objectional points of the deal." The public was offended that it took an uproar to get the city council to demand more from the Chargers.

Ray Ward, executive vice president of the Oakland-Alameda County Coliseum, warns that tremendous pressure is brought to bear on elected officials during negotiations. "The owners attempt to deal with the less knowledgeable, more pressurable type of official. They try to change what ought to be a business relationship into an exercise in macho."

"We are leaving town unless you help us" threat was leveled at the City of Sacramento by the Kings basketball team. Even though the arena consistently sold out for Kings games, owner Jim Thomas complained that the TV market was too small to support a National Basketball Association team. Thomas indicated that a $145 million city investment would keep his team in town. The city negotiated a much better package — a $70 million, 30-year loan, to be repaid with arena revenues and a $2 ticket surcharge. The Kings agreed to stay in

Sacramento for ten years and to repay the loan before they leave. Said Sacramento Mayor Joe Serna, "I wanted it to be the kind of deal that when the NBA took a look at Sacramento, this was not going to be just another city rolling over for them."

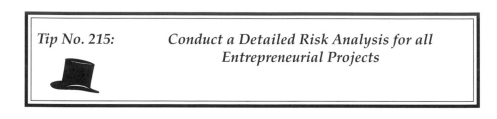

Tip No. 215:   *Conduct a Detailed Risk Analysis for all Entrepreneurial Projects*

The spectacle of the Johnson Hotel burning down brought tears to the eyes of many of Visalia, California's community members. The Johnson had stood for several decades, unifying this community of 30,000 people, that was to triple its population in the next twenty years. There was one thing that was for sure. The vacuum had to be filled with a new hotel that would serve as the centerpiece of the downtown. In the early 1970's, the city began acquiring parcels from different property owners to put together a site large enough to accommodate a new major hotel that would continue to symbolize Visalia as the preeminent town in the surrounding region.

Having acquired the land, the city began looking for a developer to build the hotel. Twice during the 1980's, the city went through the process to select a developer and in both cases, the developer failed to follow through. Frustration grew within the community. "Why is it so hard for our city officials to get a hotel?" asked the chamber of commerce.

In 1988, the city selected a San Francisco developer, William Courtney, who would lease the land acquired by the city and build a hotel on it. The community was elated. Before the ink dried on the lease agreement, however, the deal was in serious trouble. The City Manager, Don Duckworth, discovered that Courtney was unable to come up with the minimum $12 million construction loan needed to build the hotel. After intense negotiations, Duckworth and Courtney struck a deal. The city would loan Courtney $3 million initially to begin the construction and would also guarantee further loan payments if needed. In exchange for these loans, the City of Visalia would share in the hotel's revenues.

This didn't solve the problem. Since the developer still could not come up with additional construction money, the city continued to plunk its funds in to get the project built. When the hotel was completed in 1990, the city's investment was in a precarious position. Eight million dollars had been put into the project, and it sat with $12 million more in debts. The city had a choice, it could walk away and probably wind up with an empty shell, or it could acquire the hotel by picking up the $12 million debt. This did not go down well with the community. Even though they now had their new Radisson flagship hotel with 201 rooms, 100,000 square feet of meeting rooms, and would ultimately be successful, they did not like the fact that a project that was supposed to cost $4 million wound up costing five times as much.

Within a year after the Radisson opening, the clamor was so intense that the city manager had no choice but to resign. Duckworth felt victimized: "Every city council vote on the hotel was unanimous or 4-to-1, year after year. So how could I not go after it aggressively?"

Perhaps the biggest breakdown was the failure of the city staff and council to obtain a detailed risk analysis on the project before deciding to commit. Such an analysis would have provided the ranges of exposure — the least amount the project would cost, the most it would cost and the most likely cost. In this way, the governing body would have known all the risks up front before deciding to proceed. In this case, the up front homework was not done. The loftiness of the project obscured details on what things had to be accomplished to make the project viable.

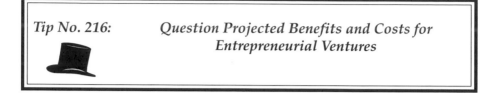

Tip No. 216:   *Question Projected Benefits and Costs for*
Entrepreneurial Ventures

Linda Paustian, a Philadelphia businesswoman, was so enraged with
the city's convention center plan that she created the anagram LOOT
(Leaders Of Our Town) to describe "the bipartisan group of people,
most of whom suffered from an 'edifice complex,' who think that
building a new, large taxpayer-financed convention center will fix
all economic woes." Paustian says that LOOT exists all over the nation, and they make grandiose claims about economic benefits that
just aren't supported by the facts.

In Philadelphia, the city decided to build a new convention center
instead of renovating an existing one that was one of the largest in
the nation. To build the new one, the city had to spend in excess of
$500 million, demolish 89 buildings on five downtown blocks and
evict 170 businesses that employed 2000 employees. Paustian noted
the following problems and issues public officials should be aware
of before undertaking similar projects:

•   Don't use convention and trade-show consultants to do the
       feasibility studies. These are the same people who will ben-
       efit from a new convention center.

•   The cost to build public convention centers is greatly exag-
       gerated when compared to private centers. The Cleveland
       Expo, a private center, cost $25 per square foot of renovated
       exhibit space as compared to public centers in Washington
       $169, San Francisco $381, Atlanta $347, and New York's Javits
       Center at $675.

•   Huge cost overruns — Chicago's McCormick Place expan-
       sion had a $60 million overrun on its $252 million project.
       The Javits Center in New York had a $110 million overrun,
       and Philadelphia's had $88 million in cost increases before
       the construction even began.

- In addition to debt-service payments on bonds, taxpayers are also responsible for operating losses. Paustian examined the operating statements of 25 public centers larger than 300,000 square feet and found that annual operating losses averaged 42 percent of revenue.

- Many convention centers hide the full extent of losses by showing public subsidies as revenue and by excluding from annual reports such costs as interest payments, employee benefits, utilities and insurance.

- Many convention centers are overbuilt. According to *Meetings and Conventions* magazine, 87 percent of all conventions require less than 100,000 square feet. Yet, many of the new ones are overbuilt to accommodate pride, not market demand.

- Public agencies use economic multipliers to project the number of jobs that are created in the tourism business. In Salt Lake City, the city used a multiplier of 3.5 — every dollar spent in the tourist industry creates three dollars and fifty cents of additional economic activity. In Philadelphia, proponents used a multiplier of 3. Paustian suggests that a demultiplier effect occurs because jobs are also displaced and that the multiplier effect is usually canceled out.

- Proponents of the Philadelphia Convention Center projected $1.5 billion in benefits over 30 years by using a flawed projection method. They inflated benefits 6 percent per year and then simply added up 30 years' of costs and benefits without discounting to compare the net present value. When properly discounted, the convention center cost the taxpayers several millions of dollars.

Several of these points can be applied to any entrepreneurial venture in which local governments engage.

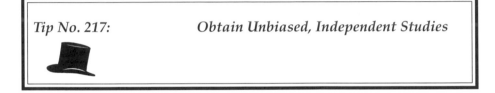

Tip No. 217:   ***Obtain Unbiased, Independent Studies***

While entrepreneurial ventures used to be the sole province of cities and counties, this is no longer the case. Squeezed by tighter budgets and criticized for a lack of creativity, school districts and special districts are initiating commercial ventures. Convention centers, stadiums, golf courses, shopping centers and other entrepreneurial ventures can become very complex. Governing board members can reassure themselves of the soundness of "deals" by hiring independent financial advisors to examine the feasibility of the project, as well as the projected benefits and costs.

For many years, the upscale City of Newport Beach, California coveted a convention and conference center. Unlike Philadelphia, however, Newport Beach hired an independent firm to assess the financial feasibility of a new center. The study, by PKF Consulting, concluded that such a conference center could not survive without substantial, long-term help from the city. According to the report, the surrounding area did not have enough hotels to generate demand for meeting rooms. The PKF report suggested that the city could do better by marketing Newport Beach as a tourist destination which would increase hotel occupancy and thus bed tax. While the results were disappointing, the study helped Newport Beach officials avoid a fiscal disaster.

The City of Long Beach, owner of the Queen Mary, found itself debating the merits of a entrepreneurial venture that would test even Michael Eisner and his Disney cohorts. Joseph Prevratil, president of the group that leased the Queen Mary, offered a "deal" to the city which would generate $40 million for badly needed repairs to the 60 year old ship. The deal involved towing the ship across the Pacific to Tokyo Bay and leaving it there for three to five years to be used as a hotel casino. During this time, the city would be paid $5 million a year in rent; and an additional $30 million would be raised for refurbishment from various sponsors, including Coca-Cola of Japan. After the five year period, the ship would be returned to Long Beach and a new wharf built.

The Queen Mary was purchased by Long Beach in 1964, for $40 million; and another $20 million was invested in it to make it usable for a hotel. Over the years, the ship became a city icon that brought tourists to Long Beach from all over the world. Unfortunately; the ship had begun to deteriorate; and the city did not have the money to make another major investment.

Prevratil stated that the ship could be towed across the Pacific with a massive flotation collar around it even without going into dry dock to make repairs. He said Lloyd's of London would insure the ship for $65 million against it being lost at sea. His estimate was that it would cost approximately $5 million to tow it to Tokyo Bay.

Investors offered the City of Long Beach $40 million to lease the Queen Mary for three to five years. They wanted to tow the ship across the Pacific in a flotation collar and use the ship for a hotel/casino.

Resisting the pressure to move quickly before the "deal" got away, the city council authorized the expenditure of $150,000 for a report from Ernst & Young to analyze the plan. A separate report on the cost of towing was also demanded of staff. The revised estimate for towing came in at $12 million, and staff also pointed out that finding experienced crew members to repair it during the journey would be difficult since the ship was launched in 1936.

After seeing the revised estimates, a skeptical city council decided to say thanks but no thanks to the generous offer and directed staff to find other alternative financing methods for repairing the grand ship. While the offer was very attractive, the bottom line was that the city council did not get convincing evidence that the Tokyo proposal was for real or that it would work.

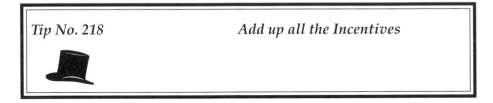

Tip No. 218   **Add up all the Incentives**

It was a competitive battle, but the State of Alabama prevailed and landed the Mercedes assembly factory in 1993. Twelve other states had tried to entice Daimler-Benz to locate within their boundaries, but Alabama's $300 million package of incentives and tax breaks won the prize. Later, after the smoke had cleared, the state started to divulge the financial details of the package. The public was not happy. For its $300 million investment, the state got Daimler-Benz to build a sports utility-assembly plant that employed 1500 people. Bottom line: It cost the state $200 thousand per job. Moreover, Alabama missed a $43 million construction payment and had to ask the State Employees Pension Fund for a loan.

Alabama is not alone. This competition for jobs and sales tax becomes an end in itself, and the actual net benefits are lost from sight. The Alabama package was three times as high as South Carolina provided to BMW in 1992, and 18 times as much as Tennessee provided for a Nissan factory in 1980.

The State of Utah provided over $200 million in incentives to Micron Technology, Inc., to construct a computer chip plant. The plant construction was discontinued when the bottom fell out of the computer chip market. The $20 million annual tax forgivnance the State of Massachusetts provided Raytheon, to convince the company from transferring jobs to other states, did not keep the company from announcing plans to lay off over 4000 workers three months later.

Tip No. 219:   *Know When to Pull the Plug on*
Entrepreneurial Ventures

After conducting a risk and cost/benefit analysis, the governing body should establish the threshold figure at which the project will be abandoned. This should be done before negotiations are initiated, as this is the time when the governing body is most objective in analyzing the merits of the project. Once negotiations begin, a "we can't lose the deal mentality" takes over, and many governing bodies wind up making concessions or contributions that they would not otherwise grant in more rational times. It happens over and over again. The fever rises to the point that the project is no longer economically feasible, but, the governing body decides to make one more concession. "We are so close: let's not quibble over a few bucks," the sentiment goes. Moreover, since concessions are made incrementally, the increase seems much smaller than it really is. Shrewd developers are very aware of the incremental build up. Retail center developer, Michael Tanaka, puts it this way, "I found that once you have gotten them psychologically committed to the project, they (elected officials) forget about the bottom line and are receptive to paying for unforeseen problems and refinements. Actually it's not too different from selling a new car."

Tip No. 220:   ***Get Ready for a Gutter Fight if You Steal***
an Enterprise

The unbelievable had happened. The tiny little City of Irwindale, California, had signed a deal with Los Angeles Raiders owner Al Davis to build a new stadium and headquarters within the city. Irwindale is approximately 20 miles from Los Angeles and has a day-time population of approximately 40,000 business people. The night time population is 1034 since there are only 300 dwelling units in the town.

Irwindale has several pits that were created from open-air quarries left unfilled by various mining companies. One of these pits was conveniently located next to a major freeway and large enough to accommodate a 65,000 seat football stadium. Irwindale City Manger Charles Martin noted that the city is always looking for ways to fill the pits. "All we have here in Irwindale essentially are holes. We figured wherever the Raiders go, they're going to have to build a hole, so why not use one of ours?" Martin added, "We plan to make this the finest sports complex the area has ever seen, and we're going to back it up with restaurants and hotels, probably even a shopping center."

How did Irwindale wind up in this seemingly enviable position? The Oakland Raiders moved to Los Angeles in 1982, and signed an agreement with the Los Angeles Memorial Coliseum to play at the site for ten years. The Raiders claimed that the Coliseum Commission promised to make stadium improvements, such as luxury boxes, but failed to follow through. This sent the Raiders looking for a new location to play their games. Upon hearing of the Raiders' dissatisfaction, several cities submitted bids. Irwindale, however, submitted the most enticing bid. The city promised to loan the Raiders $115 million to build the new stadium and support facilities and, to seal the deal, a $10 million non-refundable deposit. If Irwindale could acquire the remaining financing by November 4, 1989, the Raiders would play the 1992 season in Irwindale.

The tiny City of Irwindale not only failed to lure the Raiders football team to this site, they lost their $10 million non-refundable deposit when they could not put together a $115 million financing package.

Los Angeles was justifiably miffed by the loss of their football team. One Los Angeles city councilmember filed suit to block the sale of $90 million in revenue bonds. While this maneuver failed, other opponents took Irwindale to court for failing to conduct an environmental impact study on the project. This effort succeeded, and the Judge ruled that an environmental impact report was required. It got nastier. Conflict of interest charges were leveled at Irwindale city officials, and a probe of the entire Raiders deal was called for. Other road blocks were thrown up, resulting in Irwindale being unable to secure the required financing. The deal fell apart.

An irony of the story is that the failure of the Irwindale deal did not keep the Raiders in Los Angeles. Al Davis and the Raiders picked up their helmets and trundled back to Oakland, the city they had abandoned a decade before.

Tip No. 221:   ***Don't Let Time Pressures Void Your Good Judgment***

A larger irony is that the City of Oakland and Alameda County, fell victim to the blackmail that is so prevalent in these types of ventures. Under severe pressure to meet the tight time line for completing negotiations before the start of the 1995 football season, the Oakland-Alameda County Coliseum Joint Powers Authority accepted a deal that included a $198 million bond issuance and an up front payment of $53.9 million to the Raiders. The public was assured that the bonds would be paid back through the sale of the stadium name and Personal Seat Licenses that entitled the holders to season tickets and club and luxury suites. In the rush to put the deal together, however, negotiators used a market survey that was over one year old. Unfortunately, the market had softened; and public interest had waned. The city was not able to get a sponsor for the stadium name or sell sufficient personal seat licenses. (The personal seat licenses were the most expensive of all those offered by other NFL clubs.) As a result, revenues that were needed to meet the bond payments came in well below projections. According to the terms of the deal, the City of Oakland and the County of Alameda were required to fill the estimated first-year gap of $8 million from their general fund budgets.

The Alameda County grand jury, after analyzing the deal, did not have kind words to say, describing it as excessive; and the "financial exposure was beyond that which the county and city should have responsibly undertaken." Several officials admitted they had made mistakes in the hurried negotiations. "There's no question mistakes were made," Councilmember John Russo reflected after the grand jury concluded that the "deal was based on speculation and void of prudent thinking or adequate inquiries by elected officials."

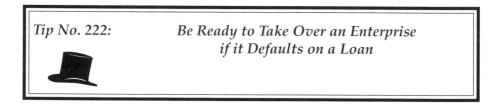

Tip No. 222:   ***Be Ready to Take Over an Enterprise***
if it Defaults on a Loan

Marine World was founded in Redwood City, California, by the ABC Television Network as a marine life and water ski theme park. In 1972, the park was sold to Resorts International, which added the animals from a wild animal park that went out of business. In 1986, Marine World-Africa USA was enticed to relocate to the City of Vallejo with a generous package consisting of municipally-owned land and a $55 million loan for site development and new attractions. The park prospered until the 1990's recession hit. Attendance began to drop from a high of 1.9 million in 1993 to 1.3 million in 1996.

The City of Vallejo reluctantly became the owner of Marine World-Africa USA after the owner defaulted on city loans.

The drop in attendance impacted revenues to the point that the owners could not make a $2.3 million loan payment. This default forced the City of Vallejo to foreclose and take over the park. All of a sudden the city of 100,000 people was responsible for a major theme park that employed over 1000 and cared for 3043 fish, birds and mammals.

Fortunately, Vallejo was able to entice a major theme park company to take over the management of Marine World-Africa USA. Premier Parks, the world's tenth largest theme park company, signed a three-year agreement to manage the park. In addition, Premier, which was given an option to purchase the park, promised to immediately invest $3 million in new attractions.

The situation Vallejo found itself in is something that all governing board members should be apprised of at the time of entering into a loan agreement with an enterprise. The local government could well wind up as the owner and operator. City Manager Ken Campo summed up the Vallejo strategy with this comment, "As soon as you confirm that the financial situation is serious, you need to take immediate and expeditious action. Don't look back — just look forward."

Tip No. 223:   ***Don't Let the "Entrepreneurial Bug"***
Derail the Primary Mission

The Los Angeles School District had a need for a 5300 student high school and with construction dollars tight, decided to develop a combined high school and commercial development. Two hundred dwelling units, a major supermarket, several retail stores and a recreation center would be built on the same site as the school. "The board wanted to try to use the momentum of building a school for developing housing and retail for the community. The project would provide important community amenities. We tried to do this in a way that no school district had done," said school board member Jeff Horton. To many observers, the board became so preoccupied with this add-on mission that the original goal of getting a badly needed school built suffered.

In the end, the project did not come together as planned. The district could not land a major supermarket or retailers, and the number of housing units were scaled back by 50 percent. More importantly, the cost of the school had increased from $60 million to $81 million; and the school opening was delayed for over 36 months.

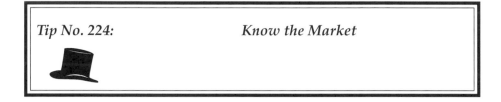

Tip No. 224:   ***Know the Market***

The story line is all too familiar. A community loses its auto center to another city or the long-term local supermarket closes its doors. The city council directs staff to get a similar replacement business. Staff meets with the involved real estate representatives and even owners of the desired use. Wooing begins with the benefits of having their facility in the city and winds up with the discussion of possible subsidies. The desired business says "no thanks" and gives one or several reasons — the demographics don't work, we're not in an expansion mode, or you're located too close to a similar use. Yet, year after year, the city council continues to push staff to find and land the business. Staff continues to spend time and dollars pursuing the improbable. All the while, the local government is blinded to other possible business ventures.

The moral of the story is that a local government cannot dictate the market; and if the desired use keeps rebuffing your courting efforts, maybe it's time to move on to another strategy.

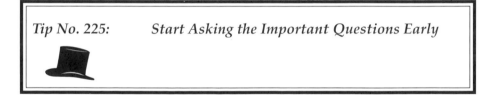

Tip No. 225:   ***Start Asking the Important Questions Early***

As an elected official, you can never ask too many questions about the "big deal." Considerable pressure can be applied, including the threat of you causing the coveted prize to go elsewhere because of your insistent questioning. Don't be intimidated. Analyze the deal early and ask the questions that the press and/or the grand jury will be asking later. This is not an exhaustive list nor do all these questions apply to each deal, but it provides a good start:

- What is the total amount of our agency's contribution over the life of the deal?
- What is the term of the deal? Can it be lengthened or shortened?
- What are all the things our agency must do to meet the terms of the deal?
- What penalties does our agency face for failure to perform according to the deal agreement?
- What is the estimated high, low and probable impact on our general fund?
- If we issue bonds, how will they be paid back?
- What is the size and term of the bond issue?
- What revenue sources are projected to be used to repay bonds?
- Who made the revenue projections and what is their track record?
- When were the revenue projections made?
- What key assumptions are being made about projected revenues?
- What up front payments are being made? Why?
- What is the developer committing to the deal? When?
- How much is the developer putting up front? How much later?
- What penalties does the developer face for failure to perform?
- What remedies are available to our agency to achieve developer compliance?
- What safeguards exist for construction overruns? Who pays for them?
- Is the owner also the developer?
- How does the deal compare to other similar local government deals?
- Which parties have conflicts of interest going into the deal? Later?

- What side deals does the developer and owner have that are related to the project?
- What is the developer's credit worthiness? Reputation?

You don't want to micro-manage, but you also do not want to be left holding the bag and reading the headline: "Grand jury blasts Raiders deal as $8 million shortfall revealed." If there is a place to delve into the detail, the "big deal" is the place to do it.

Afterword

There are over 500,000 elected officials serving on local government legislative bodies in this country. This book is written for the overwhelming majority of these officials who want their city, county, special district or school district to operate honestly, efficiently and effectively. In the author's opinion, these public officials face the most important and difficult challenges in America — education, policing, welfare, social services, and maintenance of the infrastructure.

Most local officials have dedicated themselves to improving their local government. They have discovered that guarding the public checkbook involves much more than simply cutting budgets and shunning tax increases. They scrutinize their agency's performance and are willing to take politically unpopular stands such as raising taxes or fees when convinced of the need. They also protect their agency's investment in its assets such as classrooms, sewers or roads during cutback periods, even if it means withstanding strong union pressure to focus solely on preserving employee salaries and benefits. They also:

- Build and protect an adequate fund balance.

• Issue debt only when it results in a definite payback or benefit for the agency.

• Analyze issues from a cost-benefit perspective.

• Avoid giving overly generous concessions to acquire a prestigious yet fiscally questionable commercial development, sports complex or other similar venture.

• Communicate with and educate the public about their agency's fiscal problems and opportunities.

Fiscally competent local governing board members are easy to spot. Just attend a city council, county board of supervisor's, water board or school board meeting (or watch a meeting on cable television), when the budget, treasurer's report or annual audit is being discussed. These members are concerned about their agency's fiscal condition. They seek to hold administrators accountable by inquiring, probing and analyzing. They ask the questions that elicit important budget and financial information from staff. At the same time, they become more knowledgeable about their agency's finances and budget. Their most important tools for guarding the public checkbook are an inquisitive manner and common sense.

Fiscally challenged elected officials are just as easy to detect. They shirk their responsibility by remaining quiet, not asking questions and failing to follow-up. A favorite ploy is to miss important meetings. Another is to refer the issue to committee. The primary goal is to get it off the agenda and out of sight. Delay, smoothing over, confusion and avoidance are their tactics.

This avoidance behavior used to be accepted. A new or even a seasoned governing body member could get through budget sessions by sitting back and feigning interest. With the increasing competition over every dollar, however, this tactic is no longer acceptable. The public is much more sophisticated today and they have less tolerance for elected representatives who fail to do their homework and show little understanding about their agency's finances.

For those elected officials who care about their agencies fiscal condition, they should remember the following:

1.   **Many fiscal problems have their genesis during good times**

Elected officials and administrators are most vulnerable when times are good. They are more apt to approve an overly generous retirement benefit or adopt a grant program that cannot be sustained when the grant funds run out. Everyone seems to forget that the good times will not last forever. You must be especially vigilant during these periods.

2.   **Complacency is at the root of many fiscal problems**

Most elected officials assume office with an inquisitive demeanor. Unfortunately, after a few years, many become complacent and resort to over reliance on trust and past performance. They stop inquiring and questioning assumptions. The Orange County Board of Supervisors sat complacently while the largest municipal bankruptcy in United States history occurred. You must balance trust with accountability.

3.   **The governing board's attention span is very short**

Governing bodies not only want to avoid difficult situations, they want them to go away as quickly as possible. When a fiscal problem or crisis manifests itself, everyone pays special attention. Numerous approaches and reforms are proposed. Promises are made. But as soon as the heat lessens, the attention fades. Don't let the issue disappear without satisfying yourself that the problem is truly resolved.

And finally, as you learn and master the business of governing, make notes of your experiences and lessons. Let me know where this book can be expanded or improved for future elected officials. I would love to use your tips and techniques (and black and white reproducible photographs) in future editions. Let's work together to better local government.

Len Wood

References

Advisory Commission on Intergovernmental Relations (1993). *State Laws Governing Local Government Structure and Administration.* M-186. Washington, DC: Government Printing Office.

California Taxpayers' Association (1981). *Citizens' Guide to Local Government Budgeting,* Sacramento, CA.

Carey, Patricia M. (1995). *It's 12 O'Clock: Do You Know Where Your City's Money Is?* Washington, DC: National League of Cities.

Carnevale, David G. (1995). *Trustworthy Government: Leadership and Management Strategies for Building Trust and High Performance.* San Francisco, CA: Jossey-Bass.

Gauthier, Stephen J. (1992) *An Elected Official's Guide to Auditing.* Government Finance Officers Association, 180 North Michigan Avenue, Suite 800, Chicago, IL.

Gauthier, Stephen J. (1991) *An Elected Official's Guide to Internal Controls and Fraud Prevention.* Government Finance Officers Association, 180 North Michigan Avenue, Suite 800, Chicago, IL.

Gauthier, Stephen J. (1991) *An Elected Official's Guide to Fund Balance.* Government Finance Officers Association, 180 North Michigan Avenue, Suite 800, Chicago, IL.

Glaser, Mark A. and James W. Bardo (1994). *Five-Stage Approach for Improved Use of Citizen Surveys in Public Investment Decisions.* State and Local Government Review 26 (Fall): 161-172.

Government Finance Officers Association (1995). *1995 Survey of Government Investment Practices.* Chicago, IL.

Kurish, J. B. and Patricia Tigue (1994). *An Elected Official's Guide to Debt Issuance.* Chicago, IL: Government Finance Officers Association.

National League of Cities. *A Survey of America's City Councils.* 1301 Pennsylvania Avenue NW, Washington, DC.

Osborne, David, and Ted Gaebler (1992). *Reinventing Government: How the Entrepreneurial Spirit is Transforming the Public Sector, from Schoolhouse to Statehouse, City Hall to the Pentagon.* Reading, MA: Addison-Wesley.

National Performance Review (1993). *Reinventing Government: Creating a Government That Works Better and Costs Less.* Washington, DC: Government Printing Office.

Wilson, James Q. (1989). *Bureaucracy: What Government Agencies Do and Why They Do It.* New York: Basic Books.

Wood, Len (1994). *Elected Official's Little Handbook: A Portable Guide for Local Government Legislators.* Rancho Palos Verdes, CA: The Training Shoppe.

Wood, Len (1993). *Little Budget Book: A Portable Budgeting Guide for Local Government.* Rancho Palos Verdes, CA: The Training Shoppe.

Appendix A
Sample Mission
Statements

The City of Fontana Mission Statement

The City of Fontana is dedicated to the emergence of Fontana as the premiere quality of life community in the Inland Empire.

Building upon our rich tradition of community pride, family orientation and traditional values, your City Council, Commissions and Committees, and City Staff are committed to their role in creating a community known for safety, beauty and a diversity of housing, business, and recreational/athletic opportunities and services. Above all, we recognize that it is the diverse background, cultures, and interest of our citizens that make us unique. It is ultimately their dreams and goals which will play the most important role in shaping our future as a community.

As your City government, our commitment is to wisely use our resources to provide competent, responsive and reliable services, in an atmosphere which demonstrates our commitment to accessibility, customer service, honesty and integrity. In all we do and in every decision we make, we will ask ourselves "is this best for Fontana?"

We believe in a bright future for Fontana. We are serious about our role in shaping that future. We pledge all of our efforts towards working in partnership with our citizens, businesses, community groups and neighbors as we continue to work to make Fontana a tremendous place for all of us.

Developed and Adopted by the Fontana City Council

• • • • • • • •

Tahoe City Public Utility District
Mission Statement

The fundamental role of Tahoe City Public Utility District is to serve people and their environment. We are a creation and extension of the people of the community.

Within the scope of our enabling legislation, we seek to accomplish what cannot be done effectively on an individual basis. It is our responsibility to provide water and sewer service for reasons of health and safety, and to provide parks and recreation for enhancement of the quality of life.

We are obligated to serve the public interest throughout our functions. We strive for public satisfaction with the services we offer. We are compelled to provide quality public services utilizing prudent fiscal practices. We are committed to the efficient and effective operation of all District functions.

Adopted by the Board of Directors

• • • • • • • •

Appendix B
Sample Goals
and Objectives

City of Rancho Palos Verdes
Public Safety Goals And Objectives

GOAL: A safe community in which to live and work.

OBJECTIVE:
To eliminate the perception that the City is on the decline with regard to public safety.

STRATEGIES:
- Continue to support and enhance the Neighborhood Watch Program.
- Continue to provide safety information in the Neighborhood Watch and City newsletters, public service announcements (PSA's), press releases and other public information sources.
- Provide briefing updates to newly appointed Lomita Sheriff Station Commanders to sensitize them to on-going events and issues in the community.

- Encourage participation by the Lomita Sheriff Station Commander in City sponsored communications with the public including townhall, homeowners associations and Neighborhood Watch meetings.

OBJECTIVE:
To reduce the number of traffic speed violations in the City.

STRATEGY:
- Implement new traffic enforcement programs offered by the Sheriff's Department such as motorcycle patrols and traffic monitoring by video where possible.

OBJECTIVE:
To eradicate graffiti within the City.

STRATEGIES:
- Actively publicize the Graffiti Tip Reward Program.
- Continue to support legislation that seeks to eradicate graffiti.
- Work closely with the school district to educate students regarding the effects of graffiti vandalism and to identify potential school-age vandals.
- Pursue the establishment and recruitment of persons and/or community groups as volunteers to identify and remove graffiti from various locations throughout the City.

OBJECTIVE:
To fully implement an Emergency Preparedness Program in the City.

STRATEGIES:
- Conduct regular emergency preparedness drills at City Hall. In addition to participating in drills sponsored by Los Angeles County agencies and Area G Disaster Council.
- Pursue the establishment and recruitment of a formal emergency preparedness volunteer team, including participants from the Palos Verdes Amateur Radio Club, to augment various staff emergency preparedness functions.
- Complete City Emergency Preparedness Plan.

City of Rancho Palos Verdes
City Communications, Customer Service
And Competent Workforce Goals And Objectives

GOAL: A well-informed, educated public with regard to City issues, problems and services.

OBJECTIVE:
To make more effective use of existing programs and consider, when possible, the expansion of other programs to educate the public regarding City issues and services.

STRATEGIES:
- Develop and update on a regular basis a series of department "fact" sheets that outline and explain services that are provided by the City.
- Produce the quarterly City newsletter in a more user-friendly way by shortening articles, including more photos and publishing on regular intervals.
- Avoid technical jargon when speaking with the public regarding City business.
- Continue with an on-going schedule of producing City public service announcements (PSA's) and special video programs on topics to educate the residents regarding City issues, services and programs.
- Make efficient use of telecommunications with residents and the business community.

OBJECTIVE:
To establish more opportunities for two-way communication between the City and its residents.

STRATEGIES:
- Establish a regular schedule of quarterly townhall meetings to be held throughout the community for the public with the City Council and staff to address issues of concern to the participating residents.
- Continue scheduling and conducting twice yearly community leaders' meetings.
- Solicit opportunities for the City Council and the staff to speak before community and business groups regarding City issues and services.

- Promote, encourage and assist in the establishment of homeowners associations for continued and future communication opportunities.

GOAL: A friendly, responsive and competent City government.

OBJECTIVE:
To effectively measure how we're doing and what improvements in the way we do business are necessary.

STRATEGIES:
- Establish a formal customer service program incorporating customer feedback surveys, employee training and a data base to measure improvements over time.
- Incorporate the use of telecommunications technology such as fax machines and computer modems to allow the City's customers flexibility in submitting applications, permits and other documents, where feasible, to the City.
- Participate in programs established by realtor associations and other organizations to welcome new residents in the community by creating a welcome packet of information on City services as well as response cards for ideas and suggestions.

OBJECTIVE:
To maintain and effectively utilize City staff.

STRATEGIES:
- Pursue the establishment of a general volunteer program in the City to augment various staff functions, as well as recruit persons from the community to serve as volunteers.
- Establish an employee recognition program to acknowledge outstanding service in the City.
- Continue as a budget priority the effective training of staff in various subject areas including customer service.
- Compensate employees based upon approved schedules as adopted and amended by the City Council and occasional surveys in the market of both public and private entities, when and where appropriate.

City of Rancho Palos Verdes
City Economic Development Goals And Objectives

GOAL: A community with a sound economic base.

OBJECTIVE:
To improve the business climate of the existing business districts (Western Avenue and Golden Cove).

STRATEGIES:
- Jointly pursue with the City of Los Angeles, the design and implementation of an appropriate streetscape plan along Western Avenue.
- Pursue the steps necessary to identify and investigate the possibility of establishing a redevelopment project area along Western Avenue.

OBJECTIVE:
To improve the business climate for new business operators to encourage more businesses to locate within the City.

STRATEGIES:
- Develop a general Economic Development Plan for the City.
- Assist with the development of Long Point in conjunction with City property to facilitate the construction of an eighteen hole golf course.
- Assist with the development of Ocean Trails.

City of Rancho Palos Verdes
City Finance Goals And Objectives

GOAL: A sound financial base to support and maintain vital City services.

OBJECTIVE:
To develop and maintain multiple revenue sources.

STRATEGIES:
- Adopt and retain new revenue measures until the economic development plans produce a reliable source of revenue from within the community.
- Continue to lobby state and federal representatives to protect local revenue sources, including property taxes and state subventions.
- Pursue other goals and objectives that would contribute to the City's financial base such as those outlined under the Economic Development section.
- Pursue opportunities for public and private grant funding for appropriate City programs.

City of Rancho Palos Verdes
City Infrastructure Goals And Objectives

GOAL: Reduce long-term public infrastructure costs in the City.

OBJECTIVE:
To provide for adequate public streets.

STRATEGIES:
- Complete and implement Pavement Management Study.
- Complete and implement Capital Improvement Program Plan (streets and highways).
- Analyze current Development Impact Fee Schedule to assure that new developments pay the appropriate costs associated with development impacts.

OBJECTIVE:
To extend the life of existing public facilities and replace where necessary.

STRATEGIES:
- Conduct Needs Assessment study.
- Complete and implement Capital Improvement Plan (public buildings).

OBJECTIVE:
To make more effective use of existing park facilities and consider expansion of these facilities where appropriate.

STRATEGIES:
- Adopt and implement the Los Angeles County Safe Neighborhood Parks Act ("Measure A") Expenditure Plan.
- Explore other funding sources which may be available for park acquisition and/or development (Portuguese Bend Playing Fields).
- Continue to maintain the existing park system.

Appendix C
Sample Line Item
Budget

Fund: General

Department: Public Works
Division: Building Maintenance

Expenditure Classification	Actual	Budgeted
510 – Personnel Expenses		
110 Salaries - Permanent	181,008	186,400
120 Salaries - Temporary	14,216	5,850
130 Salaries - Overtime	11,625	15,300
170 PERS	24,784	23,700
171 FICA	15,137	15,850
180 Other Benefits	44,392	44,100
190 Contract Personnel	31,454	
Subtotal	322,616	291,200
515 – Operating Expenses		
200 Utilities	98,769	96,000
221 Supplies - General	41,106	40,000
250 Tools	416	1,200
255 Uniforms	2,825	2,400
261 Periodicals	136	200
320 Equipment Maintenance	12,872	15,000
337 Vehicle Rent	6,400	6,800
350 Contract Services	12,681	7,650
440 Training	805	500
Subtotal	176,010	169,750
545 – Capital Outlay		
510 Equipment - General	4,103	
545 Other Improvements		1,550
Subtotal	4,103	1,550
TOTAL	**$502,729**	**$462,500**

Appendix D
Sample Program
Budget

Fund: General

Department: Library
Division: Public Services

Classification	Actual	Budgeted
Salaries and Benefits:	246,557	264,925
Supplies and Services:	110,772	122,035
Capital Outlay:	650	608
Total Expenditures	**$357,979**	**$387,568**

Accomplishments During Past FY

- Adult / Young People's information and research handling increased 13 percent over the previous fiscal year.

- Attendance at both Adult and Young People's events increased 25 percent over the previous year.

- Use of the Matsui Meeting Room and Art Gallery increased 90 percent over the previous fiscal year.

Goals and Objectives For Current FY

- Add a minimum of 7,500 new items in the Adult materials' collections: weed a minimum of 500 Reference collection items; add a minimum of 1,100 volumes to the Young People's material collections.

- Perform 23,000 reference/reader's advisory transactions for Adult and Young People.

- Increase the turnover rate (items held divided by circulation) for fiction and non-fiction materials by 2 percent.

- Provide 25 library tours/orientation sessions per year.

- Maintain the Matsui Meeting Room and Art Gallery occupancy of 75 percent and display space usage of 100 percent.

Appendix E
Definitions of Funds

Government Funds. There are four Government Fund types:

1.	General Fund	This fund is the chief operating fund of the governmental agency. It is used to account for all general revenue sources (property taxes, sales taxes, licenses, permits and fines) not required to be accounted for in another fund. It is usually the largest non-capital fund. There is only one general fund for each agency.
2.	Special Revenue Fund	These funds are used to account for resources which are legally or administratively restricted for specific purposes.

Examples: Federal and State Grant
Funds
Environmental Excise
Tax Fund

3. Capital Projects Funds

These funds are used to account for resources restricted for construction and acquisition of major capital facilities.

Examples: School Building
Renovation
Construction of New
Bridge

4. Debt Service Funds

These funds account for the resources used to repay the principal and interest on general purpose long-term debt, such as a new court house bond issue.

Examples: General Obligation
Bond Debt Service
Civic Center Debt
Service
Stadium Bonds Debt
Service

Proprietary Funds. There are two Proprietary Fund types:

5. Enterprise Funds

These funds are used to account for operations that are financed and operated in a manner similar to business enterprises. The accounting approach is similar to private operations.

Examples: Electric Utility
Trash Collection

6. Internal Service Funds

These funds account for the financing of goods or services provided by one department or agency to other departments on a cost-reimbursement basis.

Examples: Print Shop
Data Processing Services
Motor Pool

Fiduciary Funds. There is one Fiduciary Fund type:

7. Trust and Agency
Funds

These funds account for assets held by a governmental unit in a trustee capacity or as an agent for individuals, private organizations or other governmental units.

Examples: Pension Trust Fund
Trust Fund for
Developer Good Faith
Deposits

Appendix F
How to Tackle
a Budget

1. **Initial Flip Through**: When you receive the budget, flip through it to get a general idea of what it contains. Notice the major sections such as budget message, summary statements and detailed statements.

2. **Table of Contents**: Locate the table of contents to use as a guide to find specific items. Some budgets also contain an index which is located in the back of the document.

3. **Budget Message**: Read the budget message to obtain an overall picture of economic trends, assumptions, problems, opportunities and finances. This one item should give you the best overview

of the budget. Determine the three most important issues.

4. **Fund Balances**: Find the "General Fund Changes In Fund Balance Statement" to determine whether the budget is balanced, whether revenues exceed expenditures and how reserves will be impacted. Determine the unrestricted balances. Determine total reserves.

5. **Revenue Summary**: Find the revenue summary and compare changes from previous years. Determine total revenues.

6. **Expenditure Summary**: Find the overall expenditure summary and compare how expenditures have changed from the previous year. Determine total expenditures.

7. **Debt**: Find the debt funds. Determine your agencies total debt. Determine how much is being paid in debt service out of the general fund. Determine how close your agency is to its debt limit.

8. **Organizational Chart**: Review the organizational chart to determine the number of departments and reporting relationships. Determine which functions are provided, the number of personnel and the cost per division, unit or section.

9. **Personnel Changes**: Find the changes in the personnel chart to determine additions or deletions of positions by department. Determine total number of full-time and part-time employees. Compile full-time and part-time hours to get a full-time equivalency to compare to other comparable agencies.

10. **Individual Budgets**: Use the table of contents to locate individual budgets. Examine changes from the previous year. Focus on the objectives, are they significant and measurable. Do performance measures link to the objectives?

11. **Capital improvements**: Is this year's capital improvement program incorporated in the operating budget? Determine the total capital improvement budget.

Appendix G
Fund Balance Charts

Cities

General Fund - Unreserved, Undesignated Fund Balance as a Percent of Expenditures

Population Range	No.	Low	High	Median
<10,000	169	-17%	195%	24%
10,000-24,999	309	-11%	219%	15%
25,000-49,999	260	-17%	215%	14%
50,000-99,999	190	-8%	66%	9%
100,000-199,999	78	-37%	89%	7%
200,000-299,999	23	-2%	20%	6%
300,000-499,999	21	0%	38%	6%
>500,000	15	-8%	17%	3%

Cities

General Fund - Unreserved, Undesignated Fund Balance
Per Capita

Population Range	No.	Low	High	Median
<10,000	169	-$53	$1,230	$112
10,000-24,999	309	-$121	$794	$53
25,000-49,999	260	-$100	$636	$50
50,000-99,999	190	-$23	$302	$34
100,000-199,999	78	-$19	$546	$30
200,000-299,999	23	-$7	$135	$25
300,000-499,999	21	$0	$120	$17
>500,000	15	-$97	$337	$13

Counties

General Fund - Unreserved, Undesignated Fund Balance
as Percentage of Expenditures

Population Range	No.	Low	High	Median
<100,000	91	-5%	127%	23%
100,000-249,999	71	0%	52%	15%
250,000-999,999	75	-11%	62%	10%
>1,000,000	18	-3%	34%	5%

Counties

General Fund - Unreserved, Undesignated Fund Balance Per Capita

Population Range	No.	Low	High	Median
<100,000	91	-$42	$259	$43
100,000-249,999	71	$0	$131	$29
250,000-999,999	75	-$10	$99	$21
>1,000,000	18	-$17	$35	$11

School Districts

General Fund - Unreserved, Undesignated Fund Balance as Percentage of Expenditures

Population Range	No.	Low	High	Median
<10,000	16	-0%	9%	3%
10,000-24,999	17	-12%	17%	6%
25,000-49,999	23	-11%	23%	4%
50,000-99,999	30	-4%	68%	4%
100,000-199,999	24	-6%	38%	12%
>200,00	34	-6%	21%	3%

School Districts

General Fund - Unreserved, Undesignated Fund Balance
Per Capita

Population Range	No.	Low	High	Median
<10,000	16	$0	$172	$99
10,000-24,999	17	-$92	$146	$35
25,000-49,999	23	-$60	$146	$17
50,000-99,999	30	-$24	$263	$13
100,000-199,999	24	-$28	$290	$16
>200,000	34	-$41	$82	$16

Appendix H
Budget Document
Assessment

This assessment is designed to help you evaluate your budget from your perspective. Allocate points according to your own evaluation. For the first question, if you believe the budget message is informative and easy to read, give it 1 or 2 points. If not, no points. Continue allocating the specified points for the remaining questions. Don't spend too much time on each question — use your first reaction.

_____ Is the budget message informative and easy to read? (0-2 points)

_____ Does the budget message address major issues (assumptions, trends, problems and opportunities)? (0-4 points)

_____ Does the budget include an overall mission statement? (0-2 points)

_____ Does the budget include overall goal statements? (0-3 points)

_____ Does the budget include a section on fund balances and reserves? (0-3 points)

_____ Does the budget show goals by department or program? (0-2 points)

_____ Within department or program budgets does it include measurable objectives? (0-3 points)

_____ In your judgment, are the objectives meaningful? (0-4 points)

_____ Are the objectives measurable? (0-3 points)

_____ Within department or program budgets does it include performance measures or service indicators? (0-3 points)

_____ Are the performance measures linked to the objectives? (0-3 points)

_____ Does the format add to or detract from the document? (0-2 points)

_____ Do the charts and graphs help communicate budget information? (0-3 points)

_____ Does the budget include a table of contents? (0-1 points)

_____ Does it include an index? (0-1 points)

_____ Would an elected official feel this is a user friendly budget? (0-4 points)

_____ Would a community member feel this is a user friendly budget? (0-4 points)

_____ Does the budget address the major questions you have about the agency's issues and problems? (0-5 points)

_____ Total Points

Evaluation

Excellent	43-52
Good	33-42
Average	27-32
Improvement Needed	20-26
Revise Entire Budget	0-19

Glossary

The terms used in this glossary have been taken from local government budgets and financial reports from around the country. They represent the most common terms used in public budgeting and finance.

Accrual Basis: The method of accounting under which revenues are recorded when they are earned (whether or not cash is received at the time) and expenditures are recorded when goods and services are received.

Adjusted Budget: The current budget adopted by the government body including any modifications authorized throughout the year.

Ad Valorem Taxes: A tax levied on the assessed value of real property. Property tax.

Agency Fund: A fund used to account for assets held by a government as an agent for individuals, private organizations, other governments or other funds.

Appropriation: An authorization made by the governing body which permits officials to incur obligations and expend government resources within a fiscal year. Appropriations are made for specific amounts.

Assessed Valuation: The estimated value placed upon real and personal property as the basis for levying property taxes.

Base Budget: Ongoing expense for personnel, contractual services, and the replacement of supplies and equipment required to maintain service levels previously authorized by the governing body.

Bond (Debt Instrument): A written promise to pay (debt) a specified sum of money (called principal or face value) at a specified future date (called the maturity date) along with periodic interest paid at a specified percentage of the principal (interest rate). Bonds are typically used for long-term debt to pay for specific capital expenditures.

Bond Anticipation Notes: (BANS) Short-term interest bearing notes issued in anticipation of bonds to be issued at a later date. The notes are retired from proceeds of the bond issue to which they are related.

Budget Calendar: The schedule of key dates or milestones which an agency follows in the preparation and adoption of the budget.

Capital Assets: Assets of significant value and having a useful life of several years. Capital assets are also called fixed assets.

Capital Budget: A plan of proposed capital expenditures and the means of financing them. The capital budget may be enacted as part of the complete annual budget including both operating and capital outlays. The capital budget is based on the Capital Improvement Plan (CIP).

Capital Improvement Plan (CIP): A financial plan of proposed capital improvement projects and the means of financing them, usually prepared for a five year period.

Capital Outlay: An operating budget category which accounts for furniture and equipment with an estimated useful life of more than one year.

Capital Projects: Projects which purchase or construct capital assets. Typically, a capital project encompasses a purchase of land or construction of a building or facility, with a life expectancy of more than one year.

Cash Basis: The method of accounting under which revenues are recorded when received in cash and expenditures are recorded when paid.

CDBG: Community Development Block Grants.

Certificate of Deposit: A negotiable or non-negotiable receipt for monies deposited in a bank or other financial institution for a specified period for a specified rate of interest.

Contingency: A budgetary reserve set aside for emergencies or unforseen expenditures not otherwise budgeted for.

Debt: An obligation resulting from the borrowing of money or from the purchase of goods and services. Debts of government include bonds, time warrants and notes.

Debt Service: Payment of interest and repayment of principal to holders of the government's debt instruments.

Debt Service Fund: A fund established to account for the accumulation of resources for, and the payment of, general long-term debt principal and interest.

Deficit: (1) The excess of an entity's liabilities over its assets (See Fund Balances). (2) The excess of expenditures or expenses over revenues during a single accounting period.

Depreciation: (1) Expiration in the service life of capital assets attributable to wear and tear, deterioration, action of the physical elements, inadequacy or obsolescence. (2) That portion of the cost of a capital asset which is charged as an expense during a particular period.

Double Budgeting: The result of having funds or departments within a government purchase services from one another rather than from outside vendors. When internal purchasing occurs, both funds must budget the expenditure (one to buy the service and the other to add the resources to its budget so they have something to sell). This type of transaction results in inflated budget values because the same expenditure dollar is budgeted twice: once in each fund's budget. The revenue side of both funds is similarly inflated.

Encumbrances: Obligations in the form of purchase orders, contracts or salary commitments which are chargeable to an appropriation is reserved. They cease to be encumbrances when paid or when an actual liability is set up.

Ending Fund Balance: The cash balance remaining at the end of the fiscal year available for appropriation in future years.

Enterprise Fund: A type of fund established to account for the total costs of those government facilities and services that are operated in a manner similar to private enterprise. These programs are entirely, or predominately, self-supporting.

Equipment Rental: The Equipment Rental Fund operates as a self sufficient motor and equipment pool. Customer departments pay for the equipment used through charges billed. These charges include a form of depreciation which is accumulated as a sinking fund for future asset replacement, a factor for maintenance of the equipment, and charges for fuel.

Fiscal Year: A twelve (12) month period designated as the operating year by an entity. Fiscal years vary across the nation.

Fixed Assets: Long-lived tangible assets obtained or controlled by the agency. Fixed assets include buildings, equipment, improvements other than buildings, and land.

Float: The amount of money represented by checks outstanding and in the process of collection.

Full Faith and Credit: A pledge of the general taxing power of a government to repay debt obligations (typically used in reference to bonds).

Fund: An independent fiscal and accounting entity used to record all financial transactions related to the specific purpose for which the fund was created. There are three major types of funds: General, Proprietary, and Trust and Agency.

FTE: Full-time equivalent employee.

Fund Balance: The excess of an entity's assets over its liabilities. A negative fund balance is sometimes called a deficit.

GAAFR: "Governmental Accounting, Auditing and Financial Reporting." The "blue book" published by the Government Finance Officers Association to provide guidance for the application of accounting principles for governments.

GAAP: Generally Accepted Accounting Principles are standards used for accounting and reporting used for both private industry and governments.

GASB: Government Accounting Standards Board, established in 1985, to regulate the rules and standards for all governmental units.

General Fund: The fund supported by taxes, fees and other revenues that may be used for any lawful purpose.

General Obligation Bonds: Bonds for which the full faith and credit of the insuring government are pledged for payment.

Impact Fees: A fee assessed on new development that creates additional demand and need for public facilities.

Infrastructure: The underlying foundation, especially the basic installations and facilities, on which the continuance and growth of a jurisdiction depends, i.e., streets, roads, sewer, and water systems.

Interfund Payments: Expenditures made to other funds for services rendered.

Interfund Transfers: Monies transferred from one fund to another in order to reimburse that fund for expenditures or to finance the operation of that fund.

Intergovernmental Revenue: Revenue received from other governments, such as grants, shared taxes and reimbursements for services.

Internal Control: A plan of organization for purchasing, accounting, and other financial activities which, among other things, provides that:

- The duties of employees are subdivided so that no single employee handles financial actions from beginning to end.
- Proper authorization from specific responsible officials are obtained before key steps in the processing of a transaction are completed.
- Records and procedures are arranged appropriately to facilitate effective control.

Internal Service Funds: A fund type that accounts for revenues received and expenses incurred for services or commodities provided by that fund to user departments such as duplicating and data processing.

Liability: Debt or other legal obligations arising out of transactions in the past which must be liquidated, renewed or refunded at some future date.

Mill: The property tax rate which is based on the valuation of property. A tax rate of one mill produces one dollar of taxes on each $1,000 of property value.

Mitigation Fees: Contributions made by developers toward future improvements of government facilities resulting from the additional demand on the facilities generated from the development.

Modified Accrual Basis: The basis of accounting under which expenditures, other than accrued interest on general long-term debt, are recorded at the time liabilities are incurred and revenues are recorded when received in cash except for material and/or available revenues, which should be accrued to reflect properly the taxes levied and revenue earned.

Object: As used in expenditure classification, this term applies to the type of item purchased or the service obtained.

Per Capita: Amount per individual. Used as a comparative measure.

Prior Year Encumbrances: Money set aside from last year's budget to pay for items or services ordered during that year but received in the subsequent fiscal year. The encumbrance is removed when the items or services are received and paid for.

Program: An activity or group of similar activities organized as a sub-unit of a department for planning and performance measurement purposes.

Program Enhancement: Programs, activities or personnel requested to improve or add to the current baseline services.

Reserve: An account used to earmark a portion of the balance as legally segregated for a specific use.

Resources: Total dollars available for appropriations including estimated revenues, fund transfers, and beginning fund balances.

Retained Earnings: An equity account reflecting the accumulated earnings of the agency.

Revenue Bonds: Bonds issued pledging future revenues, usually water, sewer or drainage charges, to cover debt payments in addition to operating costs.

Special Revenue Fund: A fund used to account for the proceeds of specific revenue sources that are legally restricted to specified purposes.

Subventions: Revenue collected by the state (or other level of government) which is allocated to an agency on a formula basis.

Supplemental Appropriation: An appropriation approved by the governmental body after the initial budget is adopted.

Tax Anticipation Notes (TANS): Notes issued in anticipation of taxes which are retired usually from taxes collected.

Tax Rate Limit: The maximum legal rate at which a government may levy a tax. The limit may apply to taxes raised for a particular purpose or for general purposes.

Trust Fund: Funds used to account for assets held by a government in a trustee capacity for individuals, private organizations, and/or other funds.

User Charges / Fees: The payment of a fee for direct receipt of a public service by the party benefiting from the service.

Warrant: An order drawn by a government officer(s) directing the treasurer of the municipality to pay a specified amount to the bearer.

Yield: The rate earned on an investment based on the price paid for the investment, the interest earned during the period held, and the selling price or redemption value of the investment.

YTD (Year to Date): Total expenses incurred or revenue received since the beginning of the current fiscal year to a specific date.

Index

A

Ackerman, Debbie, 39
Advisory Commission on
    Intergovernmental Relations,
    84, 91, 243
Agnos, Art, 8-9
Alameda County, 305-306
Alatorree, Richard, 6, 138
Arnold, Jim, 75
Arthur Anderson Company, 191
Arthur Young & Company, 273
Association of California School
    Administrators, 108
Atwood, Donald, 157
Audit committees, 288-289
Audit expectation gap, 277
Audit report, 33, 160-161, 281, 288-289
Auditor, 28, 172, 191, 199, 224, 235,
    275-281, 284-287
Auditor opinions, 280
Authur, Anthony, 86

B

Barnum, Phineas Taylor, 95
Bates, Margaret, 20
Bellflower, California, City of, 183
Benchmarking, 234-235
Bernardi, Ernani, 114
Bernstein, Helen, 46
Block, Sherman, 25-28, 116

Bornstein, Irwin, 212
Boudreaux, Barbara, 268
Boston Globe, 100
Bradbury, California, City of, 119,
    121
Bradley, Robert, 88, 90
Brady, Paul, 204
Brea, California, City of, 192
Bremberg, Ginger, 15
Bressette, Randal, 210
Bridgeport, Connecticut, City of,
    95-97
Brown, Don, 45
Brown, Willie, 92
Brownridge, J. Paul, 252
Bryant, Scott, 215
Buchan, Judy, 17
Budget freezes, 113-114
Budget message, 65, 160
Budget padding, 149-152
Budget questions, 70-72
Burbank, California, City of, 152,
    158
Burke, Yvonne Brathwaite, 93
Butte County, 255-256

C

CAFR (Comprehensive Annual
    Financial Report), 10, 12, 39,
    281-283
California Municipal Bond Report,
    250
California Municipal Treasurers
    Association, 212
California Society of Municipal
    Finance Officers (CSMFO), 211
California State Auditor, 28
Camarillo, California, City of, 182,
    199-200, 202
Campo, Ken, 307
Capital Improvements Program,
    12, 101
Capizzi, Michael R., 187-188
Caporicci, Gary, 277, 279, 282-285
Carollo, Joe, 88
*Certificate of Achievement for
    Excellence in Financial
    Reporting*, 282-283
Chambers, Howard, 62-63, 66

Charlotte, North Carolina, City of, 104-106, 109, 111
Chelsea, Massachusetts, City of, 99-102, 105, 108
Chick, Laura, 6, 142
Chiles, Lawton, 88-89
Citizen committees, 117
Citron, Robert, 35, 186-187, 190-192, 194, 197, 201-203, 206, 212
Claremont, California, City of, 141, 249
Clean audit opinions, 280-281
Cleveland Plain Dealer, 201
Clinton, Bill, 15, 219
Closed-ended questions, 16
Coast Guard, 220
Colchester, Connecticut, Town of, 126
Commercial accounting, 66
Common Cause, 30
Community-Oriented Policing Program (COPS), 219, 238, 240
Complacency management, 35-36, 41
Comrie, Keith, 113
Connell, Kathleen, 155
Consumer Price Index (CPI), 76
Convention centers, 298-300
Coopers and Lybrand, 33
Corvallis, Oregon, City of, 104
Coulter, Stephen, 92
Covina, California, City of, 1-3, 157
Credit card usage, 134-135
Culver City, California, City of, 232-234
Customer surveys, 231
Cutback mistakes, 110
Cuyahoga County, Ohio, 201
Dabis, Christina, 194
Dallas, Texas, City of, 44
Dana, Dean, 156
Dearborn, Philip, 85
Deferred maintenance 258 -260
Defillo, Marion, 124
Denman Company, 184
Dingell. John, 158
Department of Education, 287
Department of Motor Vehicles, 157

D
Dixon, David, 193
Dixon, Richard, 128-129
Dougharty, Larry, 129
Dowlin, Kenneth, 92
Downsizing, 102-104
Drew, Joseph, 33, 137
Duckworth, Don, 296-297
Dumb questions, 15
Dye, Barbara, 11

E
Eastin, Delaine, 155
E.F. Hutton, 182-184
Elliott, Linda, 264
Ernst and Young, 301
Emergency Management Agency, 177
Enterprise fund, 44, 91, 114, 170, 251
Establishing the reserve level, 176
Excess property, 252

F
Falls, Tom, 3-4
Federal Bankruptcy Code, 96
Fell, May, 75
Feuer, Mike, 6, 262-263
Financial control board, 127
Financial crisis warning signs, 84
Financial gimmicks, 90-91
Financial policies, 38, 43-45, 156
Financial review board, 96
Financial statement audits, 274
Fine, Richard, 93
Fiscal crises, 84
Fong, Matt, 155
Fontana, California, City of, 40, 271-275
Forest Service, 248-249
Fort Walton Beach, Florida, City of, 169,175
French Quarter, 123-125
Fund accounting, 10, 66, 170
Fund balance, 45, 67-70, 84, 92, 165-166, 169-177, 179-180

G

GAAP (Generally Accepted Accounting Principles), 10, 274, 280-281
Garcetti, Gil, 116
General Accounting Office (GAO), 135,221, 249, 285, 288
General fund, 16, 44, 66-71, 85, 88, 91, 127, 156,161-165, 169-170, 173-174, 182-183, 190, 194, 222, 250-251, 273, 306, 309
Generally Accepted Government Auditing Standards (GAGAS), 276
Gillespie, Timothy, 92
Glendale, California, City of, 15
Goals, 5-6, 13, 33, 38, 40-43, 48-50, 56, 59, 72, 216-219, 221, 242, 272
Goins, Frances, 201
Golding, Susan, 295
Gomez, Mike, 20
Gonzales, Ron, 13
Gore, Al, 108
Government Finance Officers Association (GFOA), 170-171, 179, 192, 211, 282-283
Government Performance and Results Act (GPRA), 218-219, 221
Grants, 44, 70, 91, 99, 105, 114, 148, 157, 177-178, 221, 238-242, 250-251
Gray, Glenn, 110
Guarriello, Sal, 74
Guidelines for successful retreats, 52

H

Hahn, James, 138-139
Hagler, Patricia, 47
Hankla, Jim, 214, 217
Hanson, Ken, 209
Hargrove, Jan, 92
Hayden, Tom, 7
Hayes, Thomas, 207
Hedgecock, Roger, 294
Henderson, Bruce, 294-295
Heritage Foundation, 114

Hickey, Norman, 133-134
Hidden money, 145-148, 155-156, 159-161
Hill, Peter, 11
Holden, Nate, 122
Holton, Ruth, 30
Hon, Audrey, 120
Huntington Beach, California, City of, 192, 206
Huston, Texas, City of, 223

I

International Merchant Purchase Authorization Card (IMPAC), 135
Investment committees, 205-206
Investment pools, 209-211
Investment reports, 12,182, 184, 206-207
Irvine, California, City of, 204, 209
Irwindale, California, City of, 303-305

J

Jack Murphy Stadium, 291, 293-295
Jamison, Conny, 194
Jordan, Donald, 99
Jordan, Frank, 8-10
Josephson Ethics Foundation, 137
Josephson, Michael, 137-138

K

Karney, Richard C., 147
Klotz, Patrick, 123-124
Koch, William, 200-201
Kopp, Quentin, 155
Koretz, Paul, 74
Kosmont & Associates, 244

L

La Palma, California, City of, 285
Laguna Hills, California, City of, 209
Laguna Beach Unified School District, 79
Lakewood, California, City of, 62, 66

Lakewood, Colorado, City of, 217
Lawndale, California, City of, 183
Levels of management, 109
Leveraging, 202, 207, 211
Levitt, Arthur, 194
Library, 3, 8, 91-92, 263-266
Litigation costs, 141-142
Lockyear, Bill, 155
Lomita, California, City of, 121
Long Beach, California, City of,
    213-216, 219, 300-301
Long Beach Police Department,
    214-215, 217
Los Angeles Airport, 251
Los Angeles, City of, 5-6, 46, 113,
    122, 131, 138, 142, 157, 215, 239,
    244, 252, 261-263, 303-305
Los Angeles County, 25-28, 92-94,
    116, 128-129, 155-156, 214-215,
    222-223, 232
Los Angeles Fire Department, 131
Los Angeles Police Department, 7,
    262
Los Angeles Times, 27-28, 94, 120,
    131, 137, 139
Lungren, Dan, 155
Lundlberg, Merle, 129

M
MacKay, Buddy, 89
Management letter, 39, 284
Manhattan Beach, California, City
    of, 128-129
Mann, Zann, 250
Marine World, 306-307
Market value reporting, 204
Marley, Frank, 14-15
Mathey, Tom, 19-20
Maywood, California, City of, 183
MBIA Insurance Corporation, 211
McClain, Debra, 54
McEnery, Tom, 181
Measurable objectives, 59, 72, 222
Melbourn, Thomas, 120
Merrian, Robert, 91
Metropolitan Transit Authority
    (MTA), 33, 93, 137
Miami, Florida, City of, 87-90
Micro-management, 32-33, 35, 61,
    266

Mirabelli, Kay, 203
Mission statement, 39-40, 272
Molina, Gloria, 95
Monterey County, 267
Moody's Investors Service, Inc., 96
Moorlach, John, 197
Moran, Mary, 96-97
Moreland, Mike, 277-279, 282
Moynihan, Daniel Patrick, 76
MTA Board of Directors, 33
Municipal Treasurers Association
    (MTA), 184, 192, 203
Murphy, Dennis, 96-97
Myers, Dennis, 108
Myers, Pat, 122
National Commission on
    Fraudulent Financial
    Reporting, 288

N
National League of Cities (NLC),
    19, 29
New Britain Township,
    Pennsylvania, 237
New Orleans, Louisiana, City of,
    123-125
New Orleans Times-Picayune, 123
New York, City of, 84, 91, 120, 127,
    131, 177, 245, 268, 298
Newport Beach, California, City of,
    120, 300
Norton, Barbara, 82
Nunn, Sam, 157

O
Oakland, California, City of, 244,
    268, 295, 305
Oakland Raiders, 304-305
Oblander, Don, 208
Odio, Caesar, 87
Office of Marine Safety, 220
Open meeting laws, 21-22
Open-ended questions, 16-17, 70
Orange, California, City of, 192-193
Orange County, California, 25, 35,
    45, 53-55, 79-81, 93, 131, 181,
    186-188, 190-195, 197, 201-202,
    204, 206-208, 258

Orange County bankruptcy, 93, 191
Orange County Board of Supervisors, 55, 181, 188
Orange County Investment Pool (OCIP), 80, 186, 192-193, 206, 208-210,
Orange County Register, 54, 209
Oversight responsibility, 27, 33-36, 39, 47, 152, 184, 187
Overtime usage, 367, 131
O'Dell, Ernie, 194-196
O'Keefe, Sean, 157
O'Leary, Thomas, 4

P

Palmdale, California, City of, 183
Palo Alto, California, City of 217
Palos Verdes Library District, 263
Pena, Federico, 33
Pendergast, Bill, 54
Penny, Robert, 120
Perez, John, 108
Performance audits, 39, 275-276
Performance measures, 40, 59, 62, 216-217, 223-226, 228, 235, 287
Phernambucq, Stanley, 33
Philadelphia, Pennsylvania, City of, 131, 298-300
Portland, Maine, City of, 223
Portland, Oregon, City of, 287
Possemato, Paul, 79-81
Prince William County, Virginia, 104, 235
Program budget, 27, 61-63
Prunty, Robin, 89

Q

Qualified audit opinions, 280
Quayle, Dan, 15
Queen Mary, 301

R

Rancho Palos Verdes, California, City of, 42, 182-183, 222,
Ream, Dave, 105-106
Redondo Beach, California, City of, 194
Redwood City, California, City of, 17, 306

Reed, Sally, 27, 155-157, 223
Register of warrants, 12, 18-19, 139-140
Retreats, 48-51
Richards, John, 121
Rightsizing, 103-105, 107, 109
Riordan, Richard, 5-7, 10, 251
Risk Analysis 297
Rocklin, California, City of, 11
Rupert, Tom, 184, 192, 198

S

Sacramento, City of, 75, 295-296,
Salem, Oregon, 223
Saltarelli, Don, 53-54
San Clemente, California, City of, 192
San Diego Chargers, 292, 294-295
San Diego, City of , 291-295
San Fernando, California, City of, 35, 199
San Francisco, California, City of, 8-9, 91, 145-147, 239, 244, 255, 294, 296, 298
San Francisco Examiner, 8-9
San Jose, California, City of, 181, 201, 208
San Marino, California, 183
Santa Ana, California, City of, 105
Santa Clara County, California, 156, 231-232
Santagate, Guy, 101-102
Save Our Libraries (SOL), 265
Sarver, Linda, 1-7, 10, 13, 157
Savannah, Georgia, City of 217
Schieber, Sylvester, 129
Schneider, Ernie, 81
Seals, Gerald, 104
Seaside, California, City of, 267
Secured Assets Fund Earnings (SAFE), 201
Securities and Exchange Commission, 185, 194, 210
Serna, Joe, 296
Shenanigan's List, 155
Sher, Byron, 154
Signal Hill, California, City of, 47
Silverio, Olly, 286
Simi Valley, California, City of, 140
Sin taxes, 246

Single Audit Act, 286
Skagway, Alaska, City of, 39
Slush funds, 157-158
SLY principle, 196-197
Smith, Bill, 129
Soliciting for charity, 138
Standard and Poor's, 86-87, 89, 96
Stanton, Roger, 25
Static analysis, 245
Stein, Ted, 138
Steiner, William, 54
Stierheim, Merrett, 88
Strategic plan, 50, 215-217
Strenn, Mary, 35
Stump the Chump, 33
Sunnyvale, California, City of, 13
Sunshine laws, 20-21
Surplus monies, 166

T

Tahoe City Public Utility District, 40
Tara, Chris, 265
Tempe, Arizona, City of, 44-45, 173, 179
Ten Washoe School District, 132
Third party custodians, 198
Thomas, Sally, 145-146
Thompson, Sid, 37, 45-47
Thompson, D.J., 128
Three Valleys Municipal Water District, 200
Tokofsky, David, 269
Toregas, Costis, 41-42
Torrance, California, City of, 178, 184-185, 198,
Torrance Unified School District, 258-259
Trivial pursuit, 73
Twin Towers Correctional Facility, 26

U

Uberuaga, Mike, 206
United Teachers of Los Angeles, 108
University of North Carolina at Charlotte, 234

Unqualified Audit Opinions, 280-281
Urbandale, Iowa, City of, 174
Use of off-duty vehicles, 132-134
Utility tax, 2, 4, 247

V

Vacation liability, 130
Vague objectives, 226
Vallejo, California, City of, 306-307
Vallejo City Unified School District, 54
Ventura, California, City of, 203,
Ventura County, California, 110
Visalia, California, City of, 296-297
Vollaire, Aurora (Dolly), 119-121

W

Wachs, Joel, 291
Washington D.C., 32, 129, 219, 244
Weiss, Mark, 193
West Hollywood, California, City of, 74
White, O. Wendell, 104-105, 109
Wiggins, James, 169-170, 175
Williams, Willie, 5-6
Wilson, Keene, 121
Wilson, Pete, 154-155
Wiseman, Beau, 132
Wymer, Steve, 184-185, 198

Y

Yaroslavsky, Zev, 26, 95, 114, 157, 252

Biography

People often enter political life with a pocketful of wonderful ideas to improve their city, school district, or county. It doesn't take long, however, before they hit a seemingly impenetrable barrier that frustrates their plans—a lack of understanding of their government's budget and finances.

Instead of reigning as the successful victors of a hard fought election campaign, these financially inexperienced neophytes are treated as third stringers. Relegated to the back bench, they can only stew while their more financially savvy colleagues get programs introduced and adopted.

By not knowing how to raise red flags, fiscally challenged officials are also vulnerable to becoming unwitting accomplices in the schemes and illegal activities of dishonest colleagues and unscrupulous staff members.

It doesn't have to be that way. *Local Government Dollars and Sense* was written to help local elected officials master their oversight responsibilities. There are 225 financial tips in this book ranging from finding hidden money, to establishing fund balances, to asking the right budget questions.

Local Government Dollars and Sense is organized in an easy to follow format. Each of the fourteen chapters begins with a relevant local government vignette, followed by several related tips and techniques for exercising oversight within your organization.

Len Wood is a leading trainer and consultant to local governments who specializes in elected official, upper management, and advisory commission issues and problems.

Prior to establishing his firm, Len spent over twenty-three years in local government, fifteen of which were as a City Manager in the Cities of Rancho Palos Verdes and Claremont, California.

Len has also served as a professor at the Graduate Center of Public Policy and Administration at California State University Long Beach and Cal Poly Pomona.

He has a Master's Degree in Public Administration from the University of Southern California and a Bachelors Degree in Political Science from California State University at Long Beach.

Len is the author of three other local government books: the *Elected Official's Little Handbook*; the *Little Budget Book*; and the *Commissioner's Little Handbook*.

Order Form for Len Wood Books

The Training Shoppe
4228 Palos Verdes Drive East, Suite 200
Rancho Palos Verdes, CA 90275
310-832-5652

Please send me the following books:

	Price	Quantity	Total
Local Government Dollars & Sense	$44.95	_____	_____
Elected Official's Little Handbook	$29.95	_____	_____
Little Budget Book	$29.95	_____	_____
Commissioner's Little Handbook	$24.95	_____	_____
Tales from the Trenches	$44.95	_____	_____
CA Residents Add Sales Tax (8 1/4%)			_____

Shipping and Handling ($6.00 first book, $1.00 for additional books)   _____

Total Order   _____

Name _____

Address _____

State & Zip Code _____Phone _____

Orders must be accompanied by a check or agency purchase order.
Call 310-832-5652 for multiple copy discounts.

We guarantee your satisfaction with our publications. If for any reason you're not satisfied, return it in resalable condition within 30 days for a full refund.

www.trainingshoppe.com
LenWood@aol. com